Teaching LITERACY

balancing PERSPECTIVES

THE UNIVERSIT
RIPON AN

ROGER BEARD

teaching LITERACY *balancing* PERSPECTIVES

Hodder & Stoughton
LONDON SYDNEY AUCKLAND

British Library Cataloguing in Publication Data

Beard, Roger
  Teaching Literacy, Balancing Perspectives
  I. Title
  372.6

ISBN 0–340–56591–8

First published 1993
Typeset by Wearset, Boldon, Tyne and Wear
Printed in Great Britain for the educational publishing division of Hodder & Stoughton Ltd, Mill Road, Dunton Green, Sevenoaks, Kent by St Edmundsbury Press Ltd.

contents

CONTENTS

note about the editor

Roger Beard has taught in primary schools and in a college of higher education and is currently Senior Lecturer in Primary Education at the University of Leeds. His publications include *Children's Writing in the Primary School*; *Developing Reading 3–13* and an in-service package, *Reflections on Early Reading*. He is editor of the United Kingdom Reading Association *Literacy and Learning* Series and educational advisor for the Channel 4 *Story World* programmes.

note about the

contributors

Marilyn Jager Adams is a senior scientist at Bolt Beranek & Newman Inc. in Cambridge, Massachusetts. She holds a PhD from Brown University in cognitive and developmental psychology. In addition to her book, *Beginning to read: Thinking and learning about print* (MIT, 1990), she has published a number of chapters and journal articles on cognition and education. She was also principal author of the curriculum for Proyecto Intelligencia, a successfully validated experimental effort to enhance thinking skills among barrio students in the Republic of Venezuela.

Carl Bereiter and **Marlene Scardamalia** are both professors at the Ontario Institute for Studies in Education, where they are members of the Center for Applied Cognitive Science, which Scardamalia heads. Their research of almost a decade on the development of writing abilities culminated in the book, *The Psychology of Written Composition* (1987). More recently, their research on expertlike learning has led to development of a computer environment called CSILE (Computer Supported Intentional Learning Environment), now being field tested around North America, and to a book, *Understanding Expertise* (in press). During 1992–93 they are fellows at the Center for Advanced Study in the Behavioral Sciences, where they are part of a special project on 'Cognitive Bases of Educational Restructuring.' Their current research deals with epistemology, psychology, and discourse in the construction of knowledge in classrooms.

Peter Bryant did his PhD, based on research on children with learning problems, at the Institute of Psychiatry in London. He had a post-doctoral spell in Piaget's department in Geneva, and then worked for a year at the MRC Social Psychiatry Research Unit in the Institute of Psychiatry. Currently based in Oxford, he now carries out research on children's intellectual development, paying particular interest to the way in which children make inferences.

David Crystal works from his home in Holyhead, North Wales, as a writer, editor, lecturer, and broadcaster in the fields of language, linguistics, and general reference. Formerly Professor of Linguistic Science at the University of Reading, he is now Honorary Professor of Linguistics at the University College of Wales, Bangor. He is the author of some forty books, including the *Cambridge Encyclopedia of Language*, *Listen to your Child*, and *The English Language*, and is editor of *The Cambridge Encyclopedia*. In educational contexts, he has written several books for teachers, and been involved in the production of teaching materials, such as the *Skylarks*, *Databank*, and *Datasearch* series, and the *Language A to Z* course books for Key Stages 3 and 4 of the National Curriculum.

Margaret Donaldson is Emeritus Professor of Developmental Psychology at the University of Edinburgh. She has conducted extensive research on the development of language and thinking. Her best known work is *Children's Minds*, which has been translated into many languages. Her latest book, *Human Minds: An Exploration*, was published in 1992. She has also written for children, contributing to several language and literacy programmes for primary school, including *Link-Up*, and has published children's novels and picture story-books.

Keith Gaines works as a freelance writer, speaker and educational consultant to publishers, support services and schools. He began his teaching career in 1970 in a boys' secondary modern school in Birmingham. After working as Head of Remedial in a comprehensive school, he joined Walsall Remedial and Language Service as a peripatetic teacher in primary and secondary schools. He later worked in the Special Needs Support Service in Wakefield initially as an advisory teacher and later as Head of Service. He is the co-author of *Wellington Square*, a reading resource for junior and secondary pupils, and the author of the *New Way Easy Start* infant reading books; *Thomas Nelson and Sons Ltd*. He has written for the *TES*, *Reading* and *Education 3–13*.

Alison Littlefair works as a Language Consultant. Her particular interest is in reading and writing for information and in the publication of non-narrative books for children such as the recently published, *Reading All Types Of Writing*. She has also presented papers at national and international conferences. Previously she taught for seventeen years in primary and secondary schools including work as a language co-ordinator in a comprehensive school. Subsequently, she studied language in education at the Cambridge Institute of Education, at the University of East Anglia and researched pupils' awareness of different registers they read, at the Open University.

Jane Oakhill obtained a BEd from Sussex University before becoming a primary school teacher. Her interest in reading comprehension problems led her to return to Sussex University to study for a DPhil on that topic. She subsequently worked as a research fellow, investigating deductive reasoning in children and adults, circadian variations in cognitive performance, and adult language comprehension. She was appointed to a lectureship in Experimental Psychology at Sussex in 1990. Jane has published widely, particularly on reading comprehension problems, and is the author of

Becoming a Skilled Reader with Alan Garnham and *Children's Problems in Text Comprehension*, with Nicola Yuill. In 1991 she was awarded the British Psychological Society's *Spearman Medal* for outstanding published work in the first decade of her career as a psychologist.

Katharine Perera is currently Professor of Educational Linguistics in the Department of Linguistics at Manchester University and has worked as a teacher both in Malaysia and in Britain. She has also lectured in a College of Education. She was a member of the National Curriculum English Working Group (the Cox Committee). Her publications include *Children's writing and reading* and *Understanding language*. She is editor of the *Journal of Child Language.*

Margaret Peters was belatedly enrolled as a Chartered Psychologist over forty years after reading Psychology at Birkbeck College. She taught in schools, clinics and colleges, but for most of the time was tutor in Primary Education and Literacy at the Cambridge Institute of Education. Her doctoral research was 'A study of the factors affecting improvement in Spelling in the junior school' involving the whole school population in Cambridge throughout its junior school years. This was subsequently published (*Success in Spelling*), as was *Spelling; caught or taught?* which was completely rewritten as a *New Look* in 1985. Her work and all later writing has related to spelling in the cause of children's purposeful writing.

Jessie Reid is a former senior lecturer in the Department of Education, at the University of Edinburgh. Previously she taught English in secondary school, as well as teaching both infants and juniors in primary school. She also spent some years as psychologist at the Royal Hospital for Sick Children, Edinburgh, gaining wide experience of reading problems. Her research has focused on the development of concepts of print and on aspects of language that bear on reading progress. She has published widely in the academic field and for schools, and is the principal author of the beginning reading programme *Link-Up.*

Rosemary Sassoon has specialised in the educational and medical aspects of handwriting for many years although her early training and work was that of a scribe and a designer. The University of Reading awarded her a PhD for her work on the effects of models and teaching methods on joining strokes in children's handwriting. She lectures and researches worldwide on various aspects of handwriting as well as other letterform issues. She has collaborated in research projects with colleagues at the MRC APU, Cambridge. Her own present research interests include the causes and remediation of writer's cramp, type design in relation to children's reading, and the acquisition of a second writing system. Her main publications include: *The Practical Guide to Children's Handwriting, The Practical Guide to Calligraphy, The Practical Guide to Lettering, Creating Letterforms, Handwriting; a New Perspective, Handwriting; The Way to Teach it, Helping Your Handwriting,* and *Teach Yourself Handwriting.*

Barbara Tizard is Emeritus Professor at the Institute of Education, London. From 1980–90 she was Director of the Thomas Coram Research Unit, London. She was educated at Somerville College, Oxford, and the Institute of Psychiatry, London. She is currently writing up the findings of research, jointly directed with Ann Phoenix, on social identities in adolescence. Her earlier publications include: *Early Childhood Education*; *Adoption, a second chance*; *Involving Parents in Nursery and Infant Schools*, with J. Mortimore and B. Burchell; *Young Children Learning*, with M. Hughes; and *Young Children at School in the Inner City*, with B. Blatchford, J. Burke, C. Farquhar and I. Plewis.

Nicholas Tucker taught English in comprehensive schools in London before qualifying as an educational psychologist. He is now lecturer in Developmental Psychology at the University of Sussex, with a special interest both in children's reactions to literature and in the history and present-day status of childhood itself. He has written five books for children as well as books about children's literature, including *Suitable for children? Controversies in children's literature* and *The child and the book; a literary and psychological exploration.* He reviews books for the *Guardian* and *Times Educational Supplement*, and is a frequent broadcaster, so far appearing in over 200 editions of Radio 4's Saturday evening conversation programme, *Stop the Week*, chaired by Robert Robinson. A frequent lecturer at meetings and conferences, he has also taught in Canada and America, often drawing on the experience of being father to three children of his own.

introduction

Roger Beard

The origins of this book

This book originated as a response to the debates about the teaching of literacy in the United Kingdom and in the United States of America at the beginning of the 1990s. It does not deal with the complex issues concerning standards, but concentrates instead on the professional knowledge of language and literacy which can help make teaching literacy effective.

Of the two main branches of literacy, reading and writing, the teaching of reading has been more the focus of controversy over several decades. What has been called 'The Great Debate' has been particularly concerned with the teaching of early reading and has been between those who espouse 'meaning-emphasis' approaches (giving priority to the use of whole words and meaningful texts) and those who advocate 'code-emphasis' or 'phonics' approaches (giving priority to the teaching of sound-letter relationships). The full implications of the word 'emphasis' have not always been considered and the debate has often been over-polarised, especially in the light of the variety of strategies which children use in learning to read. As will be seen below, other more recent but related debates have also been characterised by an unfortunate lack of 'giving of ground'.

The evidence underpinning 'The Great Debate' has been thoroughly reviewed by Jeanne Chall (1967, 1983) who, in both editions of her book, concludes that, overall, code-emphasis approaches produce better results in the teaching of early reading. This is really not a surprising conclusion because the English writing system is an *alphabetic* one, an economical way of representing the speech sounds (phonemes) of English (of which there are about forty-four, depending on accent), instead of the unwieldy approach of using a different symbol for each syllable (of which there are about five thousand) or for each word (of which there are tens of thousands). Despite the occasional anomalies (e.g. 'once', 'was', 'are') the great majority of English words belong to spelling patterns of some kind (Venezky, 1970).

Nevertheless, the complexity of the debate is immediately shown by the fact that Chall's conclusion has to be interpreted with care. It can lead to well meant practices in which there is an *over*-emphasis on the code and which fail to accompany this with a concern for the quality of the *texts* used in literacy teaching. As the later chapters by Nicholas Tucker, Katharine Perera and Alison Littlefair show, there is a variety of ways of answering the question 'What makes a good book?' and it is important to keep these alternatives in mind, whatever the emphasis of the teaching. In addition, 'code-emphasis' teaching itself presents challenges: as can be seen from Peter Bryant's chapter, effective teaching depends on the teacher's knowledge of how children can be best helped to develop 'phonemic awareness' – within a context which reflects the purposes and functions of written language and how entertaining and informative the uses of literacy can be.

Chall's conclusions have themselves been questioned in recent years, on the basis of a number of lines of argument including the motivating influence of high quality picture books, the use of sympathetic 'shared reading' teaching approaches and the adoption of radical assumptions about the nature of literacy learning. Twenty years after her work was first published, her conclusion was still being challenged – and defended (Carbo, 1988; Chall, 1989).

The teaching of writing has been far less prone to extremes of debate and far less the centre of research and publications. The 1980s saw a number of innovative studies, however, which embraced several dimensions: development in writing (Wilkinson, 1980); children's use of the writing process (Graves, 1983); psychological studies of children's composing of writing (Bereiter and Scardamalia, 1987); and broad surveys of the topic as a whole (Smith, 1982; Beard, 1984). There have also been significant but less well known research studies into some of the specific components of writing. The new National Curriculum for England and Wales has recently increased particular interest in the components of spelling and handwriting by giving each of them a separate attainment target status (which is reflected in the structure of *Teaching Literacy: Balancing Perspectives*).

Of the above publications, the 'process writing' approach of Donald Graves has been most influential, involving a child-centred framework of topic choice, drafting and re-drafting, 'conferencing' with teacher and peers and eventual 'publication'. If there is room for debate, it is in relation to the research base which underlies *Writing: Teachers and Children at Work* (Graves, 1983) and related publications. Remarkably, for a project of such influence, the research base is very limited and rather vague. In fact, some critics have suggested that Graves' work is rather more evangelical 'reportage' than research. Graves' original study was based on four classes of children in a middle class community (Graves, 1975). In a review of eleven subsequent publications by Graves and his colleagues, Peter Smagorinsky (1987) notes that only thirty children are referred to: one child (Andrea) is referred to on forty-one pages; only one other child is referred to on more than ten pages (Sarah, on fifteen pages). Given that Graves uses a case study research method, questions arise about the significance of what is reported and what is not reported – there is hardly any mention of instances where the framework was found not to be valid.

In both branches of literacy, therefore, there is a broad background of debate; and by the early 1990s it was accompanied in the United Kingdom by a broader debate about the nature of primary education itself.

The wider context of professional debates

Work on this book was going on at the same time as a wider national appraisal of teaching approaches was being carried out as a whole in British primary schools, based on a Discussion Paper, *Curriculum Organisation and Classroom Practice in Primary Schools* (DES, 1992). Although coincidental, the two initiatives do share a commitment to considering teaching approaches from educational and organisational points of view rather than from 'doctrinal' ones. The initiative behind *Teaching Literacy: Balancing Perspectives* shares the argument in *Curriculum Organisation and Classroom Practice in Primary Schools* that debates about primary and elementary education need to focus on *effective* practice rather than dogmatic assertions about 'good practice', in which teaching is organised to conform to an orthodoxy of some kind. Instead, decisions need to be *informed* ones, made with reference to approaches which have been associated with speedy and successful teaching and learning or in the light of valid research findings on the processes involved. The challenge in teaching literacy is to consider widely and appropriately a variety of perspectives, to provide the kind of balanced judgements which will best help the children in our care.

In the United States of America, there has been a similar general concern about the need to reconcile tensions between different teaching approaches to reading, especially between 'whole language' and 'phonics' (Chall, 1990; Adams, 1991). The results from Jeanne Chall's research into the performance of low-income children leads her to conclude that their early reading development, like that of less disadvantaged children, is best fostered by a judicious mix of teaching approaches: word recognition skills; systematic, explicit phonics; and the use of 'connected texts' from basal readers and trade books (both story and informational). She warns that the use of 'enriched, literature-based reading programmes' may be less effective, unless they are combined with the structure and appropriate challenge provided by most 'text books'.

The very title of Marilyn Jager Adams' 1991 paper, 'Why Not Phonics *and* Whole Language?' indicates her concern that debates can suffer from misleading exclusivity. She also remarks how ill-defined the term 'whole language' is. She reports one study of sixty-four articles which referred to it: of the various defining attributes, none was referred to by two-thirds of the articles and definitions varied widely between seeing 'whole language' as an approach, an orientation, a theory, a programme, a curriculum and an attitude of mind. She goes on to welcome the enlightened aspects of the whole language 'movement', including an emphasis on constructing meaning from texts, on ensuring that language use has purpose, relevance and reward for the learner, on a flexible use of the writing process and on cooperative and interesting learning contexts. Yet, she argues, it is unnecessary and potentially damaging for 'whole language' approaches if they also make an issue of excluding phonics teaching and of assuming misleadingly that children are naturally predisposed towards written language acquisition. Both these issues are examined at length in this book.

The need for balance

Debates on the teaching and learning of literacy have spanned educational publications, the press, radio and television and no doubt have continued in school staff rooms and in teacher education courses across the UK and the USA. Such debates are a healthy part of the complex task of teaching reading and writing to children in countries throughout the world, but what gave particular impetus to the theme of *balance* in this book was the manner in which debates were being conducted. For these debates had become unduly polarised and beset by slogans whose meanings were not always clear. 'Whole language' is one of many examples. Several publications which had become very influential took a radical, plausible, but very narrow perspective on the teaching and learning of literacy. In particular, they seemed to neglect a great many insights which could be provided by significant recent work in psychology and linguistics.

But other voices were also raised. Two publications in particular acted as catalysts in the decision to bring together some more balanced perspectives, one from the UK and one from the USA. Both are represented in this volume, Margaret Donaldson's *Sense and Sensibility* and the summary of Marilyn Jager Adams' *Beginning to Read*. Margaret Donaldson's booklet was an individual response to professional debates in the UK; Marilyn Adams' book was a report commissioned by the USA government. Both were distinctive in treating early literacy education in a realistic and 'problematic' way and in being prepared to consider a range of possibilities on the basis of evidence and analysis, rather than on orthodoxy or belief.

In both the UK and the USA, debates about the teaching of literacy had been ranging over several dimensions and embracing a variety of interrelated issues. Prominent among these was the attempt to equate the psychological processes which are involved in literacy learning with those involved in the learning of a first language. This seemed to be a highly debatable assumption which deserved careful evaluation of the sources of evidence on which it was based – some of which stretched back to the 1960s. Literacy studies had also been enlivened by initiatives which concerned other dimensions: the nature of skilled reading; literacy development in the early years; approaches to the teaching of reading; the quality of texts in literacy teaching; work with children on the process of writing; and the 'developmental' aspects of spelling and handwriting. These initiatives include some attractive possibilities to teachers, but there seemed to be a danger of neglecting perspectives which stressed other aspects of literacy learning and particularly those connected with what teachers did to support and foster the skills and processes involved. There were also some dimensions where current debates were too narrow in other respects. Special needs was an example where there seemed to be a preoccupation with the labelling of learning difficulties and a neglect of children's personal experiences of literacy learning and the contexts which might best support it. Furthermore, it seemed that, with a small number of exceptions, the current field of literacy studies seemed to lack publications which presented and discussed a range of ideas, evidence and argument across these different dimensions.

The scope of this book

All this led to the feeling that a new book was needed which deliberately explored the notion of a 'balanced approach' to the different dimensions outlined above. It seemed that this could be best achieved by drawing upon three types of material: firstly, to reprint a small number of sources which had already been published and which were suitable for further dissemination; secondly, to commission specially written chapters from colleagues whose work deserved wider recognition in the context of this book; and thirdly, to invite chapters from writers and researchers whose previous publications indicated that they would be able to contribute an original chapter on the notion of 'balance' in a way which would inform classroom practices and professional thinking generally. It was very rewarding to find how much many of them felt that such a book was needed and how quickly they responded to an invitation to contribute. There is also an additional sense of balance in the backgrounds of the contributors, especially in their range of experience in working with and writing for teachers and children.

The overall plan of the book has been devised roughly to fit the literacy aspects of the National Curriculum framework for England and Wales and its Scottish counterpart *English Language 5–14*, in that there are chapters on reading, writing, spelling and handwriting. These are preceded by three chapters which examine the relationships between language and literacy. The book ends with a chapter which is based on Marilyn Adams' remarkably assiduous and wide-ranging review of the huge amount of research evidence which has accumulated on early literacy development. Most of the chapters are new and self-contained; like the three reprints this editorial introduction will set them in the context of their contribution to this volume.

Language and literacy

The book begins with a section which deals with the linguistic structure of language and with the relationship between language and literacy. The chapters in this section cover some complex material, with two of the chapters challenging some of the most influential theories of recent years, and so it may be helpful to introduce this section in particular detail.

It begins with a reminder of what language *is*. Debates on literacy teaching can easily become preoccupied with one aspect of language and can neglect its overall structure. A model of this structure is provided by **David Crystal** in the first chapter, a model which divides language into pronunciation, grammar and meaning.

Pronunciation is then sub-divided into phonetics (which is concerned with the production and transmission of speech sounds or phonemes) and phonology (which is concerned with the study of the phonemes of a particular language). As Peter Bryant's chapter shows later, debates about the direct teaching of sound-letter relationships can benefit considerably if they take account of the phonological structure of English, the system of speech sounds on which the relationships are based. This distinction is also very important to bear in mind in several other chapters, particularly the one by Marilyn Adams.

On the right side of his diagram, David Crystal sub-divides the broad area of *meaning* (or semantics) into vocabulary and discourse. The first of these, concerned with the meaning of words, is better known than the second, which is concerned with the meaning of larger chunks of text. In recent years, as can be seen in the chapters by Katharine Perera and Nicholas Tucker, there has been increasing recognition of the importance of exploiting narrative discourse in the teaching of literacy, because of the support which the underlying time sequence and structure of setting, characters, plot and resolution can give young readers and writers in the composing and the comprehending of texts. However, as the chapter by Alison Littlefair argues, it is also important to be aware of the range of non-narrative discourse and the very different demands which such texts make on young readers and writers.

Grammar is at the centre of the model, indicating the way language is centrally organised by rules. These rules can be seen operating within words (root words, prefixes, suffixes, etc.) or in the syntax between words, which Katharine Perera takes as a main point of reference in her chapter, when she discusses the linguistic features of the 'good book'. In the final part of his chapter, David Crystal indicates how models of this kind can be of help in our understanding of varieties of language. Variety in pronunciation produces different accents; variety in grammar and vocabulary produces different dialects, all of which are bound by their own rules. He goes on to remind us how important it is for beliefs and practice in professional language work to be bridged by knowledge, albeit provisional knowledge which is subject to continuing scrutiny. His reminder is a useful one for the focus of this book as a whole.

Jessie Reid's chapter examines the relationship between spoken and written language in the context of literacy learning. She confronts the view that the psychological processes involved in this learning are so closely similar to those involved in the learning of the mother tongue in its spoken form that they will, if allowed, come into play 'naturally'. This radical departure from traditional views is particularly associated with the work of Frank Smith and of Kenneth and Yetta Goodman, and has been extremely influential.

It underpins Liz Waterland's booklet on the apprenticeship approach to the teaching of reading (Waterland, 1988, pp. 12–14), the writings of Margaret Meek (e.g. Meek, 1982) and also a number of publications on emergent literacy (e.g. Teale and Sulzby, 1986, pp. vii–xxv) and on assessment (e.g. *The Primary Language Record*, ILEA, 1988, p. 23).

Criticisms of Goodman and Smith are not new, as Reid herself points out. Back in 1975, Eleanor Gibson and Harry Levin, in their major review of the psychology of reading, stressed the central role of word recognition in fluent reading, especially because the consequent reduction of alternatives renders the process not only faster, but also more determinate, efficient and satisfying (Gibson and Levin, 1975, p. 487). Elsewhere (ibid., p. 481), they point out the weakness of Goodman's 'psycholinguistic guessing game' model of reading, particularly in that it does not explain how the reader knows when to confirm guesses and where to look to do so.

In 1980, Keith Stanovich put forward an interactive model of reading, drawing on evidence that what makes a good reader is not the relatively greater use of contextual cues, but instead greater word recognition skill and strategies for comprehending and remembering large units of text. It is poor (or beginner) readers who show relatively greater reliance on contextual factors. Such criticisms have been developed over the intervening years on both sides of the Atlantic by many researchers, for instance Joyce Morris (1979), Katharine Perera (1980), Denis Stott (1981), Philip Gough (1981), Jay Samuels and Michael Kamil (1984), Jane Oakhill and Alan Garnham (1988) and Marilyn Jager Adams (1991). Indeed, as Reid remarks, it is surprising that the views of Smith and Goodman have remained so influential in teacher education for so long.

Jessie Reid adds a further dimension to the substantial body of existing criticism by looking at some of the key literature on developmental psycholin-guistics published over the last thirty years. She asks, in the light of it, whether the accounts of reading development given by Smith and Goodman actually justify their claim that the learning of written language is a direct parallel to the learning of speech. Are the key concepts in psycholinguistic theories of language acquisition taken over convincingly? Reid considers that they are not: that serious discrepancies exist which call into question the entire theoretical basis of the radical position.

She goes on to examine the other main feature of that view – the belief that language, particularly written text, is highly predictable. Drawing on a variety of sources, she finds that assumptions about predictability, and thus about the 'meaning-driven' nature of efficient language comprehension, do not stand up to the evidence. Finally, in what is perhaps the most searching part of her argument, she shows that a 'naturalistic' view and a 'meaning-driven' or 'top-down' view are actually incompatible with one other.

She argues that early literacy learning should be seen as involving the *transfer* of existing language skills to a new medium and new situations. Secondly, she suggests that teachers should not attempt to encourage precise prediction but rather various kinds of flexible *expectancy*, while at the same time accepting that fast and effortless word recognition – which for many children does not come 'naturally' – lies at the basis of skilled performance. Jane Oakhill makes a similar argument in her chapter. The later part of Jessie Reid's chapter goes on to deal with the implications for the teaching of literacy: linking teaching approaches to what children have already learned about language; lightening the load of the new learning by a judicious choice of texts (see Katharine Perera's chapter in connection with this); helping children to understand the purposes of literacy and the nature of the alphabetic writing system, build a model of the orthography and cope with the 'disembedded' language of books.

Margaret Donaldson's chapter provides further cautions about equating literacy learning with the learning of the mother tongue. She argues that, although we are biologically equipped for learning and using spoken language, we have no such natural facility for communicating with written language. Literacy depends on understanding and using symbols external to our bodies and not embedded in real situations. But Margaret Donaldson goes on to argue that skill with these symbols is particularly helpful in fostering systematic thought.

She begins her chapter by concentrating on the radical alternatives to the systematic teaching of literacy. While she shares with advocates of these views the belief that children are active and competent learners, she warns that it is misleading to denigrate active and competent teaching in support of some kind of minimal teaching movement. She also points out the unsatisfactory nature of recent debates about the use of 'real books' in the teaching of reading and the weaknesses in the view that children learn to read by reading. Like Jessie Reid, she draws attention to flaws in the arguments of Frank Smith and Kenneth Goodman and then shows how the possible bridges between spoken and written language can be used in different, but complementary teaching approaches.

Reading

The section of the book on reading begins with a chapter by **Jane Oakhill** on 'Developing skilled reading', in which she deals particularly with recent psychological work on models of reading development, the use of context and reading comprehension. She begins by stressing the *productive* nature of the alphabetic system of written English and how the sound-letter relationship enables children to read words which they have never seen before in print.

She then shows how learning about sound-letter relationships can be seen as the 'alphabetic' stage of reading development. Several different models have been put forward, but they tend to assume that children begin by reading whole words (the logographic stage) and then progress through the alphabetic stage to an orthographic stage, in which they have grasped the conventions of the English spelling system and the analogues between related groups of letters, falling back on letter-sound analysis when necessary.

The next section briefly deals with the role of phonological awareness in reading, which is more fully discussed in Peter Bryant's chapter, and then considers the use of context in reading. Like Jessie Reid, Jane Oakhill reports research findings which indicate that the use of context does not play such a central part in fluent reading as some theorists have suggested. The chapter ends with a detailed discussion of some recent research on reading comprehension.

Barbara Tizard's chapter, 'Early influence on later literacy attainment' is based on data from the longitudinal research project *Young Children at School in the Inner City*, involving thirty-three London infant schools (4–7 year olds). The chapter begins by focusing on the question of why some children are more successful than others. Evidence from this research project suggests that teachers and parents tend to give each other the credit or blame, while apparently overlooking characteristics in the children themselves. The research project's findings indicate both the significance of parental help before children begin school and of curriculum provision and teachers' expectations, thus raising questions about some of the more 'romantic' theories of emergent literary. Of particular interest are the findings in relation to children's early knowledge of alphabet letters (which Marilyn Adams also draws attention to in her chapter), their early skill at writing their names and copying words, and the influence of specific literacy teaching in reception classes (4–5 year olds).

Peter Bryant's chapter examines the role of phonological skills in learning to read. He begins by considering recent debates on early reading and some of their principal assumptions. He reminds us of the discussions on the naturalness of learning to read and debates about which aspect of language is most important in this learning. He goes on to outline the barriers created by the *phonological* aspects of reading and reviews international research in this field. Important distinctions have been drawn in this research between two aspects of children's phonological awareness: of syllables and of phonemes. In particular, research has indicated the importance of an awareness of the 'within-syllable' aspects of rhyme and alliteration and early literacy (which can develop in the pre-school years from children's experiences of nursery rhymes and games like 'I-Spy'). This awareness seems to assist the more difficult task of learning letter-sound correspondences in early reading development which, as the chapters by Jane Oakhill and Marilyn Adams show, greatly assists learning to read the alphabetic system of written English, where letters represent the phonemes of speech.

The next three chapters deal with the question of what makes a 'good book' for children, from linguistic, literary and non-narrative perspectives. **Katharine Perera's** chapter outlines some basic requirements for books which are used in the teaching of early reading: that they provide texts which will support children; that they show children that reading is enjoyable; and that they need to offer models for children's own writing. She then reports on an analysis of the story structures, sentence patterns and vocabulary from samples of reading schemes and individual books. Her findings and conclusions make an original empirical contribution to the debate about the relative merits of the use of reading schemes or 'real books' in the teaching of beginning reading.

Nicholas Tucker takes a literary and developmental perspective to the question of the 'good book', beginning with a caution about the tendency to moralise about what is suitable for children to read. He then outlines some of the dilemmas in and different ways of assessing children's literature. He concedes the values of 'light reading', but goes on to suggest a number of dimensions through which good writers provide what is best in children's books, from literary and psychological points of view. The chapter ranges over these aspects of literature – its language; the ways it can develop an understanding of the world and contribute to thinking itself; its value in imaginative play and as an insight into personality; its promotion of moral thinking, personal direction and a sense of self – and the way good books leave readers with some imaginative reconstruction to do for themselves.

The next chapter switches focus to the non-narrative aspects of the good book. **Alison Littlefair** suggests that more attention needs to be paid to competence in reading non-narrative material, which only a minority of young readers seem to accomplish successfully. She argues that we need to consider the range of genres with which young readers have to deal and illustrates some of the linguistic features of non-narrative texts which can prove challenging for children. She then discusses ways in which young readers can be supported by writers of different genres and how teachers can help them to become familiar with these different kinds of texts. She ends with a plea for teachers to 'balance the books' in what is provided in schools and for them to include in their teaching some explanation of how non-narrative books are written.

Keith Gaines uses his tongue-in-cheek chapter to show how work with children who have special needs can be distracted by 'deficit' labels, tautologies and euphemisms. He draws upon his many years of work with children to argue that teaching needs to be balanced to meet individual needs and to take account of the broader context of children's experiences of literacy. His chapter also reminds us of the political and economic perspectives within with special needs provision, including the 'Reading Recovery' programme, is resourced and evaluated.

Writing

The section on writing begins with an extract from one of the major books on writing of recent years, *The Psychology of Written Composition* by **Carl Bereiter** and **Marlene Scardamalia**. Their work has involved over one hundred studies of children's writing at the Ontario Institute for Studies in Education and adopts a more circumspect framework than that of Donald Graves, referred to earlier in this introduction. Two models are outlined which the authors have devised to explain different tendencies in writing performance and particularly the composing processes which underlie them. 'Knowledge-telling' involves producing writing in a relatively natural, unstructured way, whereas 'knowledge-transforming' involves more goal-directed planning and deliberate control over the writing, with conscious use being made of the young writer's discourse knowledge. Bereiter and Scardamalia summarise some of their main findings and end by suggesting what teachers can do deliberately to promote the kind of 'knowledge transformation' on which well-rounded writing development will depend.

Margaret Peters' chapter on spelling takes up the theme of 'balance' in relation to the continuing debate on how far spelling is best fostered by systematic teaching and how far by incidental learning. This 'taught or caught?' debate has been broadened to include visual training on the one hand and developmental writing and inventive spelling on the other. Margaret Peters provides a brief historical account of the debate and then outlines the main factors in spelling success, as identified in her own seminal research and in the work of others. She shows how an understanding of these factors can be of value to teachers when holding 'writing conferences' with children and in implementing the National Curriculum. Such an understanding is especially important in developmental approaches to spelling in the early years, when teacher intervention may be crucial in helping children to avoid becoming over-reliant on auditory 'input'. Teachers can help children to 'look with intent' at words and to learn about the structure of English spelling by other, multi-sensory methods, especially by learning a well formed style of handwriting.

Rosemary Sassoon argues that handwriting has for too long been relatively neglected in schools and in teacher education. She generally welcomes its emphasis in the National Curriculum, while denying the value of any kind of 'national model' and goes on to provide insights into how handwriting may be better understood: as a taught skill; as a motor skill; as the visible trace of a hand movement; and as a reflection of the writer on paper. Important implications stem from this: that the early stages of handwriting must be taught; and that letter forms, tools and materials must be carefully considered. Handwriting as a whole provides opportunities for informed balance: between speed and legibility; between uniformity and creativity; within and across the curriculum; and in responding to children's individual needs.

Balancing perspectives

The book ends with a chapter from **Marilyn Jager Adams**, who provides an overview of her major contribution to the literacy field, *Beginning to Read*. She describes the origins and scope of her work and suggests some of the key implications of its conclusions for primary and elementary school teachers, before leading in to the main recommendations for practice. These are drawn from the *Summary* of her book, which has been published separately. Marilyn Adams' contribution to *Teaching Literacy: Balancing Perspectives* is particularly appropriate for several reasons. Her conclusions on the main dimensions of this book are broadly but coincidentally similar to those of its other contributors. Likewise, she is prepared to challenge established orthodoxies which recent research has found to be misleading. She gives priority to systematic, reliable and replicable studies, rather than to romantic beliefs and vaguely defined cult ideas. She tries exhaustively to consider every source of evidence and argument in reaching her conclusions. This is in marked contrast with other influential publications which have been based on anecdotal evidence and drawn from studies which, although optimistically formulated, have in the end proved to be inconclusive (e.g. Meek, 1988, pp. 8 and 40; Meek *et al.* 1983, p. 223).

Overall, *Teaching Literacy: Balancing Perspectives* is a testimony to the knowledge which is now available to those who are responsible for helping children to become literate. This knowledge makes available penetrating insights into a range of dimensions – on language and literacy, on learning to read and to write, on finding entertainment and information in good books, on the composing of writing and on spelling and handwriting – dimensions along which effective teaching will allow children to be heirs to the world of learning for which literacy provides unique opportunities. For teachers especially, this book will add to their own opportunities for such learning, particularly if it is read with a reminder and a recognition: a reminder of the need to balance belief with evidence in literacy studies; and a recognition that effective teaching of literacy involves a range of practical possibilities whose validity has to be considered one against the other, as part of the systematic thought which literacy itself promotes.

language and literacy

*the structure of language**

David Crystal

The *theoretical* contribution of linguistics needs discussion, in that unless we can grasp in broad outline a picture of the way in which language is structured, it will be very difficult to find our way about the subject. We need a model of the main branches of the discipline of linguistics as a preliminary to any more detailed study. Figure 1.1 therefore shows one possible model of language structure, which attempts to interrelate the main branches of the discipline.

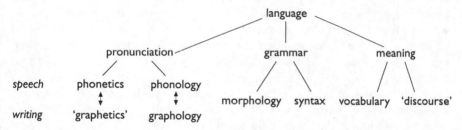

Figure 1.1 Levels of language

There are of course many possible models of the structure of language, and each has its controversial points; but all accounts agree that certain components are essential, and the figure illustrates what these are. For speech, which is in the primary medium of normal human language, three main components, or *levels* of structure are recognised: pronunciation, grammar and meaning. (This is by no means a novel analysis, of course: distinctions of this kind were made by traditional grammarians too.) 'Pronunciation' is, however, too broad a notion to be left as it is. There are two aspects to its study. Firstly, we may study the properties of human soundmaking as such – the way in which we form, transmit and hear sounds. This is the subject of *phonetics*. Apart from certain medical conditions (e.g. cleft palate), all human beings are born with the same vocal apparatus, and in principle can make the same

*This chapter has been taken from the book *Child language, learning and linguistics* (2nd edn) by David Crystal (1987), published by Edward Arnold.

range of sounds. Because of its general applicability, therefore – providing a means of analysing and transcribing the speech of the speakers of any language – the subject is sometimes called 'general phonetics'. It has to be clearly distinguished from the second term under the heading of pronunciation, *phonology*. Phonology is primarily the study of the sound system of a particular language, such as English or French. Out of the great range of sounds it is possible for each of us to produce, we in fact only use a small set of sounds in our own language – some forty-odd distinctive sound-units, or phonemes, in the case of English, for instance. Whereas phonetics studies pronunciation in general, therefore, phonology studies the pronunciation system of a particular language, aiming ultimately at establishing linguistic principles which will explain the differences and similarities between all such systems.[1]

A similar distinction might be made for the written medium, represented further down the diagram. Here we are all familiar with the idea of a language's spelling and punctuation system. The study of such things, and the analysis of the principles underlying writing systems in general, is equivalent to investigating the phonology of speech, and is sometimes called 'graphology' accordingly. Each language has its own graphological system. One might also recognise a subject analogous to phonetics (say, 'graphetics') which studied the properties of human mark-making: the range of marks it is possible to make on a range of surfaces using a range of implements, and the way in which these marks are visually perceived. This is hardly a well-defined subject as yet, hence my inverted commas, but it is beginning to be studied: typographers look at some aspects of the problem, as do educational psychologists. From the linguistic point of view, it should be possible to establish a basic alphabet of shapes that could be said to underlie the various alphabets of the world – just as there is a basic international phonetic alphabet of sounds. But this is a field still in its infancy.

On the right of the diagram we see the study of meaning, or 'semantics'. In a full account, this branch would need many subdivisions, but I will mention only two. The first is the study of the meaning of words, under the heading of 'vocabulary', or 'lexis'. This is the familiar aspect of the study of meaning, as it provides the content of dictionaries. But of course there is far more to meaning than the study of individual words. We may talk about the distribution of meaning in a sentence, a paragraph (topic sentences, for instance), in a chapter, and so on. Such broader aspects of meaning have been little studied in a scientific way, but they need a place in our model of language. I refer to them using the label 'discourse' – but as this term is not as universally accepted as the others in my diagram, I have left inverted commas around it.[2]

Sounds on the left; meanings on the right. 'Grammar', in the centre of the model, is appropriately placed, for it has traditionally been viewed as the central, organising principle of language – the way in which sounds and meanings are related. It is often referred to simply as 'structure'. There are naturally many conceptions as to how the grammatical basis of a language is best studied; and comparing the various schools of thought (transformational grammar, systemic grammar, and so on) forms much of the content of introductory linguistics courses. But one particularly well-established distinction is that between 'morphology' and 'syntax', and that is presented in the model. Morphology is the study of the structure of words: how they are built up, using roots, prefixes, suffixes, and so on – *nation, national, nationalise* etc., or *walk, walks, walking, walked*. Syntax is the study of the way words work in sequences to form larger linguistic units: phrases, clauses, sentences and beyond. For most linguists, syntax is, in effect, the study of sentence structure; but the syntactic structure of discourse is, also an important topic.[3]

All schools of thought in linguistics recognise the usefulness of the concepts of pronunciation, grammar and meaning, and the main subdivisions these contain, though they approach their study in different ways. Some insist on the study of meaning before all else, for example; others on the study of grammar first. But the existence of such differences should not blind us to the considerable overlap between them. However, before we can claim that our model is in any sense a complete account of the main branches of language, useful as a perspective for applied language work, we have to insert three further dimensions. These are to take account of the fact of language variation. Any instance of language has a structure represented by the model in Figure 1.1; but over and above this, we have to recognise the existence of different kinds of language being used in different kinds of situation. Basically, there are three types of variation, due to historical, social and psychological factors. These are represented in Figure 1.2. 'Historical linguistics' describes and explains the facts of language change through time, and this provides our model with an extra dimension. But at any point in time, language varies from one social situation to another: there are regional dialects of English, social dialects, and many other styles, as has already been mentioned. 'Sociolinguistics' is the study of the way language varies in relation to social situations, and is becoming an increasingly important part of the subject as a whole. It too requires a separate dimension. And lastly, 'psycholinguistics' is the study of language variation in relation to thinking and to other psychological processes within the individual – in particular, to the way in which

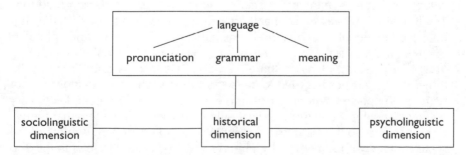

Figure 1.2 Main dimensions of language variation

language development and use is influenced by – or influences – such factors as memory, attention and perception.[4]

At this point any initial perspective has to stop. From now on, we would be involved in a more detailed study of the aims of the various branches outlined, and we would have to investigate further different theoretical conceptions, techniques, terminology and so on. But it should be clear from what has been said so far that in providing a precise and coherent way of identifying and discussing the complex facts of language structure and use, the potential applicability of the subject is very great. What must be remembered in particular is the distinction between (a) the need to get a sense of the subject of language as a whole, and (b) the mastery of a particular model of analysis to aid in a specific analytical or experimental task. The first, crucial step is to develop a linguistic 'state of mind', a way of looking at language that can provide fresh or revealing facts or explanations about the structure and use of language. From here, one proceeds to a more detailed examination of some of the main theoretical principles that underlie any scientific study of language, such as the distinction between historical and non-historical (diachronic v. synchronic) modes of language study, the distinction between language form and language content, and the importance of language variety. In the light of these principles, old problems turn up in a new light, and a certain amount of rethinking about traditional ideas becomes necessary.

Such rethinking can proceed along general or particular lines. The general viewpoint tends to give rise to fierce debate, this is the need to develop greater *tolerance* of language varieties and uses – of other people's accent and dialect, in particular. Can this be done without sacrificing the notion of the 'standard' language, without losing a sense of 'correctness' in language use, and all that many would hold dear? People sometimes accuse linguistics of throwing all standards to the wind – of wanting to say that 'anything goes', that it does not matter how we speak or write, as long as we are intelligible, expressing our ideas, and so on. This is simply not so.

The 'particular' viewpoint can be illustrated here, however, because it shows the kind of detailed thinking that needs to take place in adopting a linguistic way of looking at language. We may take any of the traditional grammatical categories, such as 'number', 'person', 'tense' or 'case' to demonstrate this. Traditionally, it was assumed that there existed a neat one-to-one relationship between the formal category and its meaning, viz. singular = 'one', plural = 'more than one'; 1st person = 'me' or 'us', 2nd person = 'you', 3rd person = 'the other person(s)'; tense = time; genitive case = possession. One of the things that linguistics has tried to do is show how such neat equations do not work. In the person system, for example, we can show this complexity very readily. Taking just one form (the so-called 'first person') we find that the *we* form *may* refer to the 1st person (as in 'We are going', where it refers to the speaker along with someone else), but it may also be used to refer to the 2nd person (as when a nurse addresses a patient with a 'how are we today?' where the *we* is equivalent to 'you'), or to the 3rd person (as when one secretary asks another 'how are we today', gesturing at their boss who has just gone into his office).

Another example of unexpected complexity is the tense system. There are many problems in the view that tense expresses time, and that time relationships are expressed by tense forms only. Visualising time as a line,

---

past time	now	future time

it might seem plausible to see the tenses fitting in neatly, as follows:

PAST	PRESENT	FUTURE
(*I walked/was walking*)	(*I walk/am walking*)	(*I will walk/be walking*)

---

past time	now	future time

But there are many examples of usage where this parallelism does not work. For instance, the present tense form *may* refer to present time, as in *I'm leaving*. But it may also help to refer to future time, when used with a future adverbial, as in *I'm going to town tomorrow*; or to past time, when used with a past narrative marker, e.g. *Three weeks ago, I'm walking down this road* . . . ; or to habitual action, when used with an adverbial of frequency (*I go to town three times a week*); or to very recent time (as in news headlines, e.g. *Sir X dies*); or to no time at all (the so-called 'timeless' present, as in *Oil floats on water*). Similar examples would arise if we were to consider the other tense forms.

It should be noticed how an examination of just one small area of grammar involves the use of a number of technical terms (even though the meanings of these terms are fairly obvious). It is evident that the need to talk at this level of detail is not far away, as soon as we approach any area of grammar. It is easy to make general, impressionistic remarks about children's usage, for example – about the 'complexity' of their sentences, or about their use of tenses or adjectives or prepositions. But such general remarks need to be carefully watched. And indeed, most of the 'obvious' features of language emerge as hiding considerable complexity, when they are subjected to analysis. Two further examples will illustrate this: the blind use of the idea of 'parts of speech', and an uncritical acceptance of measures of 'length'. The notion of 'parts of speech', for instance, seems easy enough to apply, as long as we are dealing with nouns, verbs, and other central classes. It is less easy to use when classifying such words as *yes, please, sorry, not,* and cases where words have several different uses. And we must remember that definitions of even the central classes can vary greatly from book to book. The notion of 'sentence length' provides another example of hidden complexity. This is a concept commonly used as a means of plotting language development – sentences get longer as children grow older. But how exactly is length to be measured – in syllables, words, phrases . . . ? If words, then would we count *it's* as one word or two? Would idioms (such as *it's raining cats and dogs*) be counted as having the same number of 'units' as literal sentences (such as *he's keeping cats and dogs*)? And what would we say about two sentences that were equal in length but which differed markedly in complexity (e.g. *The man and the dog and the cat were tired* and *The dog belonging to the man was in the kitchen*)? Such questions immediately arise as soon as we try to work with a simple measure of length.

Last of all – that is, after we have been motivated to accept the *general* aims and tenets of linguistic inquiry – there is the need to find and use a specific *model* of linguistic description, in order to interrelate our various observations about language structure and use. Whatever our aims (whether assessment, screening, remediation, development . . .) the need for a standard descriptive measure is paramount. There is no point in describing child A in terms of one linguistic framework, child B in terms of another, and then hoping to compare the two. (This is similar to – but infinitely more complex than – comparing two objects using two systems of measurement: if one is sixteen centimetres and the other eleven inches, which is the longer?) Likewise, an inventory, or list of 'noticeable' or 'interesting' features in someone's use of language is not an adequate account of it, and may mislead. The dangers of 'selective commentary' are threefold. *(a)* We tend to notice only what we have been trained to look for, e.g. pronouns, adjectives, tense forms; *(b)* some of the most important features of language may be omitted because they are not readily noticeable, e.g. variations in word order, elliptical patterns; and *(c)* an inventory provides no explanation, or sense of underlying pattern – for example, to make a list of features, in which item 13 was the definite article, and item 73 the indefinite article, would obviously be of little value. At some point in any grammar of English, these two items would have to be brought together, because the meaning of the one helps to establish the meaning of the other. And so it is for most areas of grammar. Grammar is not a random collection of features, nor is it learned in this way, and the same applies to other levels of language also. It is the task of the linguistic to define all the variables that make up the language *system*, and say how they relate to each other. Naturally, with such a complex system as language, there is no obvious 'best' way of doing this, and this is why there are so many competing linguistic theories. Each tries to present an explanation of language which models the way in which the system 'works'. Thus one encounters the 'generative' schools of thought associated with Chomsky, those associated with M. A. K. Halliday (first 'scale-and-category' grammar, later 'systemic' grammar), and so on. At some stage students of language have to come to grips with one of them, and learn to use it confidently, in order to provide themselves with a framework in principle consistent and comprehensive for carrying out language tasks. This is no place to argue the merits and demerits of the different positions: each model has its strengths and insights, each its weaknesses and obscurities. But there is no avoiding this final jump. Without a fund of formal knowledge to back up our general knowledge of linguistic aims and theory, there can be no bridge between beliefs and practice.[5]

1 See further J. D. O'Connor, *Phonetics* (Penguin 1973).
2 See further F. R. Palmer, *Semantics* (2nd edn, Cambridge University Press 1981).
3 See further F. R. Palmer, *Grammar* (2nd edn, Penguin 1982).
4 Introduction to the more detailed study of these dimensions are P. Trudgill, *Sociolinguistics: an introduction* (2nd edn, Penguin 1983); H. H. Clark and E. V. Clark, *Psychology and language* (Harcourt, Brace, Jovanovich 1977); W. P. Lehmann, *Historical linguistics: an introduction* (Holt, Rinehart and Winston 1962). Specifically on English, see D. Crystal, *The English Language*, Penguin 1988. Language acquisition, within psycholinguistics, is dealt with in D. Crystal, *Listen to your Child* (Penguin, 1986).
5 See further J. Lyons, *Language and linguistics* (Cambridge University Press 1981), D. Crystal, *The Cambridge Encyclopedia of Language* (Cambridge University Press 1987), *Linguistics* (Penguin 2nd edn, 1985).

reading and spoken language: the nature of the links

Jessie Reid

Reading as language learning

The view that learning to read must be treated as a language-based process is now one with which the great majority of teachers readily agree. Many might express surprise that the matter should even be in doubt. But it is only during the last three decades that learning to read has come to be widely recognised as a process in which language skills play a major role.

Most language-based views of reading that developed during this period drew support from new studies of children's speech, including particularly those studies influenced by the work of Noam Chomsky. Initially one sensed a fresh unity of vision and purpose in the new emphasis. But beneath this apparent consensus deep divisions existed, stemming from the ways in which the innovative bodies of psycholinguistic evidence and theory were seen to bear on the relationship between spoken language and its written counterpart. Disagreement is now so marked and has had such significant effects on classroom policy and practice that reappraisal seems urgent.

The radical position

Some of the emerging beliefs have represented a very radical departure from established opinion and practice. These radical views were put forward most prominently, in the early years, by two writers – Kenneth Goodman and Frank Smith – who described their positions as 'psycholinguistic' and thus linked them directly with the new post-Chomskian discipline. Goodman's three early papers (1967, 1969, 1972), asserted a close and direct parallel between the learning, and the skilled use, of spoken language and of language in print. Smith was similarly explicit in his appeal to oral communication as the only legitimate basis for a theory of what reading is and how it should be learned (Smith, 1971). He was, however, less explicit than Goodman in terms of presenting an actual model of the reading process.

The views of these two writers have been extremely influential, and have involved teachers who accepted them in trying to teach reading in an entirely new way. Perhaps even this wording is incorrect: there have been numerous expressions of the wish for it not to be described as 'teaching' reading at all. Moreover, the attempt to make this new way work has been pursued in the face of informed criticism and contrary evidence from many quarters (see pp. 7–8). It is for those reasons that it is now important to look at the validity of the underlying theory in its own terms.

The main assumptions in the radical position seem to be as follows:

1   The learning of spoken language draws on a special kind of innate ability. For normal children teaching is not necessary. The ability seems relatively independent of intelligence. Children discover for themselves how language works, and the learning can thus be described as 'natural'.

2   Reading is the exact parallel to listening, only in the visual mode. The special language-learning ability will also work for reading as children are exposed to written language and given clues about meaning. Thus learning to read is also 'natural'.

3   The systematic teaching of letter-sound correspondences is a distracting interference with those 'natural' learning processes, in that it fragments a process that must remain 'whole'.

4   The key to fluent reading is not word recognition but the use of strategies such as forming 'hypotheses', predicting (also called guessing/ expecting/anticipating) and the selecting of maximally 'productive' cues to confirm meaning. These strategies are also the basis of the skilled comprehension of speech. The text as constructed by the reader may not correspond exactly to what is on the page.

All these assumptions are represented, in one form or another, in the early writings of Goodman and Smith to which I have referred. For instance:

Reading is the direct counterpart of listening and is learned in the same natural way.   (Goodman, 1972, p. 505)

A child learning to talk looks for rules that will reduce some of the uncertainty of the world around him. In the normal progression of development he should go on to apply these same rule-discovering skills to the task of learning to read.   (Smith, 1971, p. 57)

These examples could be paralleled many times, and extended to cover all the assumptions listed above. The view of reading they represent is often referred to as 'top-down'. Is it correct?

The nature of spoken language learning

Since the nature of spoken language learning is a key issue, we should begin by turning to the psycholinguistic literature of the period when Smith and Goodman first put forward their arguments. Perhaps one of the best sources is the famous volume of papers called *The Genesis of Language*, published in 1966 and edited by Frank Smith and George Miller. How, in the view of the many distinguished contributors, did spoken language learning come about? Was a special innate ability involved, and if so, to what kinds of learning was it dedicated?

A survey of the contents of this volume makes it clear that among psycholinguists the belief in a special ability was at that time almost universal. Smith and Miller state the belief, with conviction, in their editorial introduction:

> That children can acquire language so readily can mean only that they have some innate predisposition for this kind of learning and this in turn can mean only that evolution has prepared mankind in some very special way for this unique human accomplishment.
>
> (Smith and Miller, 1966, p. 3)

The ability was given a special name – the Language Acquisition Device (LAD). But one idea dominated most speculation about its function: it was primarily the means by which young language learners *constructed for themselves the grammar of the language to which they were exposed*. Numerous attempts were made to specify the characteristics of 'children's grammar' and the stages it went through. (See, for instance, McNeill, 1966 for a typical discussion).

Chomsky himself had stated a similar opinion some years earlier in his famous review of Skinner's *Verbal Behavior*. We were, he wrote, 'forced to the conclusion that . . . the young child has succeeded in carrying out what from the formal point of view, at least, seems to be a remarkable type of theory construction.' (Chomsky, N., 1959, p. 57)

It is important to note that, in the thinking of this period, preoccupation with the acquisition of grammar almost completely dominated interest in the acquisition of word meanings. This can be seen from the index to the 1966 volume in question, where references to 'meaning' or 'semantics' or 'comprehension' are few, with some of these referring not to lexical meaning but to grammatical contrasts, such as singular/plural (see for instance McNeill, op. cit. p. 77).

The LAD and reading

We can now move to the second assumption (see p. 23) and consider the first crucially important question about psycholinguistics and reading. It is this: Is the unique innate ability on which attention was being focused in the 1960s relevant to the early stages of learning to read? When children begin to work with written language do they face the task of constructing the grammar of their native tongue all over again, as if they had never encountered language before?

If they do, then this 're-run' of the acquisition of grammar ought to be reflected in their early production of written language, just as the original learning was reflected in their early speech. Does this happen? The best evidence for or against such a re-run will obviously be found in some method of teaching beginners that enables them to bypass the difficulties found in the physical act of writing, and thus to communicate in print at a very early stage.

One such method, perhaps the best known, is *Breakthrough to Literacy* (Mackay, Thompson and Schaub, 1970). Samples of children's sentence production using the *Breakthrough* 'sentence-maker' were recorded and analysed by Reid (1974). Typical first attempts contained errors of word recognition and word order, and early sentences were certainly less compli-cated than the sentences those same children could by that age utter. But the crucial point is that there was no general stage where children produced word strings like 'daddy fun', or 'no like milk'. On the contrary they moved, once early confusions had been overcome, to composing sentences that were short but grammatically well formed.

What we see here, then, is not a re-run of spoken language acquisition but the *transfer, to the written mode, of linguistic knowledge already acquired in spoken form*. This is a very important distinction. On the other hand there was evidence that children at this early stage had to become much more consciously *aware* of the structure of sentences which they could have uttered without reflection. (See, for instance, Reid, op. cit., p. 25). Knowledge already gained was being used in a new way.

From the early 1970s onward, work on language acquisition paid much more attention to meaning, and children's innate abilities were seen as extending to the fundamental task of *constructing semantic relations* – in Halliday's phrase 'learning how to mean'. Much space is given to this aspect of language learning in the more recent collection of papers called *Language Acquisition: The State of the Art* (Wanner and Gleitman, 1982). But then we must go on to ask: Do children starting to read have to discover all over again how to map semantic concepts on to linguistic units? Once more the answer has to be that they do not. These early discoveries are already made, as in the domain of grammar. What children are ready to do at the age of five is to *transfer acquired skills and knowledge to a new medium, and to use them to support learning of a different kind*.

So we have here the first serious theoretical difficulty for Goodman and Smith, one which the two writers deal with in different ways. Goodman does not appear, in the early papers I have quoted, to make specific reference to the *construction* of grammar. He does, however, refer to children as 'predicting an underlying grammatical structure' (Goodman, 1972, p. 508) and 'using the grammatical structures implicit in the language' (Goodman, 1969, p. 17). But these references seem to be about the application of knowledge, not the acquisition of it, and they thus effectively bypass the issue of the parallel between learning to read and learning to comprehend speech.

The same may be said of Goodman's references to predicting 'meanings'. Indeed his use of expressions like 'input and meaning that lie ahead' (Goodman, 1967, p. 135) suggests that he is thinking of a stage of language development at which the encoding of meaning in a verbal form is quite far advanced. How, then, in his system, do meanings become associated with written forms in the first place? In practice they do so mostly when children have a text read aloud to them while they follow the print. But this is quite unlike the acquisition of meaning in the spoken mode, where no prior language system exists to which spoken words are seen to correspond.

Reading as rule discovery

Smith's approach is different from Goodman's in that he devotes considerable space to the nature of grammar and to language acquisition (Smith, 1971, pp. 28–59). Moreover, he commits himself early on to the view that grammar is the key to understanding language (op. cit. p. 29).

His reason for stressing the early stages of spoken language learning is, however, plain: it is because he wants to present the child as a *constructor of rules.* He seems to set aside the uniqueness of the construction of grammar and semantic concepts and to regard this achievement as merely one manifestation of a much more general ability. 'The child,' he states, 'has rules for learning rules' (op. cit. p. 55). And again: '. . . all that he needs is to discover the particular rules that apply'. (op. cit. p. 53). Yet Smith produces no supporting evidence for his claim about rule-discovering powers. Were the claim true it would have to apply to the discovery of rules in other domains, such as number or the physical sciences.

Evidence about these powers does, however, exist. Studies confirm what many teachers know from experience – that in the domain of, say, physical science the capacity to generate rules may be quite slow to develop, and that the extraordinary precocity found in spoken language learning is not matched, even when opportunities for discovery are there (see, for instance, Siegler, 1976). Indeed, many kinds of formal problem solving become possible only around puberty. Yet, as Lenneberg (1966) reports it is at puberty that the capacity to learn a first language begins to decay. The capacity to learn to read, however, remains. Different abilities are obviously at work.

It would appear, therefore, that the close parallel between learning to listen with comprehension and learning to read breaks down, whether it is based on an assumption about the relevance of the LAD or on a more general assumption about the rule-discovering skills of five-year-olds.

The question of 'natural' learning

So what can we conclude about the naturalness of learning to read? In a way, this question has just been answered at the end of the preceding section; for claims about 'naturalness' rest on the belief that learning to read can parallel the development of spoken language and draw on the same innate abilities. But part of the answer also lies in the differences between the *situations* in which the two language modes are learned. In exploring these differences Margaret Donaldson (1989 and this volume) draws attention to the fact that human beings cannot use written language as a primary vehicle of communication because they cannot produce it just with their bodies. And when they do produce it, it is visually featureless and impersonal, devoid of the expressions in the living voice and unsupported by gestures or the objects of its reference. One might describe it as the visual equivalent of computer speech coming from a tape-recorder. In addition, it cannot be taken in *simultaneously* with visual information from other sources nor produced simultaneously with other actions. It is, to use Donaldson's words, 'language on its own'. By comparison with the conversational exchanges of spoken language it is far from natural. In helping beginners, then, we have to look for kinds of introduction to written language which will provide bridges or links by which the transition to it may be eased.

The question of rule discovery is also of great importance. If it cannot be assumed that children will discover unaided the particular rules that govern the orthography, then it follows that they need help. And although Siegler's study was not concerned with reading, the kind of evidence he provides does suggest that the right kind of help can be given.

How it is to be given calls for careful thought. We must take account, for instance, of Vygotsky's work on 'zones of proximal development' (see Garton and Pratt, 1989, for an excellent exposition), and of Bruner's illuminating discussions of 'going beyond the information given' and of 'guided discovery' (Bruner, 1957; 1965). A great field of possibility lies between the one extreme of leaving children to work things out and the other extreme of feeding them rules of our own devising which may not have any real enabling power.

Goodman's cyclical model

Goodman's cycle of prediction, sampling for cues, and confirming/ disconfirming is probably one of the best known theoretical features of the radical position. It is certainly one that has been adopted with enthusiasm by those who favour the use of 'real books' and an 'apprenticeship' approach (e.g. Waterland, 1988). It calls for scrutiny here, because both Goodman and Smith link this kind of process to the comprehension of speech.

In his early discussions, Goodman uses four terms which he apparently regards as interchangeable. He talks variously of 'predicting', 'anticipating', 'expecting' and, of course, 'guessing', to refer to the way in which hypotheses are formed. But there is a problem here, for these terms are not, in ordinary usage, synonyms. When we turn on a tap we expect water to flow, but we would be most unlikely to make a prediction about it. Meteorologists make precise predictions about weather patterns, but, we trust, do not guess them! The blurring of these important distinctions in Goodman's discussions means that the status of the process Goodman is talking about – its degree of consciousness, of deliberate intent – is quite unclear.

What are readers (beginners and skilled performers alike) said to predict? At one point it is 'an underlying grammatical structure' (Goodman, 1972, p. 508). But unless the reader is well versed in grammatical terminology, such predictions cannot be verbal, conscious, or precise; they can only be intuitive and implicit. On the other hand, it seems that predicting 'a language structure that is decodable' (Goodman, 1969, p. 17) must be achieved at the level of words. If these notions are to be applied by teachers, such uncertainty is particularly troubling.

Goodman's notion of sampling the text for the 'most productive cues' needs scrutiny also (Goodman, 1967, p. 127). This phrase suggests a more precise kind of 'prediction' than some previous wording would indicate. If so, how does the reader know which cues will be most productive? Are the criteria fixed for any given word? And, more serious still, if the predicted word is not the word-on-the-page, what then? Can readers sample for the 'most productive cues' in a word they did not expect? Do they have to make a fresh prediction? The process envisaged now becomes a reiterated one, as Goodman's 1967 model actually shows. And this brings us to a question which concerns all theories of language reception: Is such a process *optimally efficient?* Is it the most economical, the quickest, the simplest way to deal with the text?

Goodman seems to believe that it is, because he believes that skilled readers have learned to make 'guesses that are right the first time' (Goodman, 1967, p. 127). But is he correct? Does language allow such learning? And is that how we process speech?

It is well established that even when the text is matched to the subjects' ability, only a proportion of responses to cloze procedure tasks correspond to the deleted words. Yet in cloze procedures the following as well as the preceding text is visible. A recent study by Abramovici and Reid (in preparation) looked at success rate when preceding text only was visible and subjects had, literally, to 'predict' what they thought would follow – a task which may be termed 'blind cloze'. The subjects were self-selected under-graduates, the text was a piece of clearly written discussion from a widely read book, and each gap required two words. The average success rate for getting both words correct was found to be a mere 11.6 per cent, and, for the first word only, 27 per cent. In normal reading, reliance on prediction that was so often wrong would obviously be a serious hindrance.

There is no reason to suppose that these findings are not typical: indeed, the figure of 27 per cent corresponds closely to that cited by Gough (1981). They therefore support a view expressed by numerous writers – that language is, in the words of Harris and Coltheart (1986, p. 170), 'essentially unpredictable'. However, there can be no question of returning to any model of reading based only on the successive recognition of separate words; so the matter of the role of 'expectancy' becomes of great importance to practising teachers. The issues are extremely complex, and call for analysis far beyond the scope of this chapter. A detailed examination of them can be found in Adams (1990). Later in this chapter I shall indicate what I see as a viable working position for teachers of beginners to adopt. The main point to be made here is that psycholinguistic theory, which 'top-down' views of reading have always claimed as their basis, emphasises the very feature of language that *makes* it largely unpredictable – namely its creativity and thus its constant novelty. Word forms are highly stable and constantly repeated. But the sentences people produce, though obeying certain rules, are nevertheless endlessly new. Goodman's theory is thus at odds with its own roots.

The work of Tyler and Marslen-Wilson has in recent years added greatly to our understanding of speech comprehension. They conclude (1982) that listeners do not guess, and that listening is not, and cannot be, top-down: that it is 'interactive with bottom-up priority'. Those conditions are necessary, they point out, in order to avoid 'hallucinating what we hear', and in order for there to be ultimate overall control by the 'signal' – the spoken words. Goodman (1967, p. 135), on the other hand, is prepared to accept that readers see 'partly what they expect to see'. According to such a view, reading would be neither like listening nor optimally efficient.

Smith's view of prediction

The index to the first edition of Smith's *Understanding Reading* does not list prediction nor any of the terms which Goodman interchanges with it. But Smith speaks (Ch. 10) of skilled readers as first identifying the 'deep structure' (i.e. the meaning) from 'features' and then using syntax to predict the 'surface structure' which is then 'confirmed'. This wording presents serious problems. The terms 'deep structure' and 'surface structure' are of course Chomsky's. But Chomsky invented them as names for elements in a transformational grammar, not for anything apprehended directly by the human mind. Lyons is very clear on this point:

Neither the earlier nor the later version of transformational grammar is presented by Chomsky as a psychological model of the way people construct and understand sentences. (Lyons, 1970, p. 85)

It seems clear, therefore, that the concepts cannot be adopted as the basis for a model of reading.

The dilemma in top-down theories

The notions reviewed here underpin the movement with which the use of 'real books' and an apprenticeship approach is associated. It is not difficult to see how they have been responsible for leading some teachers to believe that word recognition is not a crucial skill (see, for instance, Meek *et al.* 1983). But they lead to an inescapable dilemma. If reading *is* like spoken language, and thus 'natural', then it is ultimately not top-down, is not based on prediction and sampling, and involves efficient word recognition. If it is top-down, then it is not like listening, in which case the claim about natural learning is untenable, and beliefs about the true nature of the process and how it should be taught must rest on other foundations.

It is strange that a reading methodology erected on such shaky ground should have wielded so much influence. The reasons take us far beyond reading itself, into the philosophical world of Rousseau's *Emile*, of Froebel's 'kindergarten', of the whole progressive movement in primary education. Its appeal lies perhaps in its promise of a kind of liberation. Yet the last thing we want now is a violent swing to a traditional extreme where the place of language skills is ignored.

The alternative view

Is there a middle way? Is there a view of the relationship of spoken to written language which will draw on valuable new linguistic insights yet keep hold also on a realistic awareness of things that set the two modes apart? I believe that there is; and the remainder of this chapter will give some indications of how it might look.

The account starts, in a sense, from the same insights as the views which it seeks to replace. We know that, by the age of around five, children have acquired not just a stock of word meanings but the basic grammar of their native language certain rules about word order, the way sentences are composed of a subject and a predicate, the use of pronouns and prepositions, and so on. They have also discovered a great deal about what oral language is for. They have not of course thought about this knowledge and cannot speak about it. It is implicit. But they operate with it, using it to create, and to understand, endless numbers of new utterances.

As we saw earlier, they are not called on, when they start to learn to read, to do all this learning over again. Instead, the beginnings of literacy must be seen as joining on to – linking up with – the learning that has preceded them. The knowledge already in place must be given the best possible chance to transfer from language-by-ear to language-by-eye. It must play an active role in making sense of the new form which the 'signals' are taking. It must be used to lighten, as far as possible, the cognitive load that the new modality is bound to entail.

Some of the reasons for these fresh cognitive demands have already been mentioned. But a further reason has recently come to light. It has to do with the exceptional sensitivity of children, from birth, to the sounds of human speech. The most recent research has actually shown that babies can distinguish between two versions of a story – one read aloud by their mothers before they were born, the other slightly altered (DeCasper and Spence, 1986). No comparable sensitivity exists to the shapes of human writing systems. Learning these has to be altogether more conscious and aware.

Conceptual links

The linking of spoken to written language through teaching and learning has two aspects – one conceptual, one more purely linguistic. The conceptual links are those that help children to understand that language can *take a new form*, and to see, gradually, that those visual forms have their own purposes. Conceptual links help children to move from fully 'embedded' language (to use Margaret Donaldson's term) to the relatively 'disembedded' language found on the pages of books. Those links also help children to understand the nature of an alphabetic writing system. The aim is to achieve what John Downing (1979) called 'cognitive clarity'.

Among the many experiences that can foster cognitive clarity three are of special importance: becoming aware of print in the environment – at home, in school, in the street; being shown everyday uses of writing as a means of personal communication; and seeing the use of print on television. All these experiences show written language in situations where purpose is evident: the language is thus to some extent still embedded – a half-way house between speech and text on the page of a book. Sharing books with adults can help too, though here the purpose of the rows of black marks may be less apparent, for adults can tell a story when no book is present. The way the sharing is done will influence crucially the help it affords.

Children also profit by being encouraged to 'dictate' before they can write, discovering that what they say can be given an enduring form which others can read. The well established 'language-experience' approaches have thus a sound theoretical base.

Linguistic links

Experiences of a different but equally important kind can be afforded by children's early encounters with language on the pages of books. Text can be composed so as to give children the best chance to use links with their spoken language, not just in vocabulary but, more importantly, in sentence structure and idiom. The child's implicit knowledge of syntax and sense can be called into play and allowed to function rather than being frustrated and defeated by language that has not been written with beginning readers in mind. Given familiar words and predictable natural syntax, children can quickly be given the chance to start gaining meaning of a simple but specific kind from the printed page – to work out what written phrases and sentences actually *say*.

The fact that young children do transfer their implicit knowledge of syntax and sense to the reading task was demonstrated in a series of studies of early errors which became widely recognised as being of far reaching importance (Clay, 1969; Weber, 1970; Biemiller, 1970). These studies added empirical support to the belief that such transfer was possible, and indeed showed the power of the syntactic component. Children could produce errors which, though inappropriate in sense, were nevertheless an appropriate follow-on to the preceding syntax. Goodman also, of course, makes use of evidence of this kind. But there is no basis for concluding, as he does, that the processes which lead to error also underlie reading which is error-free.

Evidence of another kind had previously been obtained from beginning readers in my own work (Reid, 1958). Using a common vocabulary in sentences of varying syntactic and idiomatic complexity I was able to show that the same word could be read correctly in a simple context but prove baffling in a harder one. It was obvious that sentence structure influenced word recognition through the child's perception of what did or did not make sense.

The use of familiar sentence patterns in early reading books must not, of course, be confused with use of the surface discourse features of *conversation*. Natural-sounding utterances written down, and thus stripped of all situational support, may not make easy sense. Rather, the principle is about avoiding both 'primerese' and 'book language', providing instead language that has a simple, flowing structure particularly in the more familiar registers of description and narrative. I do not agree with those who maintain that this cannot be done, or that if it is attempted the effect on young learners will be bad (cf. Smith, 1977).

The role of expectancy

The question as to what use children should be encouraged to make of their early 'predicting' tendencies now becomes a key issue. All language-based views agree that the tendencies are present, and they are certainly supportive at the earliest stages, before children understand the function of letters, and when attention to sense must be given every encouragement. But what is their subsequent role? We have seen that, for important reasons, precise prediction (or 'guessing') is not the basis of the reception and comprehension of spoken language. We have also seen that it cannot be the main basis of reading comprehension either. The very nature of language – its degree of *un*predictability – renders such a basis grossly inefficient. That is, readers cannot learn to make, consistently, 'guesses that are right the first time'. Also, as Gough (1981) points out, the words we can most easily anticipate are those we can most easily recognise anyway.

So we have a situation where constraint and redundancy fluctuate, being at certain points more or less total, at other points almost zero, with many gradations in between. Yet, as we read, an ongoing sense of how syntactic structure and meaning are building up is crucial. Developing readers, then, must learn to be sensitive to the *degree* of constraint – in syntax or meaning – that is present at any given point, while at the same time acquiring fast and effortless word recognition. Their reading must come to entail a constant interplay between different sources of information – a moment-to-moment switching of reliance of which they will finally be unaware. Above all, they must learn *not* to predict any more precisely than the possible options allow. They must be helped to attend to the words on the page and how these are organised rather than try to make the text fit some rigid expectation. As Clay (1972, p. 162) puts it, the visual must finally dominate.

Word recognition

On the way to efficient word recognition, children must deal with the alphabetic code. They must first understand its nature and its relationship to speech. Here too cognitive clarity must be striven for; and the view that is being stated here would certainly stress the need for some degree of planned teaching of decoding strategies, for the links with speech at this level are less accessible than those made through syntax. They can only make sense to a child who has understood what speech 'sounds' are and who has begun to be able to hear them in spoken words. The recent work of Bryant and his associates (reviewed by Bryant in Chapter 6) has added significantly to our knowledge in this area. They show very clearly that there are children to whom phonemic awareness does not come easily.

The detailed relationships of spelling patterns to speech sounds must also be presented in ways which make for cognitive clarity and which allow children to generalise in the most fruitful ways. They must be represented as they are, and not falsified by over-simplification. And they must never be presented out of context, for we are aiming all the time at integrated mastery of meaning and code.

From oral to silent reading

When we read aloud, the two language modes – spoken and written – operate together. The activity is in some ways odd, because we are 'producing' the words of someone else. It is a sort of translation, and the parallel to it, going in the opposite direction, is writing to dictation. But while this latter skill is relatively late in developing, the former is required of almost all beginners. Leaving aside the benefits to the teacher in being able to monitor what a child is doing, are there also benefits to the child?

There seem to be two. Firstly, for the beginning reader, the meaning of a word (lexical and grammatical) is totally bound up with its oral form. So, always provided that the sense is easy, uttering what the print 'says' is at the same time an assertion of what it means. The extension of meaning to the visual form is reinforced. But reading aloud also serves a valuable purpose in self-correction (Clay, 1972). The early reader may be alerted to error only through auditory feedback from his or her own reading. Later, Clay believes, trials of possible solutions are done 'in the head', and heard with the inner ear (cf. my own quoting (Reid, 1958) of a child as saying 'I sounded it in my mind').

However, children should also be encouraged at a fairly early stage to read brief portions of easier text silently, reporting afterwards what they think it 'says'. The insight provided will help to throw light for them on the mystery of adult silent reading, and help also to build yet another bridge to the growth of this essential skill in their own repertoire.

There is a large body of research showing how children's spoken language learning in the domain of syntax continues beyond the age of five. (See, for instance, Carol Chomsky, 1969; Bowerman, 1982.) At the same time, in their reading and writing, children must develop their understanding, and their use, of new forms that are appropriate to written language but not to everyday speech (see Donaldson and Reid, 1982). Here innate language-learning abilities may well play a part, but these must be augmented by a new kind of conscious attention to structure and meaning. More and more of the reading is silent, and is devoid not only of the clues present in conversational exchanges but eventually, especially in fiction, even of pictorial support.

Yet one important component of success at this level is now thought to be the ability to assign, with the inner ear, some of the prosodic features (the 'expression') that the words on the page imply but do not directly convey (Read and Schreiber, 1982). Thus even mature and skilled silent reading retains its connection with the spoken tongue to which the earliest learning was linked.

sense and sensibility: some thoughts on the teaching of literacy[*]

Margaret Donaldson

Introduction

The notion has recently gained some currency that reading scarcely needs to be taught at all. No one doubts that it has to be learned and no one doubts, I think, that skilled readers can give learners help. But beyond this point dispute begins. There is deep disagreement in current thinking about the kinds of 'help' that are desirable – the kinds that truly help. And some people have come to believe that what has traditionally been known as 'teaching' is seriously damaging in its effects.

Debates of this kind are apt to become passionate, which is not a bad thing in itself if the passion arises from deeply felt concern and is an outcome of the right kind of caring about the ways in which we educate our children. But we do the children – and the future of our society – no good unless we somehow combine this caring with level-headed reflection on the facts about children and literacy, so far as these are available to us. Sense is needed as well as sensibility.

As to the presentation of the arguments in cases like this where feelings run strong, I agree with Mary Midgeley (1985) that the goal to aim for should be 'the very careful avoidance of all cheap and simple ranting which might carry people away to accept one's views wholesale, but also the full scrupulous expression of attitudes and feelings which seem to one, after thought, to be called for by the subject matter'.

The minimal teaching movement

Those who propose radical alternatives to the systematic teaching of literacy do not speak with a single voice. To say this is in no way to make a criticism.

---

[*]This chapter has been taken from the booklet of the same name by Margaret Donaldson (1989), published in conjunction with the Reading and Language Information Centre, University of Reading.

Rather it is to recognise that different writers on the subject make different emphases and that any attempt to summarise the general case will fail to do justice to this legitimate diversity. However, I think there is at least one belief that all of them would share: the belief that children are highly active and efficient learners, competent inquirers, eager to understand.

This belief is one that I hold too. I have already argued the case for it (Donaldson, 1978). More and more evidence keeps coming to support the view that it is true of human beings from the earliest months of life. Children's minds are not at any stage – not ever – to be thought of as receptacles into which stuff called knowledge can be poured. Nor do children wait in a general way for us to prod them into learning. They wonder, they question, they try to make sense. And, not infrequently, when they direct their questions at us they push to the limit our ability to answer them, as every adult who has spoken much with children knows.

A striking example of this comes from a boy called Jamie who was three years eleven months old when the following conversation took place.

Jamie and an adult were in a lane beside a house in the country. A car was parked on a concrete base.

Jamie   Why is it on that metal thing?
Adult   It's not metal, it's concrete.
Jamie   Why is it on the concrete thing?
Adult   Well, when it rains the ground gets soft and muddy, doesn't it? (Jamie nods, bends down and scratches the dry earth.)
Adult   So the wheels would sink into the mud. But the concrete's hard, you see!
Jamie   (*excitedly*) But the concrete's soft in the mix. Why is it soft in the mix?

The adult, who had not thought of this, found it very hard to explain why earth gets soft and hard and soft again whereas concrete, once set, stays hard forever.

Jamie's father worked in the building trade so Jamie was familiar with concrete mixers. He was a bright little boy but there was nothing to suggest that he was exceptional. Preschool children often show that they think spontaneously in active, searching ways, just as he did, about the world around them.

It follows directly that certain kinds of teaching can be stultifying. This truth is of ancient origin, yet it bears repeating again and again, in case we should forget. Teaching is stultifying whenever it fails to respect the minds of the learners, whenever it discourages questioning, whenever it frustrates the desire to understand.

Disgust with teaching which has failed seriously in these ways often rises strongly in sensitive people. They are then tempted to take a further step, leading on to the conclusion that the less we teach the better. After all, if children are so good at learning, why not let them get on with it? Shouldn't we just be content to provide material facilities and such encouragement as seems appropriate from time to time? Shouldn't we in fact stop being teachers and become consultants?

These arguments are attractive, seductive even. But the step of answering 'yes' to them should be recognised for the very large and risky one that it is. Some teaching is damaging; but this certainly does not lead with any necessity to the conclusion that all teaching is damaging and that we can very well do without it. Also the fact that children are active, competent learners does not imply that there is no place for active, competent teaching.

Later I shall be making a positive case for such teaching in the specific field of literacy. First, however, I want to consider how the idea that teaching should be minimal is currently being applied in that same context.

This application generally takes the form of a proposal that we should give the children 'real books' and encourage them to 'learn to read by reading'. It takes also the more negative form of a generalised rejection of anything that can be called a 'reading scheme'. Indeed, in practice the term 'real books' is often quite negatively defined: a 'real book' seems to be one that does not form part of any set of books systematically planned with the primary aim of helping children to learn to read.

I say advisedly that the term has come to be so defined *in practice.* Of course some thoughtful writers on the subject have given more positive criteria. Margaret Meek, for instance, requires that '. . . the pictures help the reader to understand the story, that the story has a shape and the author a voice' (Meek, 1982, p. 66). She does not offer this as an explicit definition, but from the way she uses the term 'real books' further down the page we may reasonably conclude that she has been saying what she understands a 'real book' to be.

Meek's criteria are good ones by which to judge the quality of fiction for young children, whether that fiction forms part of a planned programme or not. The mistake is to replace careful consideration of quality by a general condemnation of reading schemes.

This mistake is serious, and when one stops to think, it is very strange. I recently told an educator from overseas that in parts of this country books were now being judged unacceptable for no other reason than that they were published as 'schemes', and he refused to believe me.

When 'real books' are placed in absolute contrast to all reading schemes, the implications are very far-reaching. What is then being said is that books written for the purpose of helping children to learn to read cannot help them. We are not being told that some – or even all – of the books that have been written for this purpose up to now have failed to achieve it. We are being told that all such books are necessarily bad because of this property of being 'not real'. The implication is that the entire attempt should be abandoned.

It is essential to recognise that the older traditional reading schemes had grave faults, some of which are perpetuated in the less enlightened modern ones. I shall have more to say later about the nature of these faults and the reasons for them (see pages 46–47). Briefly, these reasons lay in a poor understanding of how children think and learn. But I believe we have made good progress in this regard over recent decades; and to use the old failures as a basis for rejection is like using pre-Newtonian conceptions of the natural world as a reason for no longer trying to apply physics.[1]

If we decide that children are to be offered nothing systematically devised to help them, then the gates are closed against the use of any detailed knowledge that we may have, or might obtain, about the processes by which children do in fact become literate. We are not to concern ourselves with how this is done – not at least with the aim of applying anything that we already know or might ever come to know about, say, specific difficulties that children are likely to encounter when tackling certain kinds of text. The systematic help that might derive from such knowledge is deliberately to be withheld.

Put like this, it is a curious conclusion, but I do not think I state it too strongly. The rejection of *all* published reading programmes, however good the insights on which they are based, however enlightened their guiding principles, however good the stories they contain, has just this implication.

Those who urge such a blanket rejection have certainly no desire to refuse children help. I do not doubt the sincerity of their conviction that 'real books – no schemes' will provide the best help possible. So how are we to make sense of their position? Another widely held belief is crucial to the understanding of it. This is the belief that the learning of written language is essentially the same kind of thing as the learning of spoken language.

Children, as we all know, learn to speak and to understand speech without depending on systematic instruction. They start to do this spontaneously within the first eighteen months of life, given that they are spoken to in ordinary, natural ways (which as a rule are not consciously planned). In these circumstances most children 'latch on' readily, and soon learn to make sense of the speech that is all around them.[2] So then, the argument goes, the same holds for written language. Away with schemes!

These views are made quite explicit in a paper by Goodman (1972). The paper is full of optimism about the future. It begins with the sentence:

> It is entirely possible that within the next decade virtually all children will be learning to read, easily and effectively.

All we can say, looking back, is that it may have been possible but it has certainly not happened.

Goodman thought that this achievement would follow not from better teaching but from less teaching. Universal literacy would come easily if only teachers would 'stop interfering with learners in the name of helping them'. And learners would be able to manage the task because 'reading is a language process, the direct counterpart of listening'.

Goodman offers some effective criticism of the older kinds of reading instruction that were based on inappropriate theories. He also makes some important positive emphases. But his enthusiasm for the new insights into children's power and creativity as first language learners (insights stemming from the work of Chomsky) leads him to conclusions that are seriously flawed.

The main weakness of Goodman's case lies in an over-emphasis on the similarities between speech and writing. It is true that both are 'language processes' but they are in many ways different, as Vygotsky (1962) saw clearly.[3] To my mind the notion that the differences can be ignored in educational practice is profoundly mistaken and dangerous. Much of my later argument will be concerned to explain why.

First, however, we have still to consider a further, related claim that is made by some advocates of minimal teaching in the field of literacy. It is this: *As one reads one need not attend to the words on the page.*

At this point we must go very carefully or we shall run into confusion. The sentence in italics is ambiguous. It could be taken to mean that the act of reading is not dependent on attention to individual words – that it is possible to 'get the meaning' directly, without having to be aware of the words that are its vehicle. On the other hand, the sentence could mean that attending to the words on the page is not an important thing ever to do – that it does not ever make our reading better.

On the first interpretation the sentence makes a claim (rightly or wrongly) as to fact. On the second interpretation it expresses a judgment about the value of reading in one particular way. If we confuse a factual claim with a value judgment we are in serious intellectual difficulty; yet it is all too easy to slide from one to the other without noticing what we are doing. And what can save us from this kind of sliding and slithering? Only close, thoughtful attention to the words on the page.

In the first – the factual – sense, the claim that we need not attend to individual words is well founded as it applies to skilled readers (though I very much doubt its truth when applied to beginners). Once we are sufficiently sophisticated and aware of ourselves as readers it is an option we have. We can read with more or less close attention to the words on the page before us. We can move along, when we judge this to be appropriate, making some kind of rapid sense. Or we can pause for thought, ask questions as to meanings, try to detect muddle and to avoid potential misunderstanding.

Interpreted in the second possible way, the sentence in italics would mean that the latter kind of reading is unimportant, something that we *need not* bother to cultivate, either in ourselves or in those we teach. It would mean that we should not place a high value on the ability to read reflectively, thinking about the words and their meanings, noticing how they function, how they interact; for it is impossible to give text close reflective scrutiny without attending to the words on the page. Notice that the devaluing of attention to words devalues poetry just as much as it endangers clarity of thought.[4]

Frank Smith (1978) tells us that reading without noticing the words is 'normal'.[5] This view is closely related to the notion that learning written language is much the same kind of process as learning spoken language. When children learn to interpret speech they do not for the most part consciously attend to the words they hear. This is well established. They do not concern themselves with word meanings, but rather with a perception of the total meaning of utterances in context. We may say that for young children, an utterance is *embedded* in its context, is never considered apart from its context.[6] And this embedding context includes, most importantly, what is seen as the purpose of the speaker. It is no exaggeration to say that children are concerned most of the time with what people mean, not with what words mean. Yet somehow – and this is a large part of what makes first language learning so remarkable and so intriguing – they learn enough about words at some level of consciousness to be able to put them together and express new meanings of their own.

So this is what children actually do as they learn spoken language. And at first they could do no other. It is the way human beings learn to speak. It does not follow that they can effectively learn to read in the same way.

I must now explain why I am convinced that literacy learning differs profoundly from the learning of the mother tongue.

The learning of spoken and written language

The name *mother tongue* is entirely appropriate, for language learning arises out of the earliest mutual enterprises of child and mother (or other adult in the mother's place). It arises spontaneously as interesting things occur that call for comment or action. It arises in connection with purposes, shared or conflicting; with social games; with the solving of problems where help is needed. It is combined with gesture in ways that McNeill (1987) has shown to be of fundamental importance. It has the most intimate connection with emotion – with laughter and tears, with teasing and comfort, with pleasure and anger. It is intensely immediate and personal.

In these early experiences mental life has a unified, a seamless, quality. 'Thoughts', 'language' and 'feelings' are integrally bound up with one another. And with them, too, are interwoven perception and purposive action. Young children talk at first about what they can see happening here and now, and what they are doing and feeling about it. There are extensions beyond the present into the very recent past and the very near future, extensions involving some consideration of what has just happened or what is just about to happen. But these reach at first only far enough to guarantee continuously evolving experience.

Gradually, of course, the range widens and children start to talk about things more remote in space and time. However, there is usually little of this until the third year of life is on its way, by which time a considerable linguistic competence has been established.[7]

Consider now what these facts imply for the claim that written language is learned in the same way as spoken language. If this claim were sound, then written language would also have to arise spontaneously in the course of other shared activities, with all the give and take and immediacy of speech. Reading and writing – both of them – would have to be used by adult *and by child* to communicate about ongoing events, to ask for or offer help, to question and to answer, to reproach, to amuse. They would have to be used for the spontaneous expression of human feelings – surprise, wonder, love, hate, relief, fear.

It is quite evident that they are not used in this way. But now a question at once arises: why not? Is there any intrinsic difference between spoken and written language that prevents it? A space travel fantasy may help to make the answer plain.

Let us imagine a planet inhabited by beings called Browfolk. The Browfolk are just like ourselves except that they have little windows set into their foreheads in which graphic symbols can appear, coming into view at one end and moving across to disappear at the other. Forehead symbols accompany most of the social activities of these beings, contributing greatly to the success of their cooperative endeavours. Also the symbols may appear in different colours, expressive of states of feeling. When one of the Browfolk is angry, the forehead symbols show up in fiery red. A soft blue expresses tender affection, a greyish brown expresses boredom and so on.

Sometimes a shutter closes over the window. But we are informed by returning space explorers that, behind the shutter, symbols are still regularly being produced for the private purposes of the individual concerned. Explorers also report that Browfolk children learn to produce and interpret the forehead symbols with precisely the same speed and ease as human children learn to manage the sounds of the mother tongue. They learn these symbols in the course of communicating about things that matter to them, things significant to them because of what they are seeing, feeling and doing at the time. Written symbols are, so to speak, their mother brow.

Human beings, however, do not have a mother brow. We do not use written symbols for the spontaneous expression of thoughts and emotions in our direct 'face-to-face' dealings with one another. So for us the learning of these symbols – how to produce them, how to make sense of them – is a profoundly different enterprise from the learning of speech. It is so because of our biological nature.

Links between spoken and written language

And yet we are odd creatures. Paradoxically, we have the kind of biology that sometimes lets us transcend our biology. We fly without wings, after all. So, in spite of the deep difference between spoken and written language, it is worth asking how close human literacy learning can come to the embedded learning of speech.

As Reid (1983) has pointed out, there are at least four means by which bridges, or links, can be established.

Shared reading

First, an adult and a child can look at a book together. To begin with, when the child is quite young, this is often mainly a way by which the range of knowledge of *spoken* language is extended. Some parents use books quite deliberately for this purpose. Olson (1984) suggests that such parents (who tend of course to be highly literate themselves) are actually teaching oral language 'somewhat systematically' to their children, drawing attention to the names of things and even sometimes to verbs or other parts of speech. He argues that in so doing these parents are using analytic methods taken over from the practice of teaching reading, and that they are encouraging the notion of language as something to talk about and think about, not merely to use unreflectingly. They are thus laying oral foundations for literacy. It is an important idea, to which I shall return later. But obviously early books are – and should be – used in other ways.

As children grow older they can move, within the same book-sharing context, from oral language learning to the start of reading. And to begin in this way brings advantages that have lately often been noted. These can be very significant. If all is well, the child will be sitting close to an adult with whom there is a warm, comforting, supportive relationship. This will be a pleasurable experience, there will be emotion in it. Also, as the adult reads aloud, the intonation of the voice will be used to express suspense, surprise, humour or whatever, as the story requires. This is good and helpful as a means of first encounter with those static marks on the page that must later be dealt with on their own. And it is a good informal introduction to story-telling language.

But of course not every child experiences reading shared with a friendly adult, or is likely to do so in any human culture close at hand. Further we must recognise that the advantages are diminished or can even turn into drawbacks when children are unwilling or adults unwise. Dunn (1987) found from her observation of two-year-olds that reading was often 'resorted to' by mothers when children were tired or fractious and that it was not usually 'an idyllic moment of rapport'. Similar findings are reported by Tizard and Hughes (1984) from work with four-year-olds.

The teaching of reading solely through the use of 'real books' has to involve some kind of sharing, even though the techniques of shared reading do not depend on the use of 'real books'. Thus the 'real books' movement relies on the hope that children can be given good experiences of shared reading on a regular basis in school (and of course ideally at home too). But real books have to be used by real teachers in real classrooms, where the class is likely to contain around thirty very real children. In these circumstances sustained one-to-one contact will often be hard to achieve.

So practical difficulties alone can make shared reading unsuitable as the sole way of helping beginners to learn. I do not, however, believe that it has no place in school. My thesis is that help towards literacy has to come from many sources, among which shared reading has its place. There will be times when one child can have the teacher's undivided attention. At other times the sharing can be not with a single child but with a small group, provided that multiple copies of the book can be obtained. Chosen stories can be made available on tape, so that a child can listen alone to the sound of familiar words while following the text. The help of adult volunteers or competent older children can be enlisted, and they can be given guidance on how best to handle the book-sharing. These activities now form a recognised part of the teaching of literacy in many schools.

Helping children to produce written language

The next way of bringing literacy learning closer to that of speech is the one most obviously concerned with transcending biological limitations. A big difference between speech and writing is that young children cannot produce written language easily, whereas they are well equipped with the ability to produce speech sounds. There is great merit, therefore, in the provision of a set of printed words for children to use in the construction of their own sentences.

Notice, however, that the use of words on cards to construct sentences is altogether different from the use of 'flash cards'. The practice of making children learn to read isolated words out of context dates back to old discredited associationist theories of reading and it is not a good idea. It is not a good idea because it neglects the importance of making sense. However, when children put word cards together to form sentences, making sense is precisely the aim. At the same time their awareness of language is raised in many valuable ways. They are helped to notice such features as word boundaries, word order, bound morphemes (-s, -ed, -ing, etc.) but all in the course of the expression of meaning (see the evaluation of *Breakthrough to Literacy* by Reid, 1974).

Use of print embedded in the environment

As we move on now to the third way of linking oral and written language, it will be helpful to notice that there are two distinct senses in which a word may be presented to a child in or out of 'context'. There is the sense of linguistic context which we have just been considering. However, there also exist non-linguistic contexts for language. We saw earlier the role that these play in speech, and we took stock of the fact that language on the page of a book has to manage without them (aside from the help given by illustrations). Yet there is one special circumstance in which written words, like spoken words, enjoy the support of a non-linguistic context. I refer to a form of writing that is all around us – above shop windows, inside supermarkets, on buses and bus-stops, on medicine bottles – and is often called public or ambient print. This has the merit that children see it everywhere. But it has the deeper merit of being closely related to the non-linguistic context in which it occurs. To put 'sugar' above the bags of salt or 'fire escape' above the door that leads to the linen cupboard is to invite comical or dangerous results. Assuming, however, that such errors are avoided, the setting supports understanding. Children can easily grasp the communicative purpose of printed signs, and the context helps them to get the meaning. In this respect public print – which I prefer to call 'embedded' print – is like the speech that children learn when language learning begins.

Intelligent use can be made of this fact in helping children at the very first steps of literacy learning. Many opportunities for using embedded print present themselves in the classroom where, for instance, labels and notices can be displayed. But the labels should be functional – they should serve a real communicative purpose that the children can recognise. It is good to put 'pencils' on a drawer or box containing pencils which are out of sight. It is not so good to attach a label to a chair saying 'chair'. To learn about embedded print is to learn that written language is a way in which people convey meaning to one another. This can be of particular help when one is working with children whose preschool experience of books is limited.

An interesting question now arises: if embedded print can be useful in school, could it also be used successfully with much younger children in the home? Could a child who is learning to speak – a child of two, say – be introduced to written language in an embedded form and start to learn to interpret it in parallel with speech? And would this stimulate later development towards full literacy?

A number of people who have tried this believe that it works. The method was proposed by Doman (1964) and greeted with scorn by most professional educators and academic psychologists. However, Ragnhild Söderbergh, a Swedish psycholinguist, having tried it on her own daughter and reviewed a number of other studies, is far from dismissive. She believes that a very young child may discover that written words correspond to spoken words and, like them, convey meaning. But for this to be possible '. . . a very close interaction with reading and writing people is necessary, an interaction that is meaningful to the child and where writing is adapted to the child's general cognitive and linguistic development' (Söderbergh, 1981, p. 207).

At first children who start to learn in this way tend to treat the written words as if they were the things they stand for. Thus Söderbergh's daughter, at age two-and-a-half, pushed the card for 'pram' around the floor. And another child put the card for 'Daddy' on top of the card bearing the name of a horse and said: 'Now Daddy is sitting on Dusty'.

Also at first – and not surprisingly – children seem to treat the words as ideographs. However, they gradually learn the alphabetic principle and become interested in grapheme-phoneme correspondences. That is, they start to inquire about phonics.

Söderbergh tells us that it is important to begin with the names of things that are very significant for the child: the child's own name, of course, and the names of pets, favourite toys or objects of special interest. Verbs and adjectives can follow; and 'emotionally coloured' words like *happy*, *sad* or *cry* tend to be easily learned. As with nouns, the word may scarcely be regarded as separate from what it means. Thus 'frightful' is considered frightening. This points to the profoundly embedded nature of the experience.

Söderbergh claims that, from this kind of beginning, very good later progress follows. But success clearly depends on the presence of a literate adult with a good understanding of the right guiding principles, with much patience and sensitivity and with lots of time to spare.

Use of the patterns of children's speech

The fourth way of narrowing the gap between written and spoken language is in some respects the most important of all. To appreciate its significance one must first recognise that, although writing is a means by which spoken words may be rendered visible and permanent, written language is not just 'speech written down'. Indeed, when speech *is* written down verbatim – as, for instance, when conference proceedings are transcribed from a tape recording – the resulting text makes very curious reading indeed.

The fact is that written language differs structurally from speech in a multitude of ways. There are many things which we write but would not be at all likely to say, at least in everyday informal talk. Consider, for example:

The prince, for that is who he was, took her hand.

Sue was not a girl to give up readily.

The ogre's eyes fell upon the floor.

Not all the Indians stayed upon the shore.

45

Second only to man, the great apes are the most intelligent of all animals.

Not one of these sentence forms would be regularly produced in the course of ordinary spontaneous conversation with children, or indeed in the speech of most adults to one another.

There exists, in effect, a rich and complex 'language of books'. Skilled adult readers are so used to it that they hardly notice the divergences from the spoken tongue, but it presents formidable problems for beginners because it confounds their expectations and frustrates their attempts at intelligent prediction. This is particularly true of children who do not come from highly literate homes; but the confusion and frustration are by no means confined to this group, large as it is. Novice readers from all kinds of background can be heard to stumble and falter – and often to groan in despair – when the text they are asked to read is not written in the kind of language they know, and consequently does not make sense to them.[8]

We know from many studies over the last thirty years that children bring their expectations to bear on their reading even in the very early stages (see, for instance, Clay, 1969; Weber, 1970). They try to structure and predict in highly reasonable ways, for they are reasonable beings who already know a great deal about spoken language and about the world around them. It is interesting, however, that when problems of mistaken prediction arise ('miscues' in Goodman's terminology), the children themselves are generally not conscious of the nature of the difficulties they are experiencing although they know very well that they are in trouble. Reid (1958) asked children of five to read aloud a number of sentences of which the following are examples:

(a) *I can see his face in the darkness.*

(b) *We went back to the deep mud.*

(c) *Darkness was upon the face of the deep.*

Sentences (a) and (b) were fairly easy, but (c) was very difficult. The children's own explanation was that (c) contained 'hard words' which they had not seen before – namely 'darkness', 'face' and 'deep'. They seemed to be unaware of having read the same words successfully a few seconds earlier. It is worth noting that the children in this study were attending a fee-paying school where the general standards of literacy were high.

The idea that 'hard words' are the sole source of reading difficulty is an old one, and not by any means confined to children. It used to be very widely believed that if you can read a word you can read it anywhere. In other words, linguistic context was ignored. Language structures were not thought of as important. We know better now – and Reid's study was a pioneering one on the way to our new knowledge. But we do not always apply this knowledge as well as we might. For example, as I mentioned earlier, children are still often asked to learn isolated words on cards, a practice to be deplored.

It used also to be believed that short, phonically 'regular' words were necessarily the easiest kind. One early reading scheme was based on this conviction with tragic/comic results. The first book was restricted to words containing no more than two letters.

You may ask: Is this possible? Never underestimate human ingenuity. Here are some examples:

I am on an ox. Is he on an ox? An ox is by me.

Other, less determined, writers of the early 'primers' settled for three-letter words, and we got cats on mats and sentences like 'See, see!' or 'Run, Bob, run!'.

Reading programmes that depended on these mistaken notions were, as I said earlier, very bad. They cannot be defended, except on the grounds that the truth was not obvious until the right kind of research had been done.[9]

The gross demerits of texts based on 'short easy word' theories have had much to do with the development of the stereotype of the 'reading scheme' and thus with the blanket rejection of all books written with the aim of making the beginner's task easier. But it is a very far cry from the early primers to books based on an understanding of the last of the four ways of narrowing the gap between learning to read and learning to speak. This fourth way, as will by now be evident, consists in providing text that comes close to the structural patterns of the children's speech.

I say 'comes close' because we are not, even here, dealing with speech written down. Children's actual speech, directly transcribed, would, like conference proceedings, contain features making it quite inappropriate for the printed page. There would be incomplete sentences, unexplained refer-ences to context, a lack of continuity and so on. Nor are we talking about text which contains a high proportion of conversation, even if this were edited to avoid the incoherence of actual speech. For it turns out that dialogue is at first hard to read.

The kind of text we need can be quite varied and flexible as to content, but the essential thing is that it should be based on knowledge of the kinds of grammatical structure which children commonly use and which they will therefore expect to find.

Text of this kind will give beginners the best chance of predicting intelligently, for it will enable them to use their pre-existing linguistic knowledge to the full. It will avoid, initially, those ways of expression that belong to 'the language of books' – ways which do not just use harder vocabulary but which turn sentences differently, use more complex ways of connecting ideas, shorten by deletion and obey a whole set of linguistic conventions that have to be learned. Some examples were given on pages 45–46.

Books that are free from such features yet avoid mistaken and stultifying notions of simplicity can give great support to early sense-making efforts. And as Meek (1982) says: 'The most important thing is the learner's belief that he can turn print into sense'.[10] Speaking of children who were reading the first few books in a modern programme of this kind, a wise and experienced teacher once said to me: 'It's amazing! The words just come tripping off their tongues'.

The first books in such a programme may not contain 'stories'. But they can contain language that is true to genuine and important uses of print – ways of captioning pictures, describing scenes and narrating events which do not violate accepted usage yet which stay within the grammatical constraints of children's speech. They will serve purposes that are different from the purposes of shared stories, but that complement them. If their content is relatively familiar then the children's minds are not pre-occupied with imaginative reconstruction (which is more demanding than is often recognised) and so are free to focus on sense-making of a simpler kind.

Once children have acquired some basic skill and ease at this level, the text can gradually incorporate features of book language which will enrich its resources and widen its scope.

Make no mistake, however – such books look simple but this does not make them easy to write. To be effective, they must be informed by a very good knowledge of language development. Margaret Meek likes to describe the best children's literature as 'crafted'. She is right, it is a good term. But a book of the kind we have been considering will have to be crafted too, in its own kind of way, if it is to be any good at all.

One piece of research which gave a major impetus to the study of reading book text and its relation to children's speech was a monograph by Strickland (1962). In her conclusions, Strickland emphasised the poverty and stiltedness of the old-fashioned texts by comparison with the variety found in her recordings of children's speech – a variety stemming in part from ways of combining statements by the use of connectives, especially 'and', 'but' and 'so'. The traditional use of short one-clause sentences in reading schemes often resulted in very poor cohesion, rhythm and flow. The improvement when these simple connectives are used can be very marked. But they have to be handled with discretion.

A subsequent study by Reid (1970), using some of Strickland's speech data, analysed four reading schemes which were then in common use in Britain. Focusing on the other aspect of the comparison Reid looked for structures that were common in the texts but absent from the speech samples. For example, the text might contain sentences beginning in ways that young children never use, such as: 'In the box he found . . .'. A further example concerns the handling of dialogue. As I mentioned earlier, dialogue in stories is difficult for early learners to read. First words in quoted utterances may be hard to predict. Questions may not be spotted for what they are. The switching of 'voices' can be confusing to follow. Matters are made worse when quoted speech comes before any information about who is speaking, and worse still if that information is given in the literary inverted form ('said so-and-so'). These structures do not occur in speech samples from children so they have to be learned from the printed page or from hearing stories read aloud.

One form of presentation of dialogue with a long tradition in comics and cartoons is the 'speech bubble'. This convention links the quoted words to the appropriate character in the illustration and can thus provide helpful support, especially if the quoted words are repeated in the text. What is very bad, on the other hand, is for the text to consist entirely of 'pseudo-dialogue'. This was a form much used in traditional primers, and was one of the features that laid them open to ridicule and parody (the 'Look, look, look' style of text). The same kind of thing occurs, unfortunately, in texts still in use today. One may find, scattered about on the page, words such as 'Help' which are clearly meant to be spoken by a character shown in the illustration but which are not attributed to that character in any way. The learner must therefore identify the words *before* trying to infer who uttered them. Surely this is to stand prediction on its head.

To summarise, then, the four gap-narrowers we have considered are: shared reading; devices which make it possible to produce sentences without forming letters by hand; embedded print; and the provision of books in which the language is based on the structures of children's own speech. These bridges, if they are used intelligently and sensitively, make good starting points on the way to becoming literate. Each has its own distinctive contribution, each can help. All four together can help greatly. But they are only starting points. What is to follow is a whole new kind of enterprise.

Literacy: the new enterprise

So far we have been thinking about the beginning of literacy and how this relates to what went before. We have been looking backwards to the competences that children bring to the learning task. We have been considering what is new in it for them, what is hard about it, how they can be helped to get begun.

I want now to change direction and emphasis. This will mean looking quite far ahead, while at the same time shifting the focus from problems to the long-term opportunities that literacy affords. These are evidently many; but I shall concentrate here on one kind – the kind that I think is most in danger of being obscured by current ideas about minimal teaching.

We have seen that language written down is thereby cut loose – or disembedded – from the context of ongoing activities and feelings in which speech functions and on which speech thrives. *Once on the page, language is on its own.* This gives it a degree of independence which makes it particularly apt for the development and the expression of certain kinds of thought. I have in mind thought that is about general topics with no immediate bearing on the personal life. For instance, how do birds find their way when they migrate? Or why does concrete set hard?

Human beings have in them an urge to understand. This urge carries them beyond their own immediate personal concerns towards the search for *general* understanding. It takes them in the direction of the search for truth.

The desire to understand, even in cases where understanding seems unlikely to bring any practical personal gain, certainly comes before literacy both in the history of the human species and in the history of individuals. Jamie was not literate when he eagerly wanted to know why concrete, unlike mud, is soft in the mix then stays hard forever (see page 36). But though the search for understanding does not come from literacy, literacy can greatly advance and further it. It does this in at least two ways.

The first and very obvious way is that it enables us to learn from other people whom we cannot personally know. Jamie tried to get understanding from a person who was with him but who could not help. If he had been fully literate he could have taken his question to a whole range of people otherwise inaccessible – those who have written books on 'materials science' or civil engineering. As it was, he was frustrated.

The second effect is on thinking itself – especially on the ability to sustain thought and to put thought in order. Jamie's command of spoken language enabled him to engage in a very interesting brief sequence of intelligent reflection. However, humanity has developed great *systems* of thought; and literacy is essential for anyone who is going to take any part, however, modest, in the systematic enterprise.

Engaging in this enterprise means trying to think clearly and rigorously and to hold to trains of argument. It means asking oneself questions about one's own thinking. Is there vagueness in it, or self-contradiction? Does it make the important distinctions? Is anything left out that should have been considered? In this attempt it is of the greatest help to be able to write one's thoughts down. It then becomes much easier to criticise them and re-order them in the effort after clarity and power.

What I am saying is that *the thinking itself draws great strength from literacy* whenever it is more than just a scrap of an idea, whenever there is a discussion to develop, whenever there are complex possibilities to consider. It is even more obvious that the sustained, orderly *communication* of this kind of thinking requires a considerable mastery of the written word.

The language of systematic thought

Let us now take an example of a topic that calls for thought going beyond personal experience. Consider the question of violence in modern society: Is it increasing and, if so, why? Someone who is writing about this may well have relevant first-hand knowledge. The topic may bear on her own life. There may have been some incidence of violence in her family. But what she must write – if she is to tackle the general question adequately – is not merely an account of these events. She must not just describe how Auntie Flo was mugged. She may use some of the knowledge thus gained, but she must reach beyond any personal involvement to general issues. She has first to question whether violence is indeed on the increase. If she decides it is, she must entertain hypotheses about causes. And so on.

In this sense, the thinking is impersonal. I do not mean that it is not about people or about things that matter to people. The example just given should make this clear. But it is not restricted to the thinker's own life-experiences. It goes beyond these in search of more general understanding.

There is at the moment a powerful movement in our schools the aim of which is to encourage children to write about their own experiences from a very personal point of view. It is good that they should do this. It is *not* good that they should do it exclusively. If all the prose they learn to write is narrative or descriptive then they are being deprived. They need to learn gradually, over the school years, how to participate in the impersonal modes of thinking and of linguistic expression that are such an important part of our cultural heritage.

We have seen that, compared with speech, *all* language on the page has a quality of detachment from the personal life. But the kind of written language we are now concerned with is also *more impersonal in the details of its form*. It entails the use of phrases like: 'It is possible that . . .' or 'The causes of this seem to lie . . .' or 'One reason is . . .' or 'What this means is . . .'.

The degree of this impersonality is to some extent a matter of style and it can be overdone. I reject (as my own writing – even this sentence – shows) the exaggeration which holds it improper to say 'I' or 'in my opinion' when writing on an impersonal theme. Nevertheless a repertoire of impersonal turns of phrase like the examples just given is a great help in the writing of such prose and indispensable for the reading of most of it. Language like this is a sub-class of the language of books. We may call it the language of systematic thought.

Those who cannot handle the language of systematic thought are at a gross disadvantage in every field of study from gardening to astronomy. Some striking examples are to be found in one of the core texts for GCSE history, *Conflict in Ireland* (McAleavy, 1987), prepared as part of the 'History 13–16' project by the School Curriculum Development Committee. Here, in a way that accords with current thinking on history teaching, original source

---

material is used alongside the author's text. Having been written originally for adults, this material makes no concessions to unsophisticated readers, as the following extracts will show.

> No one who has not been in Ireland during the past six weeks can possibly realise how passionate is the resentment which has been aroused by conscription. (p. 67)

> Since such benefits were not available in the south, the idea of a united Ireland as the only way to make things better began to weaken. (p. 75)

But even aside from such quotations the main text of the course calls for considerable reading maturity. In the following example, things that people demanded and thought are represented in impersonal, abstract terms:

> The call for a more 'Irish Ireland' led to the development of new political ideas. These questioned the need for any sort of link between Ireland and Britain. (p. 64)

The reader has to be able to understand that 'The call . . .' is another way of saying 'When people demanded . . .'; that '. . . led to . . . ideas' means 'people began to think differently about politics'; and that while 'These' in the second sentence refers grammatically to 'ideas' the questioning was in the minds of the political thinkers.

Again, here are two of the questions which pupils have to consider:

> How did these causes lead to the triumph of Sinn Fein? (p. 64)

> What impact has Ireland's conflict had on the wider world? (p. 86)

Once more the language is highly impersonal.

In many subjects that are studied in secondary school there are also special language problems connected with the precise definition of terms. Often these terms are ordinary words that have been given a particular meaning, like *wave*, or *work*, or *power*. Pupils studying physics have to detach the word 'wave' from everyday notions of (say) the seaside, and the word 'work' from all associations with 'a job'. The precise definition has to be attended to and learned, not just by rote but within the limits of its scientific context. In mathematics the notion of *'raising a number to a power'* must similarly be detached from everyday expressions like 'the power of the law'.

Is it then reasonable to suppose that the majority of children will be able just to 'pick up' the language of systematic thought, especially if their reading experience consists mainly of stories? I think not. The argument for giving well planned help with the learning of this kind of language throughout the later primary years and into the secondary school seems to me to be very strong.

A good example of sense and balance in regard to the teaching of English is to be found in the revised arrangements for the Scottish Standard Grade examinations (1987) (the equivalent of GCSE) where it is recognised that:

> Language skills do not simply mature in the fullness of time; their development requires conscious cultivation. (p. 4)

The document argues for explicit teaching of the main ways in which 'sentences are constructed and punctuated', 'devices of structure and style are used', 'spoken language differs from written forms', 'language is manipulated for different purposes'. Yet the aims are in no way narrow. To quote from the document again: '. . . they (the pupils) need experiences of language which will extend them intellectually, imaginatively, morally, emotionally'. I can only agree.

Laying the foundations of literacy

Now teachers of young children may feel inclined to say that all this has nothing to do with them – that the problems involved arise later and can be dealt with later. I can understand this attitude but I think it is mistaken, for it underestimates the importance of what happens in the early years. It does not sufficiently recognise the significance of *the way in which children are first taught to read*, and in particular whether this is such as to encourage them to be thoughtful about language right from the start and to look on it as a flexible system over which they can gradually extend their power. The ability to deal with sophisticated impersonal prose of the kind we have been considering does not leap up suddenly when needed like the genie from Aladdin's lamp. It is the outcome of years of sustained direction towards an ultimate goal. If primary teachers do not recognise this they are failing to see the scope and reach of their own importance.

Written language has been used for many purposes in different cultures since it was first invented. For instance, Shirley Brice Heath (1986) cites the Tuaregs of the Sahara as using it only for graffiti on desert rocks, for talismans and for brief love notes. She also makes the point that, within a given sub-culture in a modern western society, the generally accepted uses of literacy may not include those usually emphasised in school; and further that good initial teaching of children should not fail to take account of their community norms. This is true. We must recognise, therefore, that 'literacy' can quite properly be defined in a variety of ways. However for the purposes of the present discussion I think it is hard to improve on the definition proposed by Olson (1984).

Olson defines literate people as those for whom 'language is known as language'. Literate people are aware of language as an artefact – a structure composed of words and sentences which, as Olson puts it, is 'somewhat independent of the meaning intended by the speaker.' Such people are used to regarding language as an object that one can talk about, study, analyse.

In a metaphor which has become deservedly famous, Courtney Cazden

(1974) spoke of language as being either transparent or opaque. When it is transparent, as it typically is in ordinary use, we see meanings *through* it. But when we learn to make it opaque we can look *at* it and think *about* it. This is close to what Olson is saying. Literate people know how to make language opaque when it suits their purpose to do so. And they tend to encourage their children to do this while the children are still learning to speak, before reading has begun. That is, they talk to their children about words, not just with words, helping them to notice what is being said and what they themselves are saying. Olson argues – and I agree with him – that this kind of background experience stands children in very good stead when they make their first serious attempts to deal with the written word, for they already have some of the attitudes to language which are most appropriate and helpful.

It follows, of course, that such children are at a great advantage – as we know them to be in practice – by comparison with those from homes where literacy, in Olson's sense, is lacking. And the latter tend to be the least privileged among us in other respects as well. However, all children can benefit from positive help in learning to handle written language in ways fitting to its nature and to its scope as an instrument of thought. This help must be given bit by bit and with sensitivity in the early stages; but I believe that, with this proviso, the sooner it is begun the better. The teacher of reading can start quite early to encourage conscious, reflective ways of considering the written word. This may not be essential at first, though it can be very helpful even then, but it unobtrusively lays the foundations for much that is to follow.

Once the earliest stages are over and children are at ease with text that is fairly simply structured and does not present too many perplexities of wording, there comes a long period, extending through the primary years, when they must gain increasing mastery, as readers, of the language of books, including the language of systematic thought. They need now to enlarge their under-standing of the many ways in which words can be handled with skill on the printed page – handled to achieve economy, or elegance, or emphasis, or surprise, or cohesion between sentences, or logical clarity in a sustained argument, to name only a few of the aims that may concern an author.

In learning about the meanings which these novel ways of wording carry, and about the power they bring, children will also begin to make them their own – part of their repertoire as writers. And the chances of their doing this effectively will be greatly increased if they can develop the ability, as they read, to switch at will to a close examination of unfamiliar or puzzling sequences, while at the same time making their best hypothesis about what the meaning might be.

In trying to lay the foundations of literacy we should never underestimate the difficulty of the task we set children in the secondary schools. We require of them a kind of thinking that does not come spontaneously to the human mind. The urge towards it is there, but the possibility of its mature develop-ment depends on a long cultural heritage; and of this heritage the special literate ways of handling language form an essential part. Primary teachers have a crucial role to play in ensuring that the bases of this kind of competence with the written word are well established when a child crosses the secondary school threshold for the first time. If it is not done by then, it will very likely be too late.

Literacy and social power

The arguments in this section so far may seem to lack balance – and, indeed, as I have managed to state them so far, they do lack balance. But one cannot say everything at once. I used to have a teacher who, without reading further, seized on the first sentence of every essay and criticised it at great length for what it did not contain! I must now try to correct what would otherwise end up as a poor representation of my own views.

I do not hold that preparation for later schooling should be the only goal of the early school years. These have their own intrinsic claims, justifications and satisfactions. And I most certainly do not hold that the development of the intellect is the only, or even the main, long-term educational goal. Whitehead begins his book *The Aims of Education* with the famous sentence: 'Culture is activity of thought and receptiveness to beauty and humane feeling.' Even this first sentence does not say everything but it is a nutshell packed unusually tight. I believe that all of these are, indeed, attributes of the well-educated mind. However, I do not take Whitehead's order of mention as the true order of importance. We need not assume that he intended it so himself.

It may seem strange, then, that I have been placing so much emphasis on the intellectual, disembedded modes of thought. The explanation lies in the following argument.

Our kind of society needs these modes of thought, if for no other reason than that they underpin all our science and all our technology, giving us great practical power. It is power that we often abuse. For instance, it enables us to make bombs. Thus, though it serves good ends also, it is a highly dangerous power for us to have; and yet I see no realistic prospect that we shall willingly give it up. We might, just possibly, learn to use it more wisely, with greater restraint and foresight. That is the best that can be hoped for.

If the argument is accepted so far, then the next step is to consider who is to have this power. In my view, it is of extreme social importance that it should be widely spread. I certainly do not mean that we should all, or most of us, become scientists. But we should not feel overwhelmed by science and technology – not daunted or shut out. We should know ourselves *capable* of the kind of thinking in which scientists and engineers professionally engage. Otherwise their activities are apt to seem as mysterious as those of the high priestly caste in a primitive tribe.

And likewise we (as many of us as possible – and certainly many more than at present) should feel ourselves capable of thinking like a philosopher, or like a specialist in any intellectual discipline – literature, politics, economics, education – at least to the extent of reading an introductory book on the subject and reflecting seriously on the arguments it contains.

I do not suppose that most people would want to read such books as a habitual activity, or even at all. I am talking about feeling confident that one could. It is the conviction of inability that is damaging. This is the deep damage – or part of the deep damage – that results from what we call 'educational failure'.

Widespread literacy at this level is evidently remote. But I am sure that we could move closer to it – and equally that we could find ourselves moving much further away. In this connection, any set of beliefs or values is damaging that leads teachers to neglect the *study* of language.

On the other hand, it is a grave error to suppose that what happens in school is the only thing affecting the outcome. This is a tempting mistake for those outside the schools – for society at large – to make. It offers society an easy way out of responsibility, making it possible to blame failure if not on lazy or stupid children then on misguided or incompetent teachers. But the truth is that children will not study language – or anything else – effectively if, for example, they are short of sleep, or if they have come out without breakfast, or if they have been abused and frightened, or if they belong to a sub-group that is given little credit for intellectual potential. Those who try to teach such children are constantly reminded of this fact. The rest of us should constantly remind ourselves.

Methods and the individual child

I want now to guard against another misunderstanding, among the many that are always possible. When I argue for active, systematic teaching in the furtherance of literacy I am not arguing for regimented uniformity. Whatever we do, we should respect the individuality of the children we teach. Even if a way of teaching is good for the many, some may fail to thrive on it. When this becomes apparent, other ways should always be tried.

But notice that this is true no matter what method is being used. For instance, while most children enjoy stories rich in fantasy, some want fact because it interests them more. And some find fantasy terrifying. A famous example in this last category is the philosopher, Jeremy Bentham, who, by his own account, was an anxious child with an overly vivid imagination. Ghost stories, he tells us, were among the torments of his life. But even the story of Robinson Crusoe disturbed him, for he was not sure at first whether the Goat of the Cave might not be the devil. And fear of the devil made him quite unable to read *The Pilgrim's Progress*.[11]

Bentham's fears were extreme and seem to have been deliberately fed by the servants in his father's household. The fact that a few children are particularly vulnerable in this way does not mean that, as a general rule, we should offer only a bland story diet guaranteed never to provoke a shiver along the spine. I have a personal memory of reading John Bunyan's *The Holy War* at a fairly early age and of being intrigued rather than frightened by the story of how Diabolus and 'that mighty giant Beelzebub' laid siege to the city of Mansoul. I think the book was made specially memorable for me by two things. First, it was a beautiful old edition with illustrations that caught my imagination. And secondly, as I read it I had my first dawning awareness of the nature of allegory: I came to suspect that Mansoul was not just a name on a par with Manchester. This was an insight that made a deep impression and opened up before me a whole new range of possibilities. But another child might have found it quite unexciting.

Who is to say in advance what will make a reading experience memorable for a given human being? For I also remember the delight I felt when I first managed to read, by myself, the name of a local cinema in a newspaper advertisement. I would be hard put to it to rank these two very different reading experiences in any order of significance in my mental life.

We cannot legislate for such flashes of delight; but we can work systematically to provide conditions that favour them. However no teaching programme, even if well founded, should be followed slavishly. This is a principle of the utmost importance. A good teacher is always on the look-out for children with special attitudes and sensitivities and tries to respect these, as far as material and emotional resources allow.

Conclusion

Certain conclusions as to the development of the impersonal modes of thought seem inescapable: first that, if things are to improve, the foundations of intellectual competence should be laid early; second, that becoming literate in Olson's sense is one of these foundations; and third, that almost all children will become literate more easily and fully if they are given systematic help which is based on a good understanding of the nature of the enterprise but which never fails to respect them as individual learners.

However, this is not all that matters. Literacy learning has – should have – many strands. The 'bridging' experiences that I discussed earlier are of varying kinds, fulfilling different functions. Shared reading serves to capture the imagination, attune the ear and develop the sense of story. Embedded print fosters and clarifies important concepts about the communicative functions of written language. Materials which allow children to compose their first phrases and sentences without the need for pencil and paper open up a means of effective communication in written form. They focus attention on the role of individual words and bound morphemes, and on many basic features of sentence structure such as word order. They provide opportunities too for beginning to talk about language.

Then there is certainly a most important place for the reading of text which is very simple, but which is not stilted in its sentence forms and is linked to familiar and interesting themes. Its use gives a progressive sense of mastery over the new medium. It provides models for children's own written sentence production. It helps to lay the foundations of one of the main components of skilled reading, which is rapid and effortless word recognition. And it allows for an early introduction to easy non-fiction prose.

This blend of varied experience can continue right through the primary school, as shared reading gives way to independent reading of both fiction and non-fiction, and writing skills develop. While these processes go on, the children can also be encouraged to think about language, oral and written, and to extend their awareness of its structure. They can begin the sytematic study of the language of books, a study valuable in itself and crucial for the maturing of literacy in the fullest sense.

'Nothing too much' is the best guiding principle (though notice that this does not imply 'anything goes'). The different strands should combine in different ways at different times. Boundless enthusiasm for any one of them is unwise. The general conclusion has to be that the receiving of systematic help with literacy learning – involving the use of good reading or language programmes – does not preclude and should not obstruct the experience of reading good books of all kinds for the joy of it. These complement one another. In educational debate, for some curious reason which I do not fully understand, we are constantly being led to suppose that we must choose either a or b when we urgently need both – and can perfectly well have both.

There is, most fortunately, no incompatibility between developing a love of literature, with all the personal enrichment which that brings, and developing the ways of handling language that favour clear, sustained rational thought. These can – and should – develop side by side, through the school years.

---

1 A recent paper by Hynds (1988) provides an example – a rather extreme one – of how the inadequacy of earlier theorising is being used now to try to discredit all reading schemes. Hynds says: 'Thinking of the rats, well-intentioned educators . . . devised reading schemes'. The rats that he has in mind are those used in behavioural learning studies. He then goes on to give the impression that all reading schemes are based on behavioural concepts of the nature of learning.

This is just not true. It is not true now, and it was not true even when the influence of behaviourism was at its height. For instance, one reading scheme was written back in the 1950s by I. A. Richards, the distinguished literary critic and poet, and he was deeply opposed to behaviourism in any form. Unfortunately this scheme did not turn out to be one of Richards' most successful enterprises. Its guiding principles were logical rather than psychological.

I do not suppose that Hynds is guilty of deliberate distortion. I believe rather that his paper provides an example of the way passionate commitment can restrict what the mind admits as knowledge. It is a very general human problem. Think of the Holy Office and Galileo.

2 Research has established that most parents do speak to children in somewhat special ways, sometimes called 'motherese'. What is much less clear is the extent to which children are helped by various kinds of 'motherese' at various stages of development. The issues are highly complex and the evidence that would resolve them is not easy to obtain. (See Gleitman *et al.*, 1984.)

3 Goodman was certainly not alone. The times in which he wrote were heady ones for developmental psychologists and for educators influenced by them. What should have been more often recalled as a corrective was Vygotsky's work dating from the early 1930s (though not published in English until 1962). Vygotsky was in no doubt about the distinction between speech and writing (or what he called 'oral speech' and 'written speech'). As he put it: 'Written speech is a separate linguistic function differing from oral speech in both structure and mode of functioning' (Vygotsky, 1962).

4 It is worth remarking at this point how much emphasis is given to reflection on wording by the writers of the recent Kingman Report (DES, 1988). The Report talks of '. . . examining words and how each contributes to the meaning of a sentence' (p. 9). It argues over and over again for the raising and extending of children's awareness of how language is structured and how it functions (Ch. 2, passim). There is no doubt that the writers believe that children should learn to attend closely to what is on the page.

5 'Normal' is itself ambiguous. It can mean 'average' with no value judgment implied; or it can carry an implication of desirability, as is evident when one thinks of the connotations of 'abnormal'. Smith also uses the word 'need', not in the exact sentence that I have used for illustration but in the same kind of way, for example as follows:

> . . . we need be no more *aware* [his italics] of the words than we are of the paper [i.e. the paper they are printed on] if we are concerned with meaning.

6 Young children do sometimes seem to 'play' with words, as in pre-sleep monologues, but it is hard to be sure of the significance of this. What I have said about the role of context relates to the use of speech in interpersonal communication.

7 Earlier examples do occur. Dunn (1987) provides one from the speech of a child just twenty-one months old. At breakfast there had been a distressing battle over food. Later in the day the child started a conversation with his mother by referring to this event:

Child   Eat my Weetabix. Eat my Weetabix. Crying.
Mother Crying, weren't you? We had quite a battle. 'One more mouthful, Michael.' And what did you do? You spat it out!
Child   ('*cries*').

I believe it to be significant that this early backward reference expressed strong remembered feeling. Notice that it did not depend on an ability to use the past tense.

8 Söderbergh (op. cit.) makes the same point:

> When it comes to syntax *the difference between spoken and written language may be considerable, and a syntax that is too much deviant from that which the child uses in his spoken language may make the text impossible to read for him [sic].*

9 Some people, however, were in advance of their time in this respect, as is usually the case in the history of ideas. See, most notably, Huey (1908).

10 In fairness I must point out that Meek does not use this judgment to support the same conclusions as my own.

11 For an account of Bentham's fears and the effect of them on his later thinking see Ogden (1932).

reading

developing skilled reading

Jane Oakhill

Introduction

There has been a very large amount of research into children's reading – how they should be taught to read, how reading develops, differences between good and poor readers, and how to improve children's reading, to name but a few areas. However, the vast majority of this research has explored how children read (or fail to read) *words*. Far less work has been done on children's reading *comprehension* and how it might be improved. In this chapter I will discuss not only the development of children's ability to read words, but also the development of comprehension skills. The aim of the chapter is not to produce an overview of the psychological research into children's reading development but, rather, to survey some areas of research and theory from psychological work on reading development that are particularly relevant to teachers.

Models of reading development

Alphabetic systems of writing, such as that used for English, capitalise on the fact that speech is already associated with meaning. The alphabetic principle is the key to a *productive writing system*: an indefinitely large number of words can be produced from a small, reusable, set of letters. Once children have grasped the alphabetic principle, they will gain independence in reading, since they will be able to read words that they have never before seen in print. In particular, children need to learn the rules that relate written letters or groups of letters to sounds. These rules are called *grapheme-phoneme correspondence* rules (GPC rules) because they state the relation between small units of written language (graphemes) and small units of spoken language (phonemes). However, although alphabetic systems result in economies in the amount to be learned (unlike the Japanese Kanji system where each symbol represents a unit of meaning and has to be learned as a visual pattern), they can also be a source of confusion for beginning readers.

In English, in particular, GPCs are by no means regular, and there is often no one-to-one correspondence between letters and sounds. In addition, young children may find it very difficult both to conceptualise and to identify phonemes for reasons which we will discuss below.

Because of these difficulties in perceiving and conceptualising phonemes, most children begin to learn to read words as visual patterns, often recognising their own name or common logos like *Lego* and *Coca-Cola*. In recognising these first words, they often rely on salient features: the first letter, the overall shape for instance, but this strategy soon proves unreliable as the number of words they try to recognise increases. Learning every single word as a separate visual pattern would put an enormous burden on memory (the Japanese need until early adulthood to develop a reasonable working knowledge of Kanji characters). So, it makes sense to start learning letter-sound correspondences so that new words can be deciphered. Learning such correspondences will also be the key to independent reading. This progression from recognising words as visual patterns to a more analytic approach has been captured in stage models of reading. There are several different stage models, which differ in their finer details, but have the same overall approach. For instance, Frith (1985) proposed three stages of development, each of which builds upon the previous one. In the first, 'logographic' stage, the child treats words as logographs, recognising them as visual patterns, very much as Japanese readers recognise Kanji characters. In this way, the child is only able to recognise a few familiar words by using salient features, such as first letter or word length. Thus, if they recognise the word 'daddy', they may claim that any other word beginning with 'd' also say daddy. At this stage, the child has no means of deciphering new words. In the second, 'alphabetic', stage the child begins to learn letter-sound correspondences, and thus acquires the ability to decode unfamiliar words and pronounceable non-words. In the final, 'orthographic', stage, the child learns the conventions of the English orthography, and can identify words by making use of larger orthographic units and analogies between such units, without the need for grapheme-to-phoneme conversion. This is the stage at which skilled adult readers operate although, of course, they can fall back on earlier strategies if necessary (for instance, using GPCs to decipher words that may be in their spoken, but not in their reading, vocabularies). The existence of such stages has been supported by evidence from research. Initially, children often confuse words that they can read with other words beginning with the same letter, or which are similar in length or some other salient feature. By around seven or eight there is evidence that children are capable of beginning to use GPC rules. They are more accurate in reading words with regular grapheme-to-phoneme mappings than irregular ones (a visual, or salient feature method of identification would predict no such difference). By about nine to ten years, children tend to be more flexible. They are equally accurate on regular and irregular words, indicating a decrease in reliance on spelling-to-sound rules, and make extensive use of orthographic cues and analogies as well as graphemic information.

Phonological awareness and reading

In order to apply GPC rules, the child has to be able to break words into their component parts (segmentation), determine the corresponding sounds, and blend these together to produce a pronunciation for the word as a whole. However, the use of these rules demands at least an implicit knowledge of the phonemic system of the language, and this poses a number of problems for young children. We have already considered a general difficulty above: the GPC rules for English are complex, and there are a number of irregular words. In this section, we will discuss further difficulties. Before they can apply an analytic strategy to word decoding, children must become aware of the phonemic segments into which words can be divided. However, experiments with young children have shown that they find the segmentation of words into phonemes almost impossible, even though they are perfectly able to *perceive* differences at the level of phonemes (i.e. they know that words that differ by one phoneme, such as *cat*, *rat* and *bat*, do not sound the same, and have different meanings). Children of around five or six have great difficulty with tasks that require them to make fairly subtle phonemic distinctions between words, such as deciding whether two words begin with the same sound, or rhyme (for further details, see Chapter 6). Pre-reading success on these tasks predicts later reading ability. Young children also perform poorly when asked to say what remains when a particular sound is removed from a word (e.g. /p/ removed from 'pill'). Children with a mental age below seven years are unable to do the task. Again, performance on this task has been shown to correlate with early reading ability. Even such young children are much better at segmenting words into syllables, and putting syllables together to form words. For instance, they can do a task that requires them to say 'cowboy' without 'boy': in one experiment, about 80 per cent of five-year-olds could delete one syllable from two-syllable words. These data show clearly that young children have difficulty in making explicit the phonemic distinctions necessary for some approaches to reading.

Young children's difficulty in this area is probably related to the fact that phonemes, unlike syllables, do not have acoustic boundaries separating them in speech, and the concept of a phoneme is, consequently, a very abstract one. Phonemes overlap in speech because of a phenomenon known as *coarticulation*. The way the parts of the mouth move means that, for example, the articulation of /b/ will depend on the following vowel – how a phoneme sounds is dependent on context, particularly the vowels that precede or follow it. The first part of *bat* is pronounced differently from that of *but* because the very first bit of the word contains information about the vowel as well as about the /b/. Thus, when a word is broken into its constituent sounds, and these are said individually – for example, *cat* into /k/, /a/ and /t/ – only approximations to the underlying phonemes can be derived. No matter how fast the consecutive sounds are spoken, they will not blend together to form *cat* unless they are distorted. So, strictly speaking, it is misleading to teach a child that the letter '*p*' corresponds to the sound /p/, because the sound cannot be said! However, although it is important to be aware of the potential problems, Adams (1990) argues that the advantages of encouraging children to articulate the 'sounds that letters make' will outweigh the disadvantages.

It must always be borne in mind that, although correlations have been found between performance on various tasks that measure phonemic awareness, and subsequent reading ability, there is not necessarily any causal link between the two: the data do not show, for instance, that high ability on a phoneme-deletion task results in a child becoming a good reader – there may be some third factor (general intelligence or an interest in verbal materials, for instance) that accounts for ability in both, and perhaps also performance on a variety of other tasks that may also correlate with reading, but to which one would not necessarily wish to impute any causal role.

There are data from a variety of sources that address the question of whether there is a causal link between phonemic awareness skills and reading. Chapter 6 surveys this research, so it will only be mentioned relatively briefly here. In an important study, Bradley and Bryant (1978) compared ten-year-old backward readers not only with normal readers of the same age, but with much younger normal readers (six-year-olds) who had the same reading age as the backward readers. They required the children to pick the odd one out in sequences of four spoken words (either on the basis of alliteration, or of rhyme), and to produce words that rhymed with other words that were read out to them. The ten-year-old normal readers performed best, but the important finding was that the backward ten-year-olds were poorer on these tasks than even the younger normal readers who had, presumably, had far less experience of written language. Thus these results support the idea that the phonemic skills that Bradley and Bryant's tests measured are causally implicated in reading ability, and do not just arise as a by-product of the development of reading ability and familiarity with written material. In a later longitudinal study, Bradley and Bryant (1983) provided further support for their causal hypothesis. They showed that performance on the odd-one-out task at age four or five was a good predictor of reading achievement, but not of mathematical ability, three years later. But it is possible that there is a relation in the opposite direction – learning to read might improve phonemic awareness. Other work (Ellis and Large, 1988) suggests that this is so – learning to read improves sensitivity to the sound properties of spoken words, particularly after the initial stages of learning to read. Ellis and Large's study showed that the relation between reading and phonemic skills changes over the first few years of schooling. They tested a variety of phonemic skills: syllable- and phoneme-segmentation, and rhyming and blending tasks. In a longitudinal study, they found that the phonemic skills of those children who were non-readers at age five predicted their reading ability at age six. However, once reading begins to develop, it seems to foster the development of phonemic skills. For those children who had begun to read, reading skill at age five, and again at six, predicted phonemic skills one year later. Ellis has suggested that when children begin to read, this 'makes sense of' sound skills and fosters their development. Research with adults also suggests that learning to read using an alphabetic system fosters the development of phonemic awareness. Chinese adults who were fluent readers, but only in a logographic script, did poorly on phonemic segmentation tasks by comparison with those who could read an alphabetic script. Similar results have been found when illiterate and ex-illiterate adults are compared on segmental analysis tasks (Morais *et al.*, 1979). The finding that illiterates performed poorly on such tasks suggests that learning to read can have a causal role in the development of phonemic awareness. A reasonable conclusion might be that some aspects of phonological awareness (such as awareness of onset and rime, see below) can precede reading and can be helpful in the beginning stages of learning to read, whereas others are fostered by learning to read (see Chapter 6). However, whatever the precise relationship between such skills and reading, it is clear that young children should find approaches to teaching reading that demand explicit phonemic awareness very difficult.

There is an apparent paradox here. On the one hand, considerable evidence now exists to show that a phonics approach to teaching reading produces the most rapid advances in early reading ability (see Johnson and Baumann, 1984 for a review). In addition, a recent report by HMI found: '. . . a clear link between higher standards and systematic phonics teaching. Phonic skills invariably formed a part of the repertoire of those children who showed early success in reading' (DES, 1991a). On the other hand, the evidence outlined above suggests that beginning readers will have considerable difficulties with such an approach because phonemic analysis is so difficult for them. However, phonics approaches do not necessarily have to use segmentation and blending, at least in the initial stages. As Goswami and Bryant (1990) point out, there are speech units other than the phoneme. Onset and rime (respectively, the initial consonant or consonant cluster, and the end of the word, e.g. b-eak, str-ing) are more comprehensible to young children. Goswami and Bryant present convincing evidence to show that this type of connection between phonemic units and strings of letters plays an important role in children's reading. Even beginning readers can make analogies based on rime to help them read unknown words. For instance, if five-year-olds are told what *beak* says, they are able to read *weak* by analogy. Goswami and Bryant stress the importance of children's knowledge of rhyme in their beginning reading skills:

> 'They become adept at recognising when words have common rimes or common onsets. So they form categories of words and when they begin to read they soon recognise that words in the same categories often have spelling patterns in common and that this spelling sequence represents the common sound. As soon as they realise this, they can make inferences about new words, and they do' (p. 147).

On the basis of this evidence, Goswami and Bryant argue against discrete stages in reading development, and suggest, rather, that children just gradually get better at using strategies they use at the beginning stages of reading. Perhaps phonics instruction works well for beginning readers not because it teaches them GPC rules in the first instance, but because it fosters their awareness of other units of speech and the way in which these can be mapped onto written words.

Reading development and the use of context

The role that context plays in skilled reading and in learning to read has been much debated in theories about how reading should be taught (see Chapter 2). However, before we can address the question as to whether increasing reading skill is reflected in increasing proficiency in using context, we need to distinguish between different ways of using context. First, context can be used to prevent or correct errors in reading – seeing whether a first guess at a word 'fits in' with the text. Second, context might be used to facilitate word recognition itself. In general, the evidence from research shows that older and more skilled readers are better able to use context to make predictions (e.g. guessing what the next word in a text might be) but make *less use* of context to help them recognise words. Frank Smith (e.g. 1973, 1988) argues that, since adults can derive the meanings of words *directly*, without recourse to phonological recoding, there is no reason why children should be taught this 'unnatural' method, and that it may even be harmful. Others (e.g. Mitchell, 1982; Adams, 1990; Reid, Chapter 2 of this book) have pointed out the errors in Smith's writings – many of his theoretical ideas are misguided or just plain wrong. For instance, there is no evidence that learning to read draws on an innate ability in the way that learning to speak does, and substantial evidence that it does not. Here, we will focus on his views on the role of contextual information in reading. Skilled readers pay far more attention to individual words and letters than Smith suggests, and do not rely on context to help with word recognition in the course of normal reading – they don't need to. Smith has argued that children will learn to read by themselves if exposed to enough meaningful and interesting language that will allow their natural hypothesis-testing talents to operate and that, like skilled readers, they should determine the meanings of new words from context, not by using rules to decode them. In fact, all the evidence from studies of word recognition show exactly the opposite pattern – the word recognition ability of skilled readers is so fast and automatic that preceding a word with a portion of relevant context does not help, and neither are they slowed down when the word to be recognised is preceded by an incongruous context ('the dog ran after the CAT' vs. 'the girl sat on the CAT'). However, the younger the subjects, the more affected they were by context; their ability to recognise words was speeded by a congruous and slowed by an incongruous context. Stanovich (1980) has argued that the contextual and perceptual ('top-down' and 'bottom-up') information in reading work together (interact), and that the primary use of context in poorer readers is to compensate for the fact that they cannot recognise words from the perceptual properties alone. Thus, context can provide hints about a word's identity to poorer readers, but better ones don't need to use context – it is quicker and more efficient to recognise words from the graphemic information on the page, without going into time-consuming guessing and hypothesis-testing procedures. West *et al.* (1983) extended this finding to meaningful stories – they used contexts taken from children's books. Again, it was the younger, less skilled readers who showed the larger effects of context.

Finally (even if Smith's view of how adults read were correct) there is no reason to believe that the best way to teach children to read is to train them in the skills used by adults. As we saw above, developing reading ability seems to progress through a series of stages that reflect children's developing cognitive abilities: they cannot learn to use GPC rules until they have some phonemic awareness, and it is not for some years that they will come to develop the flexible use of graphemic and orthographic skills and analogies available to the skilled adult reader. Reading cannot simply be some sort of sophisticated guessing game. Although some children just seem to work out the alphabetic principle for themselves (see Margaret Clark's book, 1976, about children who learned to read before going to school, many self-taught) most do not. This is not to say that the ability to predict likely words from context, and the use of context to monitor the suitability of candidate words is unimportant: it is simply not enough. As Adams (1991) puts it: '. . . skilful readers are able to concentrate on meaning only because they have learned to process the words and their spellings very quickly and nearly effortlessly. But such automaticity grows from a history of having read words – not from skipping, ignoring, or guessing at them'.

Comprehension skills

It is usually, but not always, the case that once children have learnt to decode words reasonably efficiently, comprehension will follow automatically. As children learning to read have been using and understanding their native language in its spoken form for some years, one would expect the skills they have learnt to transfer to understanding language in its written form. However, although reading comprehension ability correlates highly with word recognition skill, a small but substantial minority of children have a specific comprehension problem. In some cases children who have reading comprehension problems also have listening comprehension problems. In other cases, children may have comprehension problems that are specific to reading. In this section, both of these possibilities will be discussed.

One important point is that writing is not simply speech written down. The 'language of books' is a particular register that children may not be familiar with unless they have had many books read to them in their early years. If children are to learn to read with understanding, they need to be initiated into book language. In addition, written language does not have all the supporting cues (stress, intonation, gestures and facial expressions) that accompany spoken interactions.

A second problem that is specific to *reading* comprehension is that children may be so preoccupied with word decoding that they may not have the cognitive capacity to carry out comprehension processes at the same time. In addition, the rapid loss of information from short-term memory makes it difficult for very slow readers to 'hold' information from early on in a sentence so that they can relate it to what comes later and understand the sentence as a whole. Since decoding skills will improve with practice, children will be able to devote more attention to comprehension as they become more skilled. However, beginning readers may think that the point of reading is to 'get the words right', and may not connect this activity with deriving meaning from a text, as happens when stories are read to them. Until children's word recognition skills are relatively fast and automatic, they may not be able to give sufficient attention to comprehension. Once again, the importance of efficient decoding skills needs to be emphasised. Obviously, comprehension is important too, and the two skills – word recognition and comprehension – should be developed in tandem.

In other areas, there is likely to be some overlap between the understanding of written and spoken language (of course, some of the common processes may be more difficult to carry out in the case of written text, for the reasons given above). Understanding a text (whether written or spoken) results in a mental representation of the state of affairs that the text describes – a *mental model*. Even after the individual words have been identified and grouped into clauses and sentences, a number of other skills will also be necessary to construct such models. The meanings of the individual sentences and paragraphs must be integrated with others. Inferential skills will be needed to go beyond what is explicitly stated in the text: a text that required no inferences to make sense of it would be long and tedious in the extreme, and authors necessarily leave some of the links between parts of a text implicit. Second, proper under-standing of the text depends on an understanding of the main point, and on sensitivity to the relative importance of other information in the text. Third, readers need to monitor their own comprehension; to be aware of whether or not they have adequately understood a portion of text and to know how to remedy any breakdowns in comprehension.

Inference making

Inferences are important for comprehension in many different ways (for a review, see Oakhill and Garnham, 1988, Ch. 2). In particular, inferences are crucial to the process of connecting up the ideas in a text to build a coherent representation of the whole. The emerging mental model of the text can be used to guide such inferences – it should indicate where the gaps are, and which of the myriad of possible inferences need to be made. There have been numerous studies of children's developing ability to make inferences. In general, these studies show that younger children have the ability to make the same sorts of inferences as older ones (once differences in world knowledge are taken into account), but that the younger ones tend not to make inferences spontaneously, and only exhibit their ability when prompted or questioned explicitly.

Understanding text structure

The information in a text is usually arranged in a hierarchical structure. The text is focused around one or more main ideas, with subsidiary ideas and trivial details subordinated to the main ones. Children's ability to pick out the main point of a text, and to judge the relative importance of different aspects of the text, increases markedly during the primary school years. But even by age twelve, children are only able to distinguish explicitly between the highest and lowest levels of information (and not between intermediate levels). By contrast, children's recall of text is sensitive to level of importance from a very young age. Even five-year-olds are more likely to recall more of the important events in a text than the trivial details. The discrepancy between awareness of levels of importance and the influence of importance on recall may be related to children's developing metalinguistic skills (see below). Although children cannot explicitly identify which are the more important ideas in a text, they still pay more attention to those ideas.

Another important component of understanding text structure is seeing how the ideas in a text are related, and one way to assess children's understanding of the logical structure of texts is to ask them to tell stories themselves. Such reseach has shown that children's ability to produce coherent narratives develops gradually but that, like adults, they have certain expectations about the sorts of information that should be present in stories from a very young age. The ability to understand how ideas in a story are related probably develops even before children learn to read providing, of course, that they been read to extensively.

Metalinguistic skills

Comprehension processes are more dependent than word recognition on meta-level knowledge (knowledge about knowledge). An important meta-linguistic skill in comprehension is the ability to monitor one's understanding. In general, younger readers are less likely to realise that they do not understand a portion of text, or to know what to do about it even if they do realise (for a review, see Garner, 1987). They are, for example, unable to detect that crucial information is missing from text, or to spot even gross inconsistencies. However, the direction of the link between comprehension ability and metalinguistic skills is not clear. It may be that the process of learning to read increases children's language awareness, rather than the other way around.

Why are some children good 'readers' but poor comprehenders?

Our own work (for a review see Yuill and Oakhill, 1991) has shown that children who have a specific comprehension problem (i.e. those whose comprehension is poor in relation to their word recognition ability and chronological age) differ from good comprehenders in their ability to make inferences and integrate information from different parts of a text). They could be characterised as fairly literal readers – they seem to process the text sentence by sentence, and tend not to derive the gist of the whole, or go beyond the literal meaning. Such children do *not* have general memory problems, although they do have deficient working memory capacity (the sort of memory that is used in doing, say, complex mental arithmetic, where simultaneous demands are made on both processing and storage capacity). Since working memory is important in making inferences and in the construction of a meaning representation from a text, it is not surprising that poor comprehenders are deficient in these text comprehension skills. Other text-level skills differentiate between good and poor comprehenders. Poor comprehenders, like younger children, do not have a clear awareness of what comprehension is and when it has been successful – they often fail to realise that they have not understood a text properly. There is evidence that their problems arise, at least in part, because they fail to make use of comprehension monitoring strategies (see Garner, 1987). Again, working memory may play a part in such processing and readers with deficient working memories may have little scope for the sorts of processes required to monitor comprehension. In general, we have found that children who are poor at understanding written text are also poor at listening comprehension, and even at understanding and narrating the main point of picture sequences.

Conclusions

As I argued at the beginning of this chapter, the key to reading is learning the alphabetic principle of our writing system. To do this, children need to learn about the correspondences that hold between spoken words and written symbols. Unfortunately the majority of children *don't* just 'pick up' the rules of written language. They need explicit and persistent help if they are to crack the code which, in an alphabetic system, relates letters or small groups of letters to the sounds of spoken language. Furthermore, early and systematic training in phonics benefits not only children's word recognition, which is only to be expected, but also their comprehension (Chall, 1979). I am not, of course, arguing that children should be taught phonic rules before they learn to read, though there is an indication that some phonological skills can speed reading development (sensitivity to rhyme, for example). Learning to read and becoming aware of the sound system of the language probably go hand-in-hand. Indeed, recent research has shown that learning to read itself facilitates children's understanding of some aspects of the sound system of the language and its relation to the alphabetic code of the writing system.

Efficient use of context is by no means enough, even for beginning readers. Again and again studies have shown that proficient readers do not need to guess words that are already in their reading vocabulary – their word identification skills are so fast and automated that they can recognise words from the perceptual information (in a bottom-up manner) far more rapidly and accurately than they can guess them from context. This is not, of course, to say that top-down processes (using context to help identify words) do not play a part in reading. They do, both in the stages of reading before word recognition becomes highly proficient (and even for skilled readers when the words are for some reason difficult to decipher). The denial that context is all important is completely independent of the sorts of books used to teach children to read. It does *not* mean that children must necessarily be taught using carefully controlled and boring reading materials. Since beginning readers are comparatively poor at both word recognition and use of context, it makes sense to present them with both interesting and predictable reading material so that their chances of successfully using context are maximised, and can be used to support their developing word recognition. Such material has the added advantage of emphasising reading for meaning from the beginning. It also makes sense to use attractive books and exciting stories if only from a motivational point of view. There is nothing wrong with reading schemes, so long as they meet these criteria. However, since proficient readers recognise words primarily from bottom-up information, and we know that many children have difficulty learning to do this, we must also teach children strategies for decoding words.

One very general implication of our own work, on reading comprehension, is that it stresses the importance of recognising that a significant proportion of young children may have a specific comprehension problem. Although, in general, children who are good at one aspect of reading will be good at others, comprehension skills do not necessarily develop automatically, and it is possible to find children who can 'read' a story, and who know the meaning of all the words in it, but who, nevertheless, have no understanding of the text as a whole. Such children are often not recognised as having any reading difficulties. They are good at decoding words, and often read aloud with a surprising level of fluency given their lack of comprehension. This underlines the necessity of assessing children's comprehension abilities, as well as their word-recognition skills, from an early age, and fostering comprehension from the outset.

Reading is a complex skill with many components. Hence, any sensible approach to teaching reading will itself be multifaceted. Insistence on one point of view, to the exclusion of the other, can only be damaging – both to children and to the advance of knowledge.

early influences on literacy

Barbara Tizard

A research project in London infant schools

Why are some children more successful at school than others? When we asked this question of parents and reception class teachers, most of them had a definite theory about what leads to educational success – only 3 per cent said they did not know. But they tended to give rather different answers, each group giving the credit, or the blame, to the other. The most frequent answer given by teachers (48 per cent of them) was that parents were mainly responsible, whilst only 18 per cent of parents gave this answer. They were more likely to say (42 per cent did so) that the teachers, or the school and family together, were responsible, whilst only 10 per cent of teachers gave this answer. Surprisingly, only 12 per cent of parents and 16 per cent of teachers thought the children themselves were the most important factor (Tizard *et al.*, 1988, p. 82).

My colleagues and I tested these theories by following children through primary school, relating their attainments to three types of influence. The first were family influences – both background factors such as the child's ethnic group, mother's educational qualifications, and family income, and the home 'educational' practices, such as the amount of time parents spend helping their children, or reading to them, their contacts with the school, etc. The second type were school influences, including the teachers' expectations and practices, the curriculum presented to the class and to each child. The third type of influence was concerned with the characteristics of the children, e.g. their gender, verbal ability, and behaviour in the classroom.

Before we could study the children's progress, and relate it to these influences, it was crucial to begin by finding out how much they knew about reading, writing and maths before they started school, since it seemed likely that many would have already acquired some knowledge of literacy and numeracy. In order to get easy access to them at the preschool stage, we decided to study children attending nursery classes attached to infant schools.

At that time, the majority (63 per cent) of three- and four-year-olds within the Inner London Education Authority (ILEA) were attending a nursery class or school. In the summer term before they started infant school we tested all the children in thirty-three ILEA schools who were going up from nursery class to infant school the following September. Because the ILEA had a termly intake, this involved testing about ten children in each school, who were then aged about four years and nine months. The schools we selected were almost all in disadvantaged multiracial areas. All had at least one boy and one girl of Afro-Caribbean origin amongst the ten 'nursery leavers'. Altogether, we tested 171 white children and 106 of Afro-Caribbean origin.

The proportion of manual workers amongst the children's parents was much higher than the national average; their average income was low, and only 16 per cent were owner-occupiers. Because of the areas in which we worked, there were very few non-English speaking children in the sample.

There are no standardised tests of reading and writing available for four-year-olds so we put together our own test battery. (In this chapter, I will omit an account of the maths tests and maths progress.) We wanted to assess, not 'reading readiness', but the child's acquisition of the first stages of reading. Our first test of early reading skills was an adaptation of Clay's *Concepts about Print* test (Clay, 1979). This is concerned with whether children know the basic conventions of written language, which are essential for reading. These include knowing that print goes from left to right, from line to line, from page to page, and that it is the print in a book which we read, not the pictures. It also includes being able to distinguish between a letter and a word. To test these skills, we used a *Mr Man* book, with a picture on one page, and print on the other, and asked the children such questions as 'Can you show me what we read?' and 'Where do we start reading?' 'Can you show me a letter?'

The second early reading test was word matching. This does not require the children to read, but to point to one of four words which is the same as the word in the right-hand margin. The third test involved showing the children cards on which were written all the letters, in both upper and lower case, and asking them to name or sound as many as they knew. Finally, we presented them with ten common words to see if they could read any of them.

We tested writing ability by asking the children to write their first name, without a model, and to copy a phrase ('on the ground'). Their efforts were scored according to the stage they had reached in learning to write. In order to assess the children's spoken language skills we also used the *WPPSI* (Werhsler Pre-school and Primary Scale of Intelligence) vocabulary test. This asks them to define words, e.g. 'What is an apple?' 'What is a bicycle?' Higher marks are given for abstract definitions, e.g. 'An apple is a fruit' than for more concrete ones, e.g. 'You can eat it'. The test is therefore often considered to be more a test of verbal intelligence than of vocabulary.

All the tests were individually administered, and we found that the children almost always enjoyed them. It is sometimes argued that children so young cannot be tested reliably – that they do well one day, but badly the next, or vice versa. To check on this, we tested nineteen of the children twice, about a week apart, and found that in fact the agreement between their scores on the two occasions was very high, 0.88 for reading, 0.86 for writing.

Level of preschool literacy skills

Even though few of our children came from middle-class families, we found a wide range in their attainments. On the whole, they had acquired few reading skills. On average, they could identify five letters, although 12 per cent could identify at least twenty. Very few could distinguish between words and letters, less than a third knew that print goes from left to right, and only 20 per cent knew that in reading one proceeds down the page, from one line to another. Less than 3 per cent could read any of the words in our test. As to writing, a quarter could write their first name correctly without a model, whilst some could not copy any letters recognisably. The average score of the group on the *WPPSI* vocabulary test was slightly below the national norm.

Our next task was to discover what factors were associated with better developed literacy skills. It was certainly not a matter of which nursery class the children attended, since there was no difference in the average score of the children in the different schools. We looked, therefore, for an explanation in the characteristics of the children and their families, using information we had obtained from our tests, and from interviewing the mothers during the summer holidays. The most important parental influences turned out to be the level of the mother's educational qualifications (just over half had none); the extent to which the parents had tried to teach the child to read and write (almost two-thirds had made some attempt, generally not frequently or regularly); and the extent of the child's experience of books. We measured this by the number of children's books in the home, which we counted ourselves (about a quarter had ten or less), the frequency with which the child was read to (39 per cent of the parents said they did so daily) and how that reading took place (e.g. whether a complete story was read, whether it was discussed, etc.).

In addition, we found that two characteristics of the child were associated with higher literacy attainments – their gender and their verbal ability. Girls were more proficient at writing than boys, and children with a higher verbal ability, as measured by the *WPPSI* vocabulary test, were also more proficient at both reading and writing. Both the parental and the child influences were statistically significant at the 0.001 level (and were therefore highly unlikely to happen by chance) and all were independent of each other. (There was no significant difference between the early literacy skills of the black and white children.)

Relationship to later reading ability

It might be thought that these findings are of little importance, since children are not expected to be able to read and write before starting school. Indeed, we found that a quarter of the reception class teachers in our study strongly disapproved of any attempts by parents to teach preschool children to read or write, whilst most of the others had serious reservations about it. They feared that parents would use the wrong methods, and confuse the children, or put too much pressure on them, so that they lost interest.

The parents did indeed often use what the teachers believed to be the 'wrong' methods, in that many had taught the names rather than the sounds of letters, and had taught upper case rather than lower case letters. If the teachers had been right, children who had been taught at home should make less progress at school than those who had not. But the opposite proved to be the case. We re-tested the children with an extended version of our preschool tests at the end of the reception year, when they were aged five-and-three-quarters. Every year, for the next three years, we used a group test – the *Young's Reading Test*. This test is divided into two sections: the first requires the child to match words to pictures; the second to complete sentences, which involves reading for meaning. For the top Infant year, when the children were seven-and-three-quarters, we used both a reading and a writing test. We devised our own group writing test which required the children to write an ending to an unfinished story they had just been read, and to write a sentence describing each of three pictures. Their work was scored for the quality of their story, the range of vocabulary used, and their transcription and grammar skills.

When we compared the children's test scores over the four years, we found that the correlations were quite high, and increased from year to year.

Table 5.1   Correlations over time for reading and writing

	Nursery (age 4) & age 5	Age 5 & 6	Age 6 & 7	Age 7 & 8	Nursery (age 4) & age 7
	(N = 247)	(N = 346)	(N = 288)	(N = 256)	(N = 205)
Reading	0.57	0.78	0.85	0.89	0.56
Writing	0.50	NA	NA	NA	0.49

Correlations are very easy to understand. In order to correlate one year's scores with another, all the children's scores at, say, the preschool level are put in order from best to worst, and this order is compared with the one obtained at, say, the end of the first year in school, when the children were aged five–and–three-quarters. If the order is exactly the same on the two occasions the correlation would be one, although, because of measurement error, it is very unlikely to exceed 0.9. If there is absolutely no relationship between the order in which the children come on the two occasions, the correlation would be zero.

As Table 5.1 shows, the correlation for reading scores over that first year was, in fact, 0.57, and each year the correlation between the children's scores at the beginning and end of the year got larger. Between the ages of six and seven the correlation was 0.85, which meant that the children's order hardly changed at all over those two years; their attainments relative to those of their peers became more and more fixed. Also, the correlations between the nursery (age four) and age five scores were the same as the correlations between age four and age seven. This means that the children who started school with some grasp of the literacy skills measured by our nursery tests were likely to be doing relatively well at the end of infant school when they were aged seven-and-three-quarters. Although some children lacking these skills on entry caught up later, it was a good deal more likely that they would still be behind three years later.

In the last year of Junior School, when the children were aged eleven-and-three-quarters, we retested them, using the *Suffolk Reading Test* which involves comprehension of sentences. The correlations between the nursery (age four) reading scores and the age eleven scores was 0.38, and between age five and age eleven, 0.61. The children who did well at the nursery stage (age four) also did well at age eleven, but there were some children who did poorly at the nursery stage who did well at eleven.

Which early literacy skills were the best predictors of success at age eleven?

A finding which surprises many teachers is that the best predictor of reading achievement at ages seven and eleven years was the number of letters the children could identify, and their skill at writing their names and copying words, at the nursery stage (see Table 5.2). Identifying letters and handwriting skills were independent predictors of later reading achievement. They were much better predictors than the children's *WPPSI* scores for verbal ability, or the extent of their preschool experience with books or the frequency with which their parents read to them (Tizard *et al.*, 1988, p. 109; Blatchford and Plewis, 1990).

These findings do not necessarily mean that later good achievement at reading was *caused* by parents teaching their children to read and write in the preschool years. Causality cannot be determined from a correlational study. This is because some factor that has not been measured may be responsible for the association. For example, it could be the degree of the children's interest in literacy that led some of them to acquire literacy skills early, perhaps through asking their parents for letter names, or help with writing. If this interest continued, it would also lead to more advanced skills at a later

Table 5.2 Correlations across time for specific reading skills

	Nursery (age 4) & age 7	Nursery (age 4) & age 11
Letter identification	0.61	0.45
Handwriting skills	0.49	0.48
WPPSI vocabulary	0.36	0.31
Word matching	0.31	0.23
Concepts about print	0.27	0.15

age. Or it is possible that the higher attaining children had parents who were more *effective* in helping them with school work both before and during primary school (we measured the amount of parental help, but not its effectiveness).

Despite these caveats, there are two reasons for believing that it is likely that knowledge of letters and other early reading skills *do* bear a causal relationship to later reading attainment. First, although children can make some initial progress in reading without recognising the shape of individual letters, the ability to recognise them is an important aid in the development of word recognition (see Chapter 14). Second, those children assessed by the reception class teacher as having some early reading skills would be likely to be given reading books, whilst those who enter school with very rudimentary literacy skills are often seen by the teacher as needing a long preliminary period of looking at books and gaining experience with pencils by drawing, etc. The rationale for this lies deep in the ideology of British primary school practice. But the consequence is that unless the teacher then gives a good deal of attention to the less advanced children, the gap between the children which was present before they started school would inevitably be maintained or increased. To a considerable extent, throughout primary school the children kept their place on a moving escalator.

Can the inequalities be redressed?

Our evidence also suggests that the children's experiences after entering infant school could influence their progress. In statistical terms, the children's preschool test results explained about half of the variation in their top infant test scores. We found that the children's progress depended not only on their preschool skills, although this was a very important factor, but also on two factors within the infant school – teacher expectations and the school curriculum. We found a consistent relationship between the teachers' expectations of individual children, and the curriculum they introduced them to. Those children of whom the teachers had high expectations, often children they considered to be 'a pleasure to teach', would be introduced to a wider curriculum than children who had similar skills at the beginning of the year, but who they did not expect to do so well.

We found that teachers had expectations not only of individual children, but of the class as a whole, which influenced their overall curriculum for the year. There were major differences in the curriculum taught in different schools. For example, during the reception year a third of the teachers had not asked any of their children to write a word (other than their name) without a model. In contrast, a third had introduced the use of word-book dictionaries, and had encouraged the children to write at least one sentence on their own without copying from a model. It is important to remember that the average literacy skills of the children on starting school were very similar in all the classes, so these curriculum differences were not due to the teachers responding to differences in the children's attainments, but to their differing expectations of 'children in this area'.

We had some evidence that the reception year has a particularly large effect on progress. Table 5.1 shows that the correlations between the children's scores at the beginning and end of the reception year were a good deal lower than in subsequent years. That is, the children were more likely to change their order in that year than at any later year; some children who started the year with very limited skills overtaking those in other classes. This fits in with another finding, that the difference between the average reading scores in the different schools was greatest in the reception year. Reception teachers have very varying aims. We found that the majority put most emphasis on settling the children into school, teaching classroom discipline, etc., and only a fifth said that academic progress was one of their two main aims.

Our evidence suggesting that the reception year may be of special importance for children's progress is supported by an interesting study made by three US researchers (see Pederson, Faucher and Eaton, 1978). Pederson *et al.* discovered that children who had been taught by a particular first grade teacher, Miss 'A', had higher educational attainments as adults than those who had attended parallel classes in the same school. It was said of Miss 'A' that 'it did not matter what background or abilities the beginning pupil had, there was no way that pupil was not going to read by the end of grade one . . . She invariably stayed after school to help the slow learners . . . and could remember every pupil by name even after an interval of 20 years.' The initial boost she gave the children was present in their reading attainment at the end of elementary school, and this appears to have given them an advantage throughout secondary school.

Implications for parents and schools

Teacher expectations and the curriculum offered to the children can both be changed. Not all teachers are as gifted or as dedicated as Miss 'A', but the account of her work is consistent with our finding that high expectations and a defined reading policy at the very outset of schooling may greatly benefit subsequent progress. There seems to be enough evidence to suggest that rather than leaving those children who enter school with very low levels of literacy to accumulate more experience with drawing, and looking at books, definite academic targets should be set for them, and a defined strategy for attaining the targets.

Teachers often worry that such a course would lead to labelling children at an early stage, and that in any case children who are slow to start often 'take off' later in their own good time. This may, indeed, happen, but the large correlations we found between the children's test scores from year to year suggest that it is a relatively unusual occurrence. It seems likely that there is more danger in waiting for children to 'take off' than in giving them extra help at an early stage.

Higher expectations of reading attainments may well require that children spend more time at school on reading. Our observations in the top infant year showed that on average only 4 per cent of classroom time, that is, 2 per cent of the school day, or eight minutes, was spent on reading. This included silent reading, flipping through books, reading to the teacher, reading to another child, and playing reading games. Eight minutes was an average over the schools; in some schools, the children observed did no reading, in others they read for as much as thirty minutes. The greater part of the working time in class was spent on oral language work (23 per cent) art and construction (21 per cent) writing (20 per cent) and maths (17 per cent) (Tizard *et al.*, 1988, pp. 51–4). Yet at the end of infant school two-thirds of the children were below average on our reading test, and 25 per cent were definitely poor readers, with reading scores of 84 or less.

So far as parental teaching at the preschool stage is concerned, although our findings do not necessarily mean that it leads to later success, one can safely conclude that it is unlikely to do harm and, indeed, is likely to be helpful. Teachers' worries about the methods parents use – teaching upper case letters and letter names – are unnecessary. According to Adams (1990) the essential first step in reading is to ensure that children are highly familiar with the shape and names of letters, and whether they begin with upper or lower case letters is of no importance. In fact, although the parents did tend to teach the names of upper case letters, in some respects parents were using more up-to-date teaching methods than the teachers. Only about a quarter used reading books or flash cards. Much of the teaching seemed to take place in the context of very meaningful activities, pointing out letters in the environment, writing names on birthday cards, etc.

Our research, by focusing on formal skills, may seem to undermine the current understanding amongst infant teachers that reading is about extracting meaning from texts, not decoding symbols. But this is a false dichotomy.

Decoding can be taught in the context of meaningful activities, both at school and at home, and teaching letters does not exclude the need for other reading related activities. Reading aloud to children is an important way to stimulate their imagination, increase their vocabulary, and arouse their interest in books. But reading aloud on its own, especially to a group, does not ensure that children will make a connection between meaning and print, or have any understanding of written language.

phonological aspects of learning to read

Peter Bryant

The debate

Arguments over the best way to teach children how to read usually reflect fundamental differences about the nature of reading and of learning to read. That is certainly the case with the current interesting dispute about the effectiveness of the 'real books' approach, or of the 'whole language' approach, as it is often called in America (Liberman and Liberman, 1990). On the surface the discussion is about teaching methods, but the deeper disagreement is about what it is that children have to learn in order to be able to read.

The case for real books, as I understand it, is in the end based on the idea that learning to read is a natural development. The idea has actually been with us for some time, for it has been eloquently championed for many years by Kenneth Goodman (1967; 1982). He argued that learning to read is not all that different in kind from learning to speak. Children learn to read by being exposed to written language in much the same way as they learn to speak by being exposed to spoken language. The only real difference is that they can use their knowledge of spoken language and its constraints to help them to decipher written text. So, when they meet a written word whose meaning defeats them they can use their understanding of the meaning of the rest of the sentence to help them to reach a reasonable conclusion about that particular word although effective reading will probably depend on recognising its specific identity.

One important claim made about this psycholinguistic guessing game, as Goodman called it, is that it not only helps children to read an unknown word; it also helps them to learn to recognise that particular word next time without having to rely on the contextual prop of the rest of the sentence. Thus the fundamental force behind learning to read is the children's knowledge of spoken language and their use of context to help them to learn new words. Written language is a natural extension of spoken language, and the most sensitive, enjoyable and effective way of teaching children to read is to allow them to use their undoubted linguistic skills to the full during the process of learning. That takes us to 'real books', in which the written language provides 'authentic' literary patterns for children to relate to.

The contrary position (for the moment I am just dealing in extremes) is different on the surface and just as different under the surface. It is that children need to be taught phonics first of all: children, it is claimed, have to be thoroughly at home with letter-sound relationships before they can make any real progress in reading or writing. People who hold this view argue for a different teaching method, and they do so because of their view of the nature of learning to read. That view, to use Gough and Hillinger's striking and amusing phrase (1980), is that learning to read is 'an unnatural act'. The claim for unnaturality is based on the simple assumption that in order to understand the alphabet children have to learn to do something which in a sense goes against the psychological grain. They have to begin to analyse the sounds in words: they have to break up words into phonological segments – usually phonemes – because these are the sounds that alphabetic letters represent. The reason for thinking that this is an unnatural task is that it is plainly a very difficult one for young children (as we shall see from evidence given later on in this chapter) and that it is virtually the opposite of what, up to that point, they have been doing very skilfully with spoken language. Up to that point they have had to treat words and even phrases as wholes, because that is where their meaning lies.

There are two fundamental differences between these extreme positions. One difference concerns *which aspect of language* plays the most important part in learning to read. The first position concentrates on syntax and semantics, and the second on phonology. The other difference is over the issue of *naturalness.* One position holds that learning to read is a natural outgrowth of learning to speak, and the other that there are obstacles for children who are learning to read which their knowledge of spoken language will not help them with. One position holds that their experiences of spoken language will provide the natural platform for learning about written language. The other states that many of the children's previous experiences with spoken language will actually make it difficult for them to come to grips with the entirely new demands imposed by their first encounters with the alphabet.

It is worth pausing for a moment to consider the coincidence of particular views about language and reading with particular views about the naturalness of learning to read. Those who are most impressed by the role that children's grammatical skills play in reading also argue that there need be no natural barriers to learning to read. In contrast, those who argue for the importance of phonological skills make the claim for unnaturalness. Why should this be so? The answer surely must have something to do with the apparent ease of syntax and the apparent difficulty of phonology for young children. They talk grammatically, but as we shall see they often flounder in phonological tasks. Phonological demands therefore seem to constitute more of a barrier than syntactical ones: hence learning to read is considered a natural development by those who concentrate on the (apparently easy) syntactical demands, and an unnatural act by those more concerned with the (apparently difficult) phonological aspects of reading.

Children's phonological awareness

Children's difficulties with phonemes

It is often quite difficult for people to see why phonology should be a genuine barrier to reading. After all, children seem to have mastered the phonology of their language superbly well in their first five years. They string phonemes together into real words with no difficulty; they distinguish words like 'cat' and 'hat' on the basis of single phonemes. Why should there be any problem at all?

The answer came in a series of experiments which began in the 1960s and which tested children's ability to make explicit phonological judgements. The story of these experiments has often been told (Bryant and Bradley, 1985; Goswami and Bryant, 1990; Liberman et al., 1989; Gombert, 1992). But the difficulties that the tasks in these experiments posed for young children still have some of the same kind of surprise value as, for example, young children's mistakes in Jean Piaget's conservation tasks have (Piaget, 1952). The younger children's performance in these tasks showed that by and large they are quite incapable of making distinctions which are transparently clear to any literate adult. One of these tasks was devised by David Bruce (1964). He gave children between the ages of five and nine years a 'subtraction' task, in which he asked them to say what a word like 'sand' would sound like if a particular sound ('n' in this example) were removed from it. This proved an extraordinarily difficult assignment for the younger children. The mean score for five-year-olds was actually 0, and six- and seven-year-olds were correct only 6 per cent and 29 per cent of the time respectively. Even by the ages of eight and nine the children's scores (55 per cent correct and 89 per cent correct respectively) in this apparently simple task were nowhere near perfect.

The apparent difficulty that these children had in making explicit judgements about phonemes was confirmed in another well known study by Liberman et al., (1974). They devised a tapping task. Four-, five- and six-year-old children had to learn to tap out either the number of syllables or the number of phonemes in a word spoken to them by the experimenter. The phoneme task was a great deal harder than the syllable task at all age levels, and in fact was quite impossible for the youngest group: they simply could not learn to tap out the number of phonemes in even the simplest of words.

The striking difficulty that Liberman et al., demonstrated in children who have to estimate the number of phonemes in a word was confirmed in another version of this task where children had to set out the same number of counters as the phonemes in one condition or as the syllables in another condition in a series of words that were spoken to them (Treiman and Baron, 1981). Once again the phoneme task was extremely difficult for young children and far harder than the syllable task.

The apparently consistent difficulty that children in their beginning years at school have over making explicit judgements about phonemes may have serious implications for the question of learning to read. The authors of these studies claim that young children are quite unaware of the phonemes which they produce and which they use to distinguish words. They use these phonemes, but they are not consciously aware of the way that words consist of, and thus can be broken down into, these small phonological units.

How seriously anyone concerned with reading takes this claim depends on his or her views on the importance of the alphabet and of learning grapheme-phoneme correspondences in reading. For if children are unable to break words down into their component phonemes, they will be quite unable to learn about the alphabetic code. A child who cannot work out that the word 'cat' can be broken down into three constituent sounds will be at sea with the alphabet. This might be serious, but then again it might not. If alphabetic knowledge plays little part in reading, it will not matter very much whether children can learn about grapheme-phoneme correspondences when they begin to read.

The evidence however suggests that this last possibility is a slim one. There definitely does seem to be a connection between children's skills in phoneme tasks and the progress that they make in learning to read. This evidence takes three forms. First there are strong correlations between children's success in phoneme detection tasks and their reading levels, and these correlations hold even after stringent controls for differences in IQ (Stanovich *et al.*, 1984a; Stanovich *et al.*, 1984b; Tunmer *et al.*, 1988; Lundberg *et al.*, 1980). Secondly there is some evidence that children who are particularly backward in reading are also particularly unsuccessful in tasks in which they have to manipulate grapheme-phoneme correspondences. Two studies show that dyslexic children read a series of real words as well as other (younger) children who have achieved the same level of reading, but are much worse than this control group when it comes to reading pseudo-words (e.g. 'wef' and 'slosbon') (Frith and Snowling, 1983: Baddeley *et al.*, 1982). Since it is likely that the only way to read these pseudo-words is by grapheme-phoneme correspondence it seems likely that these studies show that children who have difficulty with reading are also less able than most to break words up into their constituent phonemes.

Finally, there is an impressive intervention study. Lundberg *et al.* (1988) gave a group of Danish kindergarten children prolonged extra phonological experience, a great deal of which involved breaking words into phonemes and constructing words from phonemes. These children eventually learned to read more successfully than other children in a control group who had received as much extra attention, albeit of a non-phonological kind.

How children learn about phonemes

These results add up to a strong case for two claims: one is that children have to surmount a phonological barrier, and the other is that their success in doing so will play a large part in the progress that they make in learning to read. The implication of these data as far as teaching is concerned is that children will benefit from being taught about phonological segments.

The issue of teaching, however, raises another question. We need to know how children get over the barrier – what it is that eventually makes it possible for them to see that words and syllables can be broken down into constituent phonemes. One possible hypothesis – and it is the hypothesis which most strongly supports the idea of 'phonics' teaching – is that children become explicitly aware of phonemes because they are taught about them when they are learning how to read. This is the view taken by Jose Morais *et al.*, and it is based on the results of some impressive studies on illiterate adults and on people who learn non-alphabetic scripts.

Morais *et al.*, carried out two studies (1979; 1986) in Portugal at a time when illiteracy was quite common there – especially in rural areas – so that one could easily find competent and effective adults who nevertheless were unable to read. Both studies took the form of comparisons between adults who were illiterate and others who had been illiterate most of their lives but who had quite recently taken literacy courses and could now read. In one study these people were given tasks rather similar to those devised by Bruce (1964): they had either to work out what a word would sound like if the first sound were removed ('purso – urso') or if a particular initial sound were added to it ('alacho' – 'palacho'). The illiterate group was a great deal worse at these tasks than the 'ex-illiterates'.

In the second study, illiterate people and people who had recently become literate were given the same kind of phoneme task but were also given other tasks: in one of these they had to judge whether words rhymed or not and in another they had to make musical discriminations. Again the illiterate people were at a particular disadvantage in the phoneme task, although their scores were lower than those of the literate people in the rhyme task as well.

These two studies certainly show that adults who have not learned to read but are in other respects adapted and effective people have much the same difficulties in tasks involving explicit judgements about phonemes as young children at the beginning stages of learning to read. The conclusion that Morais *et al.*, drew from their striking results was that explicit awareness of phonemes is not a natural development at all: it is, they claimed, a product of being taught to read. People become aware of phonemes because they are taught about the alphabet. This is a claim with powerful implications for the teaching of reading: for, if it is correct, it means that it is entirely up to teachers to remove the barrier to explicit awareness of phonemes.

If Morais *et al.*, are right, then one should be able to find similar insensitivities to phonemes among people who are literate but who have learned to read a script which is not alphabetic. One such script is the traditional Chinese orthography. This is a logographic script, in which individual symbols represent whole words. Although many of the logograms contain 'radicals' which give some information about the sound of the word, Chinese is definitely not a script in which individual elements represent individual sounds that add up to the total sound of the word. It is very far from being a system of grapheme-phoneme correspondences.

However, in China today most people are taught an alphabetic orthography as well. This is 'Pinyin' which represents the Chinese language in Roman letters. Thus there are some Chinese people who know just the traditional orthography because they were taught to read before the introduction of Pinyin, while others know this orthography and also the Pinyin script.

Read *et al.* (1986) decided to give people from both groups phoneme addition and subtraction tasks which were precise analogues of those that Morais *et al.*, used in their first study. The results of this Chinese study fit well with the claim made by Morais. The people who could only read the traditional orthography were far worse at these phoneme tasks than those who had learned Pinyin as well. This is a remarkable result because it establishes that there are people who are perfectly literate, albeit with another alphabetic script, but who nevertheless seem to be quite out of their depth in a simple phonological task.

Japan provides us with another instance of a non-alphabetic orthography. The Japanese read a mixture of two kinds of script: one is logographic, and the other syllabic. These syllabaries (there are in fact two Japanese syllabaries) are of course phonological, but they work at a grosser level than the phoneme, since most Japanese syllables involve more than one phoneme. Thus, according to Morais' hypothesis, Japanese people who have not also learned an alphabetic script should be relatively insensitive to phonemes. This was the claim that Virginia Mann (1986) tested in a comparative study of six-year-old Japanese and American children. She gave them the Liberman phoneme and syllable tapping task, and also two subtraction tasks – in one they had to work out what a word would sound like without its initial phoneme and in another what it would sound like without its initial syllable.

Mann found that the American six-year-olds were considerably better than the Japanese in the phoneme tasks but not in the syllable tasks. This result agrees well with the study by Read *et al.*, and in general with the idea that people only become aware of phonemes as a result of learning to read. But the results of another experiment in the same study suggest the need for some caution here. Mann also gave these tasks to nine- and ten-year-old Japanese children who, she claimed, had never learned an alphabetic script. She reported that by this age they had no particular difficulty with the phoneme tasks. So it seems that Japanese children fall behind American children who are being taught an alphabetic script in phoneme tasks, but eventually are able to make explicit judgements about phonemes without the benefit of having learned an alphabetic code.

But why, one must ask, are these Japanese children able to make the kind of judgement which defeats Chinese adults who have not learned an alphabetic script? One possible reason for the difference is that the experience which the Japanese children have when they are being taught the syllabary eventually leads them to an awareness of phonemes. Typically these syllabaries, when presented as wholes, are arranged in a matrix form in which each column contains all the syllables starting with a particular consonant (e.g. 'ka', 'ko', 'ki') and each row contains all the syllables ending with a particular vowel ('ka', 'na', 'ta'). Teachers apparently draw the children's attention to this pattern. Thus, even though the syllabic symbols which these children learn do not represent phonemes, the experiences that they have while learning a syllabary may draw their attention to the fact that syllables can be broken down into constituent phonemes. So, in the end, Mann's study provides much support for, and no strong evidence against, the idea that children become aware of phonemes because they are taught about them.

The claim that children who are coming to grips with an alphabetic orthography must be taught how to disentangle phonemes seems from this series of studies to be a very plausible one indeed. There is no doubt at all that the work of experimental psychologists over the last decade has, by and large, provided us with a convincing rationale for 'phonics' teaching.

But this rationale depends on a simple assumption about the nature of the phonological task in learning to read. Morais *et al.*, make the assumption very clear: it is that the grapheme-phoneme correspondence lies at the heart of learning to read – that children have to master the connection between alphabetic letters and individual phonemes. That is why they lay such stress on phoneme tasks, and one must accept that if grapheme-phoneme units are so important their case is a convincing one.

Rhyme and the preschool years

If there is a phonological barrier and if learning to read is consequently an unnatural act, the barrier must be at the level of the phoneme. Young children, we have already seen, do not have much difficulty over disentangling syllables, and they are also reasonably at ease with another kind of phonological unit which lies somewhere between the phoneme and the syllable.

Long before children go to school and have any formal experience with reading many of them become quite adept at juggling the sounds in their language. The most striking instance of this is to be found in their awareness, and evident enjoyment, of rhyme and alliteration. This goes almost without saying, but there is plenty of empirical evidence to support it (Dowker, 1989;

Lenel and Cantor, 1981; MacLean *et al.*, 1987; Bryant *et al.*, 1989). Preschool children do quite well, and consistently above chance level, in rhyme detection tasks and they are quite good at producing rhyming and alliterative poems. These, it should be noted, are rather general statements, for it is also clear that there is quite wide variation among children in their performance in these various tasks. Nevertheless, three- and four-year-old children are able to work out whether two words rhyme or not quite well, even though they are unable to read or write.

What significance has this fact for the question of learning to read? If one assumes that the only important phonological requirement in learning to read is to master grapheme-phoneme correspondences, then the answer to this question is that there can be very little connection between children's early acquaintance with rhyme and their later experiences with reading. After all, rhyming sounds usually comprise more than one phoneme: the rhyming sound in 'sand' and 'hand' for example is 'and' and it consists of three phonemes. This view of the general unimportance, as far as reading is concerned, of the preschool skill of rhyming and detecting rhyme is actually the one taken by Morais *et al.* (1987), and this is no surprise because the view is completely consistent with their two claims – that the main phonological task in reading is learning about grapheme-phoneme correspondences, and that children acquire the ability to understand these correspondences as a result of being taught to do so at school.

However, something must be wrong with this hypothesis. It cannot be completely right because there is now considerable empirical evidence of a strong link between children's ability to detect rhyme and alliteration in the preschool period and their success years later on in reading. Several longitudinal studies have shown this. One such study was by Lynette Bradley and myself (1983) where we gave four hundred four- and five-year-old children rhyme and alliteration tests before they had begun to learn to read, and then followed their progress in reading and also in mathematics over the next three to four years. There was a very strong relation between the rhyme and alliteration measure taken at the beginning of the project and the children's reading scores (but not their mathematics scores) at its end when they were aged eight to nine. This relation was stronger even than the relation between IQ and reading and it remained significant after stringent controls for differences among the children in intelligence and in vocabulary.

This study also contained an element of intervention. A small group of six- and seven-year-old children was given extra practice with rhyme and alliteration over a two-year period, and this experience had an effect (albeit a modest one) on their reading. When reading was tested later these children fared better than a comparable control group who had been given as much extra attention, but not in the areas of rhyme and alliteration.

A later study (Bryant *et al.*, 1989) confirmed the strong longitudinal connection between children's early rhyming skills and their eventual progress in reading. In this study the first measures of rhyme and alliteration were taken when the children were three-and-a-quarter years old, and yet proved to be extremely powerful predictors of reading, even after controls for differences in IQ, in vocabulary and in social background. There is no doubt now about the connection. The more sensitive children are to rhyme and alliteration before they begin to learn to read, the better on the whole their progress in reading will be. This means that there is a definite link between a preschool and presumably untaught phonological skill and learning to read.

As a result, we face a real conflict. On the one hand we have the claim that it is quite hard for children to learn about grapheme-phoneme correspondence and that they only become aware of the way in which words can be broken up into phonemes as a result of being taught to do so at school. On the other hand we find a definite connection between a phonological skill which they acquire without the help of formal teaching long before they go to school and their success in reading.

The significance of different speech units in children's reading

The dispute that I have just described is about the significance of the phonological experiences that children have before they go to school. There is no disagreement on the importance to reading of children's phonological skills in general, or on the benefits of phonological instruction.

Fortunately this is a dispute which can be resolved, but the solution to it involves broadening one's idea about the role of phonological skills in learning to read. Hitherto we have concentrated on children's awareness of the phoneme and, when it comes to reading, on their learning about grapheme-phoneme correspondence, and we have seen that children only seem to become properly aware of phonemes when they begin to learn to read and probably as a result of reading instruction. But there is no reason why phonological codes in reading should operate just at the level of the phoneme. There are other regular correspondences between sound and script. Since, as we have seen, children have a lively sense of rhyme before they learn to read, let us turn to rhyming sounds. 'Hand' and 'stand' rhyme and the rhyming sound 'and' is spelled in the same way in both words.

The frequency with which rhyming sounds are spelled in the same way in different words is a striking feature of the English orthography. The relation is not an entirely regular one, since many rhyming sounds in pairs of words, such as 'fight' and 'white', are spelled differently. But there is certainly a great deal less variation in the way that rhyming sounds are spelled than in the way that the same phoneme is represented in different words.

These rhyming sounds of course often consist of several phonemes. In fact, they usually represent a speech unit which lies somewhere between the phoneme and the syllable. 'Sand' and 'hand' are monosyllables and the rhyming sound is only part of each syllable. The possibility that these shared rhyming sounds represent a speech unit has been taken seriously by linguists and psycholinguists, who now talk of 'intrasyllabic speech units'. Halle and Vergnaud (1980) claimed that within syllables there is a natural distinction between the 'onset' and the 'rime'. The onset is the opening consonant or consonant cluster if the syllable does begin in such a way and the rime consists of the vowel sound and any following consonants: every syllable therefore has a rime though not every one has an onset. So, 's' is the onset and 'and' the rime of 'sand'; and 'str' the onset and 'ing' the rime of 'string'.

There is now a great deal of empirical evidence that the onset/rime division does play a significant part in the way that people analyse speech sounds. Don MacKay (1972) showed that the division appears to determine the nature of many people's speech errors. For example, when people mistakenly produce a hybrid word, formed involuntarily from two words, the new word typically consists of the onset of one and the rime of the other: they will say 'don't shell' (shout/yell) rather than 'don't shoull'. Also when people are asked to construct new words from constituent sounds in different words (from the beginning sound in one and the end sound in another) they do so more easily if the beginning sound is the onset and the end sound the rime (Trelman, 1983).

What about young children? We have already made a tentative connection between their rhyming skills and the onset/rime distinction. In fact, there are strong empirical grounds now for believing that this distinction plays a crucial part in children's early phonological awareness. It also seems that the main developmental change in the nature of children's phonological skills after they go to school is that they progress from being able to divide words into intrasyllabic units (onset and rime) to being able to analyse them in terms of their constitutent phonemes.

The results of a study by Kirtley et al., (1989) suggest this development strongly. The point of this study was the fact that these intrasyllabic units frequently only consist of one phoneme. It follows that children, who can distinguish onset from rime but can make no finer phonological distinctions than that, should be able to identify phonemes when these represent an intrasyllabic unit, but should not be able to do so when they are only part of such a unit.

In the Kirtley et al., study a large group of children, whose progress in reading was being monitored in a longitudinal study, was given an oddity task when they were five years old. In this they heard, in a series of trials, four words, three of which contained the same particular phoneme, while the fourth did not. In some trials this shared sound was the words' onset ('peg' 'land' 'pin' 'pot') while in others it was the last sound ('sit' 'dot' 'pet' 'car') and therefore was only part of the rime. Children who can manage the onset/rime distinction but cannot make finer phonological distinctions should do well in the first condition and badly in the second, since in the first they have only to analyse onset while in the second they have to take apart the rimes in each word.

One can make another prediction: if children begin to be able to detect phonemes as a result of being taught to read, then those who have made no progress in reading should be quite unable to do the end sound task while those who have should do reasonably well in it.

Both predictions turned out to be right. In general the beginning sound task (onset) was a great deal easier for the children than the end sound task (part of the rime). Furthermore, when the children were divided into those who could read no words at all in a reading test and those who could read some words, the first group produced scores above chance level in the beginning sound task only and chose randomly in the end sound task. The second group, on the other hand, did manage to perform above chance level in the end sound task, and therefore were able, to some extent at least, to divide the rime into its constituent phonemes, though they too did much better in the beginning than in the end sound task.

This last result is further evidence that children begin to be able to break words up into constituent phonemes as a result of learning to read. But does that leave any role for the awareness of onset and rime which quite clearly precedes by quite a long time the experience of learning to read? Usha Goswami and I (1990) have come to the view that this form of awareness also plays an important part in learning to read. Our starting point is the observation, already described, that children's rhyming skills predict their success in reading, but we now know much more about this connection.

Goswami (1986; 1988a and b) has shown that even beginning readers are aware of the fact that particular letter sequences symbolise sounds which often contain more than one phoneme. She worked with relatively difficult words like 'beak' and 'peak' – words which on the whole six- and seven-year-old children do not read successfully. Her technique was to tell them the meaning of one of the words like 'peak' and then to ask them to read other words, some of which contained the same spelling sequence such as 'beak'. She found that children were more likely to read new words with the same spelling sequence than they were other words such as 'lake' with different letter sequences and different sounds. So children make this inference about the relationship between complex sounds and spelling sequences right from the start, and it is interesting to note that further work by Goswami also established that they do so when reading stories and when they are writing as well.

The developmental sequence therefore seems to be a remarkably clear one. Before they go to school children show a degree of phonological awareness, but the speech units that they can make explicit judgements about are not phonemes: they are intrasyllabic units – onset and rime. These speech units are spelled in a reasonably regular manner, and young children seem to become aware of this regularity as soon as they begin to read. Their sensitivity to onset and rime thus affects their progress in reading and writing. When they have made some progress in reading and writing their experience with alphabetic letters makes it possible for them to begin to break words up into their constituent phonemes. Thus phonological skills at one level (that of onset and rime) are a cause of reading, and at another level (that of the phoneme) its result.

The implications for teaching that stem from this set of conclusions are plain. Teachers have to make sure that children are aware of the phonological connections in reading. These connections will be important for them on at least two levels – the intrasyllabic units and the phoneme. It is plain that children are more likely to need help with conquering the phoneme than with learning how to use their already considerable knowledge of onset and rime. But the now undoubted need to teach children about phonemes and grapheme-phoneme correspondence should not obscure the educational significance of the larger speech units. Though children on the whole are aware of these units, there is evidence now that they are helped considerably by being taught about the connection between letter sequences and onset and rimes (Wise *et al.*, 1990). Phonological instruction helps children at several levels.

Conclusion

Most psychologists who have argued for the importance of phonological skills in reading have also thought that children need to be taught about phonemes. This view is based partly on data that children have difficulty over making explicit judgements about phonemes, and partly on the assumption that learning about grapheme-phoneme correspondence is the basis of learning to read.

There can be no doubt about the immense difficulty that phoneme tasks pose for young children. But there are now good reasons for questioning the assumption that grapheme-phoneme correspondence is all important. Children also learn about the relationship between letter sequences and relatively large speech units, such as onset and rime, and there are good reasons for thinking that they take quite naturally to doing so because of their early sensitivity to rhyme and alliteration.

So the belief that the phonological skills involved in reading have to be taught because they do not come naturally to children is not completely true. Children possess some of these phonological skills (but to a varying degree) long before they go to school: but other skills do have to be taught at school. However both the early and the late skills are extremely important in reading and deserve to be encouraged.

the 'good book': linguistic aspects

Katharine Perera

What is required of early reading books?

Ideally, the reading books that are available for children in their first year or so at school need to be able to do three things. First, they need to provide the kind of text which will support children as they begin to learn to read. Secondly, they need to show children that reading is enjoyable and rewarding. And thirdly, they need to offer good models for children's own writing.

The first requirement is necessary unless children have already acquired the foundations of literacy at home, or unless the teacher teaches reading using other means, such as the published 'Language Experience' approach *Breakthrough to Literacy*. In practice, in many schools the reading books that children are given provide the main basis of their reading instruction. The second requirement – that books should be enjoyable – is important for all children but particularly for those who have had no experience of books and story-telling at home. If the first books they meet are dull, pointless and unappealing, it is hard to see how they can discern any reason for making the effort to learn to read. The third requirement – that books should be well written – is justified by the evidence (e.g. Eckhoff, 1983) that children tend to write in the style of the books they are currently reading.

Taking these three requirements as a starting point, and focusing in this chapter solely on stories and only on their linguistic aspects, it is possible to outline in broad terms some features that characterise good books for beginning readers.

Some linguistic features of good story books for beginning readers

1 Stories should have a recognisable story structure. Typically, stories are written in the past tense and include characters, a setting, an action or event

95

or situation that motivates what follows, and a satisfying conclusion. Such a structure encourages the reader to keep going because it holds out the promise that the effort of reading will be rewarded. This plays a very important part in making reading enjoyable. It also provides a necessary and valuable model for the young writer.

2 Stories should be written in flowing, rhythmical language as this is pleasant to read aloud and, again, provides a good model for the young writer. There is also a case to be made for the use of the kind of sentence patterns that children are likely to hear, and to use in their own speech. This case rests on the evidence from research by people like Rose-Marie Weber (1970) that beginning readers who are reading aloud say what they expect to find rather than necessarily what is printed. This suggests that familiar language patterns will lead to more successful prediction and, therefore, to a greater sense of achievement.

However, the structure of written language has characteristic differences from spoken language (there is an account of these differences in Perera, 1984). One aspect of children's development as writers is their growing ability to use appropriately those structures that are more common in writing than in speech. This grammatical ability is acquired chiefly through experience of a literary style in books – first by hearing stories read aloud and then by reading them for themselves. Therefore, at some point in children's literacy develop-ment, there is a place for stories written in language which does not depend exclusively on an oral style. Teachers who are sensitive to their pupils' level of language development and knowledgeable about their experience of listening to stories will be in a position to decide when that point has been reached. For some children at least, a judicious blend of familiar and more literary grammatical structures will be just the right combination.

Whether the language of early reading books is familiar or more literary, what is important is that it should be language that people really use, rather than a kind of language, sometimes known as 'readerese', that occurs exclusively in books written to teach children to read.

3 Stories that are to be used by children who are beginning to learn to read should have a higher level of vocabulary repetition than is usual in books written for proficient readers. It is partly by seeing the same word many times in different contexts that children gradually develop the essential skill of rapid and effortless word recognition (Juel and Roper/Schneider, 1985). But word recognition is also aided by familiarity with frequent spelling patterns and their pronunciation. Marilyn Adams, who has carried out a thorough review of the research literature, says this:

> *Proficient reading depends on an automatic capacity to recognise frequent spelling patterns visually and to translate them phonologically. Differences in this capacity are principal separators of good from poor readers.*
>
> (Adams, 1990, p. 293; see also this volume, p. 207.)

Therefore, children are likely to be helped if their reading books contain at least some words that demonstrate a consistent relationship between spelling and pronunciation. We can note at this point that this does *not* mean language of the 'Can Nan fan Dan?' variety; indeed, Marilyn Adams herself comments that such language is 'inordinately difficult to process' (1990, p. 322). Rather, it means that if a book contains, say, the word *reading*, it will be more helpful if it also has words like *leader* and *teacher* than if it includes other *-ea-* words with a different pronunciation, such as *head* or *great*.

To fulfil all these criteria is very difficult. It is hard to write entertaining stories in natural, rhythmical language using a limited and constrained vocabulary. Therefore, the selection of reading books will often involve some compromise.

Reading books examined

In order to discover how far different kinds of reading books do meet the criteria, I have analysed the language of a number of books that are used with children in the early stages of learning to read. These books come from the following five reading schemes: 'New Way', 'Reading 360', 'Oxford Reading Tree', 'Story Chest' and 'Book Bus'. In each case, I have examined between 1000 and 1200 words. I have also looked at roughly 1200 words from books that do not form part of any scheme and have not been written with the aim of teaching children to read; they are the kind of books that are used by many teachers to supplement or, in some cases, to replace a reading scheme. (They are often called 'real books', but I believe that this is an unfortunate label as it implies, misleadingly, that any book that is written with the purpose of helping children to read is not real. I prefer to call them 'individual books', as what they have in common is that they stand alone and do not form part of any set of graded or sequenced books.) The selection of these books was made by a children's book specialist, who has considerable experience both as a teacher of reading and as an adviser to teachers who want to replace a reading scheme with individual books.

Between them, the forty-five stories I have examined represent a range of different views about the kind of reading material that should be presented to beginning readers. We can reveal the extent of that range by seeing how many of the characteristics that are typically associated with a reading scheme are displayed by each of the six sets of books. Archetypal reading schemes are sets of books with most or all of the following objective characteristics: (1) they are produced with the aim of teaching children to read; (2) they are explicitly and finely graded into ascending levels of difficulty; (3) they have strict vocabulary control within and across books; (4) they focus on consistent spelling patterns; (5) they feature the same set of characters in all the stories; (6) they have a common authorship; (7) they have a uniform format; and (8) they are supplemented by other activities, materials and a teachers' manual.

The early stages of 'New Way', 'Reading 360' and 'Oxford Reading Tree' display most of these characteristics, with slight differences of emphasis. 'New Way', for example, gives more prominence than the other two to consistent spelling patterns but does not use the same set of characters in all the stories. The early stories in 'Story Chest' have some reading scheme features (notably (1), (3), (6) and (8)) but the books are not finely graded for difficulty; they come in different formats; they are written in different styles about completely different characters; and they do not aim to teach consistent spelling patterns. (Sound-spelling relationships are taught separately in this scheme by means of rhymes.) The stories in the 'emergent' and 'early' phases of 'Book Bus' have been broadly graded and put together by the publisher to provide teachers with a collection of individual books that can be used to teach reading. Other than that they have none of the characteristics of a reading scheme: they are written by different authors; they have different formats; there are no shared characters; there is no vocabulary control between books; and there is no focus on spelling patterns. As the five schemes differ in the extent to which they can be considered archetypal reading schemes, I shall from now on refer to them collectively as 'publishers' schemes' rather than 'reading schemes'. The individual books are not written with the aim of teaching children to read, and they are published by different publishers so, not surprisingly, they have none of the objective characteristics of reading schemes.

In order to make the comparisons between these six rather different sets of books as fair as possible, I have used the measure of the number of different words within any one story and have restricted the selection of stories to those which contain fewer than 120 different words. (Many individual books that are in use with beginning readers use over 200 different words.) More detailed information about all of the stories is given in Appendix 1 at the end of this chapter.

In the rest of this chapter I shall use the analysis of the language of these forty-five stories to illustrate in more detail the linguistic features I have already outlined.

Story structure

We can consider some stories which, despite being very simple, nevertheless demonstrate in an embryonic way the characteristics of well-formed story structure.

In *Lots of Caps* ('New Way'), a cap-seller puts all his caps on top of his head and then sits down under a tropical tree and falls asleep. While he is sleeping, monkeys in the tree steal all the caps except one. When he wakes up he stamps his feet in anger but the monkeys merely imitate him. He is so cross that he throws down his remaining cap – and the monkeys imitate that too and the cap-seller retrieves all his caps. So the story presents a character in a clearly defined setting who has a problem that is solved in a satisfyingly humorous way. There is also a humorous ending to *New Trainers* ('Oxford Reading Tree'): in this story a boy gets a new pair of trainers and then plays in them so that they get wet and muddy. His father is so preoccupied with telling him off that he doesn't notice that he is walking into wet concrete in *his* new pair of shoes. Here the conclusion depends on a pleasing role reversal.

Sometimes the conclusion is signalled by a change of language after a number of repetitions. For example, in *Sleeping Out* ('Story Chest') some children are sleeping out in the open with their mother. Every time they hear a strange noise they ask her what it is and she tells them, e.g.

> *What's that going sniffle, sniffle?*
> *A hedgehog. Go to sleep.*
> *What's that going yowl, yowl?*
> *A cat. Go to sleep.*

The last strange noise is 'zzzz-zzzz':

> *What's that going zzzz-zzzz?*
> *It's Mum. She's gone to sleep.*

Caspar's week (Individual) uses the same technique. Caspar is an accident-prone cat who creates a different kind of havoc on every day of the week:

> *On Monday . . .*
> *Caspar fell in the toilet.*
> *There was water everywhere!*
> *On Tuesday . . .*
> *Caspar knocked a plant off the windowsill.*
> *There was dirt everywhere!*

The story ends with a departure from the pattern that has been established:

> *Tomorrow is Sunday . . .*
> *Maybe Caspar will rest!*

Not all early reading books handle story structure well, though. It may be that the characters are not properly introduced at the beginning. For example, the story *At the Zoo* ('Reading 360') begins like this:

> *'This is the zoo, Ben,' said Tom.*
> *'You will like it here.'*

Mum appears on the next page but it is not until another four pages further on that it becomes apparent that Dad is there too, when Ben says, 'Come here,

Dad.' This is rather disconcerting at this late stage in the story and is similar to what children sometimes do in their own story writing.

Another weakness is when there are sudden, unsignalled shifts of time or setting. There is an example in *The Storm* ('Oxford Reading Tree'):

> *It was bedtime.*
> *Biff was in her room.*
> *Biff looked outside.*
> *There was a storm.*
> *It was time for school.*
> *Wilf and Wilma came.*

The last two sentences would read more smoothly, and would provide a better model for children's own writing, if they were written like this: The next day, when it was time for school, Wilf and Wilma came.

Sometimes there is inconsistency in the use of tenses. For example, *Bear hunt* (Individual) begins like a typical story with a formulaic opening and past tense verbs:

> *One day Bear went for a walk.*
> *Two hunters were hunting.*

When Bear is in danger, the narrator addresses him directly, e.g. 'Look out! Look out, Bear!' Such interventions are sometimes followed, appropriately, by the past tense, e.g. 'Quickly bear *began* [my italics] to draw'. But sometimes they are followed, rather oddly, by a present tense verb, before the narrative reverts to the past again, e.g.

> *Look up, Bear!*
> *Bear is caught.*
> *But Bear still had his pencil . . .*

Given children's tendency to muddle tenses in their writing anyway, it is unfortunate if what they read reinforces that tendency.

Probably the most serious failure of story structure is the absence of a satisfying and clearly final conclusion. In *At the Zoo* ('Reading 360') the children go to see the goats:

> *'Hello, little goat,' said Ted.*
> *'What do you want?'*
> *'Can't you see,' said Kay.*
> *'It wants to play.'*
> *'No,' said Ted.*
> *'It wants something to eat.'*
> *'But we can't feed the animals,' said Tom.*
> *'The zoo man will feed the goats.'*

And that is the end of the story. It simply stops, without there being any sense that it is complete and rounded off. The same is true of one of the individual books, *If I had a sheep*. Here, a young girl fantasises about the things she would do if she had a sheep: she would teach it to count, play games with it where they would pretend to be grown-ups or pirates or princesses, and so on. The story ends like this:

> *If she fell over . . .*
> *. . . I would make her better.*
> *I would read her a story . . .*
> *. . . and take her to bed.*

As the fantasies have not been confined to a single day, there is no reason why going to bed should signal the end of the story – it would be perfectly possible for it to continue the next day. Having a satisfying conclusion matters so much because it gives a point to the story. Without one, all that has gone before is undermined: if there is no point to the tale, then why tell it? And, even more, why read it? In a study of children's oral story-telling, Arthur Applebee (1978) found that fewer than half of his five-year-old subjects gave their story a formal conclusion, although nearly all of them handled the other aspects of story structure successfully. This finding emphasises how important it is for children's reading books to provide good examples of well-concluded stories.

Rhythmical language

The rhythm of English derives from the alternation of stressed and unstressed syllables. Typically, nouns, verbs, adjectives and adverbs are stressed while the articles, prepositions, auxiliaries and pronouns are unstressed. In the following sentence the words that would normally be stressed are printed in capital letters, the unstressed words are in lower case:

THIS is the BEAR who FELL in the BIN.

When children first begin to read, it is very common for them to give all words equal stress, so the sentence sounds like this:

THIS – IS – THE – BEAR – WHO – FELL – IN – THE – BIN.

Although beginning readers tend to stress every word, they do not generally stress every syllable, so 'parrot' and 'elephant' are pronounced PARrot and ELephant, not PAR-ROT and EL-E-PHANT. Therefore, an excellent way to introduce the alternation of stressed and unstressed syllables into children's oral reading is to give them books that contain polysyllabic as well as monosyllabic words. I counted the monosyllables and polysyllables in each of the forty-five stories to see what the proportion of polysyllabic words was. Some of the early books in 'New Way' and 'Reading 360' contain only monosyllabic words. This is likely to lead to jerky reading with too many strong stresses, e.g.

> BEN – THE – DOG
> WENT – DOWN – THE – HILL.
> LOOK – AT – ME.
> LOOK – AT – ME – SAID – BEN.

(*Down the hill*, 'New Way')

None of the stories analysed in these two schemes has more than 20 per cent polysyllabic words. In contrast, the other four sets of books each has at least one story with more than 25 per cent polysyllabic words. This should lead to more rhythmical reading, even if the child is still stressing the grammatical words that are unstressed in adult speech, e.g.

> 'GET TEDdy,' SAID KIPper.
> BIFF COULDn't GET TEDdy.

(*By the stream*, 'Oxford Reading Tree')

Language that children use or hear

Variety of sentence length

We can expect that children will read more readily language that they themselves either use or hear, than language that no one is likely either to say or to read aloud for pleasure. A number of grammatical features contribute to natural-sounding language. The first to consider is variety of sentence length. Taking the individual books as a yardstick (since their authors have not been constrained by ideas about what makes sentences readable), we can see in Table 7.1 the kind of variation in the length of written sentences that occurs naturally.

Table 7.1 Variety of sentence length in 'individual' books

Title	Range of sentence length in words	Mean	s.d. (standard deviation)
Have you seen the crocodile?	2–24	10.8	8.0
Rosie's walk*	32	32.0	—
Caspar's week	3–11	6.1	2.6
Bear hunt	1–11	4.1	2.2
You'll soon grow into them, Titch	4–22	11.2	5.5
If I had a sheep	8–14	9.5	1.9
Charles Tiger	5–16	10.6	3.4
Mr Gumpy's outing	4–52	9.8	10.8
Mr McGee	6–15	11.2	2.8

*This story consists of one 32-word sentence.

It is clear that there is considerable variation of sentence length within most of the books. *Mr Gumpy's outing* is highly unusual in having a difference of 48 words between the longest and the shortest sentence, but it is not abnormal for there to be a difference of 10 or 11 words (e.g. *Charles Tiger*). The comparable figures for the publishers' schemes are given in Appendix 2. The 'Book Bus' selection is very similar to the set of individual books, even containing one very unusual book, *The pet show*, which has a difference of 48 words between the longest and the shortest sentence. The other publishers' schemes generally have rather less variation of sentence length within each book, with a difference of 6 or 7 words between the longest and the shortest sentence being normal.

The figures in Table 7.1 and Appendix 2 also reveal the fact that sentences are, on average, longer in the individual books than in the publishers' schemes. Mean sentence length in *Charles Tiger*, for example is 10.6 words, whereas in *Fat Pig's car* ('New Way') it is 5.7; in *Help me* ('Story Chest') it is 5.2; and in *The storm* ('Oxford Reading Tree') it is only 4.7. As sentences are units of meaning, it may be that a heavy concentration of long sentences impedes understanding and is rather daunting for those children who are reading slowly and with some difficulty. Where short sentences are interspersed with occasional longer ones, the variation makes the language sound natural, while the general pattern of fairly short sentences probably makes the young reader's task easier. The closing sentences of *The sports day* ('New Way') illustrate this:

> Tom got up.
> He went very fast.
> 'Hello Tom,' said his Dad.
> You have jumped fast but
> you have jumped back
> to the start.

In contrast, an unrelieved sequence of short sentences – particularly when they have a similar sentence structure – can sound rather stilted, e.g.

> The witch opened the door.
> Gran pushed the witch.
> Chip took the witch's keys.
> They ran out of the room.
> Chip locked the door.

> (*Castle adventure*, 'Oxford Reading Tree')

Appropriate use of pronouns

Another grammatical characteristic of natural-sounding language is the appropriate use of pronouns. Once we have mentioned someone or something in a conversation, we generally refer to them after that with a pronoun, so long as the reference is clear, e.g. 'I saw my sister yesterday. She was looking well. She's just come back from a cycling holiday.' It would be very odd to say, 'I saw my sister yesterday. My sister was looking well. My sister has just come back from a cycling holiday.' Yet this is what happens in some early reading books, e.g.

> Jill said,
> 'We want to help the tortoise.
> What can we do?'
> Miss Hill said,
> 'What do you think the tortoise wants?'
> 'The tortoise wants a home,' said Kay.
>
> (*The tortoise*, 'Reading 360')

Here it would be more natural if one or more of the tortoise phrases were replaced by 'it'. The under-use of pronouns is not confined to reading schemes, however. The individual book *Mr Gumpy's outing* begins like this:

> This is Mr Gumpy.
> Mr Gumpy owned a boat and his house
> was by a river.
> One day Mr Gumpy went out in his boat.
> 'May we come with you?' said the children.
> 'Yes,' said Mr Gumpy,
> 'if you don't squabble.'

Although it might be argued that this is a special kind of repetition of the proper noun Mr Gumpy, characteristic of a particularly literary style, it seems likely that the following literary example, with its combination of the proper noun 'Mr Wolf' and the pronoun 'he', provides a more helpful model for young children's own writing:

> Along came old Mr Wolf.
> He went up to the house made of straw.
> And old Mr Wolf said,
> 'Little pig,
> little pig,
> let me come in.'
>
> (*Let me in.* 'Story Chest')

The appropriate use of pronouns also entails avoiding them when their reference would not be clear. In their writing, young children sometimes use a pronoun without the necessary noun having been explicitly mentioned. There is an example of this in *I don't like fish* ('Book Bus'):

> 'Hello, Seal. What's your favourite food?'
> 'Fish of course,' said Seal.

'What do you think about fish, Walrus?'
'Fish are FANTASTIC,' said Walrus.
'Do you eat fish too?' said Polar Bear.
'Sometimes, but beans on toast is best!'

The last 'you' in this extract refers to an Eskimo boy, but this is only apparent from the picture. It is obviously unfortunate when a reading book provides a misleading model for children's own writing.

Reduced forms

In speech, we generally use the reduced forms of words like 'is', 'are', 'have', 'will' and 'not' unless we want to emphasise them. So we are more likely to say, 'I don't know if she'll like the present I've bought her' than, 'I do not know if she will like the present I have bought her'. In the individual books these speech-like reductions are used extensively, e.g.

'We'll walk home across the fields,'
said Mr Gumpy. 'It's time for tea.'

(Mr Gumpy's outing, 'Individual')

'Oxford Reading Tree', 'Story Chest' and 'Book Bus' also generally use reduced forms, e.g.

'I don't like witches,' said Gran.
She put a net over the witch.
The witch couldn't get out.

(Castle adventure, 'Oxford Reading Tree')

In the other two publishers' schemes there is some inconsistency. For example, in Fat Pig's birthday ('New Way') 'don't' is given in the reduced form but 'it is', 'I will', 'will not' and 'did not' are all given in full:

It is Fat Pig's birthday.
I will have a party,
said Fat Pig.
Don't forget to come
to my party, said Fat Pig.
We will not forget,
said Meg and Ben.
. . .
Look, I did not forget
to come to the party, said Deb.

If that passage is read aloud with reduced forms throughout, it sounds rather less stilted. It would be easy for publishers to replace unreduced forms with reduced ones when books are reprinted; in some cases, the resulting increase in naturalness would be quite marked.

Vocabulary control

The real challenge that faces authors of early reading books is to produce interesting well-structured stories written in rhythmical, natural-sounding language while using only a strictly controlled vocabulary and endeavouring to repeat the most important words frequently enough for children to be able to become familiar with them. Some stories are unappealing to read at least partly because they contain unmotivated repetition. By that I mean repetition that does not contribute to the story but is there purely to provide reading practice, e.g.

> *Ben can run.*
> *Look.*
> *We can run.*
> *We can run like this.*
> . . .
> *We can run.*
> *We can run fast.*

> (*Ben and Lad*, 'Reading 360')

In the forty-five stories I have examined there is very little of that kind of repetition. Authors seem to take considerable pains to use *motivated* repetition – that is, repetition which plays a key role in the telling of the story. For example, when Charles Tiger searches for his lost roar, his quest leads him to different places and different creatures:

> *He looked in the long grass*
> *and found a snake*
> *– but no roar.*
> *He looked in a deep river*
> *and found a crocodile*
> *– but no roar.*

Here there is repetition both of vocabulary and of grammatical structure, with the pattern 'He looked in a *adjective noun* and found a *noun*' occurring again and again. Not only does this nicely reflect the insistent nature of his search; it also makes possible the breaking of the pattern at the end off the story when the lost roar is found:

> *Under a stone he found a spider*
> *– and his*
>   *great*
>   *big*
>   *roar.*

> (*Charles Tiger*, 'Individual')

Some of the publishers' scheme stories have a similar kind of motivated repetition. For example, in *Bad cow* ('New Way') when a cow gets into the garden, Ben tries to chase her out without success:

Moo, said the cow
but she did not go.

He then enlists the help first of a dog and then of a horse, each time with the same result. The pattern changes, though, when a bee intervenes:

The bee buzzed round the cow.
Buzz, buzz, buzz, said the bee.
The cow ran out of the garden.

The motivated repetition in *Charles Tiger* means that each different word is repeated, on average, 2.1 times. but some of the individual books have much lower word repetition rates than this, e.g. *Bear hunt* – 1.5, and *Rosie's walk* – 1.3. In contrast, the publishers' scheme books have higher word repetition rates, e.g. *Bad cow* ('New Way') – 3.2, *Gran* ('Oxford Reading Tree') – 3.5, *Two little mice* ('Story Chest') – 4.0, and *At the zoo* ('Reading 360') – 6.2. But at least as important as these figures are the repetition rates *between* books. Not surprisingly, the individual books share very little vocabulary with each other. So if a child were to read *Charles Tiger* (which has 66 different words) and then to read *You'll soon grow into them* (with 62), he or she would find only seven words (11 per cent) in common between the two books. In this respect, the books in 'Book Bus' are more like individual books than reading scheme books. Between two of the 'Book Bus' books – *There's a monster in my house* and *The enormous turnip* – there is an overlap of 16 per cent. In contrast, the overlap between the pairs of books I examined in the remaining schemes ranged between 24 per cent (*Fat Pig's car* and *Looking for a letter*, 'New Way') and 45 per cent (*Two little mice* and *Let me in*, 'Story Chest'). When children move from one book to another within a scheme, they are to some extent building on what they already know. When they move from one individual book to another they may well be virtually starting afresh each time. Clearly this is possible only if there is a great deal of adult support available, either in the classroom or at home.

Conclusion

As Roger Beard (1990, p. 91), and many others, have demonstrated, it is very easy to catalogue the weaknesses in the earlier generation of reading schemes, with their dull, pointless 'stories' and their unnatural language. If we imagine a situation where an infant teacher is stocking her bookshelves from scratch but is forced to choose between such a scheme and individual books, then we may predict that she would reject the old-fashioned reading scheme. But, fortunately, the choice is not so stark. Recently published schemes have benefited greatly from some of the ideas that have gained currency during the last twenty years or so. These ideas include the centrality of meaning in the reading process; the importance of story structure; the need for natural-sounding language that can be read, and re-read, with pleasure; the interplay between words and pictures; the contribution that print in the environment can make to learning to read, and so on. In spite of the marked improvements in the newer schemes, much current discussion about books for teaching reading still draws a sharp dividing line between reading schemes on the one hand and 'real' books on the other.

I have tried in this chapter to show that, by examining a range of books and relating their linguistic features to the needs of children who are beginning to learn to read, it is possible to identify the strong and weak points of both kinds of book and to recognise the contribution that both kinds can make to the learning process. If the teacher knows there is enough adult support available to make it feasible for her pupils to learn to read solely from individual books, then she may choose this approach, and the children will encounter some appealing books. Even so, those of average and below average ability may find the sentences in some books dauntingly long and the rate of introduction of new vocabulary unmanageably rapid. If, on the other hand, the teacher chooses to use a good reading scheme which has well-constructed interesting stories written in reasonably natural language, then she can still try to keep a sizeable number of the best individual books in the classroom, so that the whole class can enjoy them together at storytime, or so that children can read them by themselves when they are ready to. It is worth making the point that the greatest need for the simplification, structure and support offered by a reading scheme is in the early stages, when there is so much to be learnt at once. After that, once children can read simple stories fluently and independently, many of them will be ready to enjoy for themselves the rich delights offered by individual books.

Appendix 1 READING BOOKS EXAMINED

Scheme	Publisher	Date	Author(s)	Title	Level	Total no. of words	No. of sentences
'NEW WAY'	Macmillan Education	1987	Anonymous	Down the hill	2	60	12
			"	Sam wants to play	2	68	12
			"	Help me	2	56	10
			"	The sports day	3	114	21
			"	Fat Pig's birthday	3	125	16
			"	Lots of caps	3	194	31
			"	Fat Pig's car	4	212	37
			"	Looking for a letter	4	221	30
			"	Bad cow	4	168	28
						1218	197
'READING 360'	Ginn	1978	H. Keenan-Church T. Clymer	Ben and Lad	2	68	23
			"	The tortoise	3	469	84
			"	At the zoo	4	402	75
			"	The hare and the tortoise	5	166	27
						1105	209
'OXFORD READING TREE'	OUP	1986	R. Hunt	A new dog	2	52	12
			"	New trainers	2	34	9
			"	By the stream	3	71	16
			"	Nobody wanted to play	3	80	16
			"	House for sale	4	109	23
			"	The storm	4	188	40
			"	Gran	5	309	58
			"	Castle adventure	5	306	57
						1149	231

Scheme	Publisher	Date	Author(s)	Title	Level	Total no. of words	No. of sentences
'STORY CHEST'	Arnold-Wheaton	1982	J. Cowley & J. Melser	Feet	Get ready	18	4
				Who's going to lick the bowl?	Ready, set go	16	6
			"	Plop!	Ready, set go	30	6
			"	Sleeping out	Ready, set go	49	15
			"	Mrs Wishy Washy	Read together	102	14
			"	Help me	2	170	33
			"	Two little mice	2	302	48
			"	Let me in	3	354	43
						1041	169
'BOOK BUS'	Collins	1990	K. Hayles	I don't like fish	Emergent	76	15
			S. Wilde	Yum, Yum!	Emergent	85	17
			M. Shepherd	The enormous turnip	Early	302	35
			S. Andrews	Greedy Stanley	Early	192	26
			R. Green & B. Scarffe	The pet show	Early	274	9
			D. Blackburn	There's a monster in my house	Early	91	12
			E. Reeves	Flower shop Fred	Early	196	24
						1216	138
'INDIVIDUAL'	Walker	1986	C. West	Have you seen the crocodile?	—	151	14
	Puffin	1970	P. Hutchins	Rosie's walk	—	32	1
	Macdonald	1988	C. Ward	Caspar's week	—	85	14
	Scholastic	1979;	A Browne	Bear hunt	—	81	20

Publisher	Year	Author	Title			
Puffin	1982 1983; 1985	P. Hutchins	*You'll soon grow into them, Titch*	—	191	17
Macmillan	1988	M. Inkpen	*If I had a sheep*	—	104	11
Collins	1987; 1989	S. Dodds	*Charles Tiger*	—	138	13
Puffin	1970; 1978	J. Burningham	*Mr Gumpy's outing*	—	283	29
Puffin	1987; 1989	P. Allen	*Mr McGee*	—	202	18
					1267	137

Appendix 2 **VARIETY OF SENTENCE LENGTH IN PUBLISHERS' SCHEMES**

Scheme and title	Range of sentence length in words	Mean	s.d. (standard deviation)
'NEW WAY'			
Down the hill	3– 7	5.0	1.5
Sam wants to play	5– 7	5.7	1.0
Help me	4– 7	5.6	1.0
The sports day	3–12	5.4	2.0
Fat Pig's birthday	5–12	7.8	1.9
Lots of caps	2–15	6.3	3.3
Fat Pig's car	3–10	5.7	1.7
Looking for a letter	4–14	7.4	2.5
Bad cow	1–13	6.0	2.6
'READING 360'			
Ben and Lad	1– 7	3.0	1.3
The tortoise	1–14	5.6	2.5
At the zoo	1–10	5.4	2.0
The hare and the tortoise	3–11	6.2	2.3
'OXFORD READING TREE'			
A new dog	4– 6	4.3	0.7
New trainers	2– 5	3.8	0.8
By the stream	1– 7	4.4	1.6
Nobody wanted to play	1– 6	5.0	1.4
House for sale	3– 7	4.7	0.9
The storm	3– 8	4.7	1.2
Gran	3–10	5.3	1.6
Castle adventure	2– 9	5.4	1.3

'STORY CHEST'

Feet	4– 6	4.5	1.0
Who's going to lick the bowl?	1– 6	2.7	1.8
Plop!	3– 6	5.0	1.1
Sleeping out	2– 5	3.3	1.2
Mrs Wishy Washy	4–12	7.3	3.0
Help me	2–10	5.2	1.5
Two little mice	1–13	6.3	2.5
Let me in	4–20	8.2	3.8

'BOOK BUS'

I don't like fish	2– 8	5.1	1.8
Yum! Yum!	4– 9	5.0	1.3
The enormous turnip	5–21	8.6	4.0
Greedy Stanley	3–15	7.4	3.0
The pet show	8–58	30.4	16.5
There's a monster in my house	5–12	7.6	3.1
Flower shop Fred	3–17	8.2	4.2

the 'good book': literary and developmental aspects

Nicholas Tucker

Introduction

Children's literature has always been subjected to strongly judgemental criticism from the adult world. In sympathy with Walter de la Mare's belief (1941, p. 11) that 'Only the rarest kind of best in anything can be good enough for the young', concerned adults have often agonised over the possibility that such sensitive plants should ever receive anything other than the purest literary nourishment in order to grow up straight and true. Literary critics, for example, constantly offer strong value judgements about the children's books they are reviewing, whether at length or only over a couple of lines, in a way they would never dream of doing when reviewing most adult fiction. Developmental psychologists have also joined in here when it comes to assessing a book's appropriateness to the stage of development of its intended young reader. So while no one would ever dare describe D. H. Lawrence's *The Rainbow* as 'Highly suitable for those at present considering the ups and downs of married life', it is still common to read recommendations for children's stories 'especially aimed at those about to start school'.

Moralists also continue to keep an extra watchful eye out for good and bad examples set in children's books, with authors like Roald Dahl once regularly in hot water over this or that detail from one of his many books. Critics from sociological backgrounds, meanwhile, tend to discuss children's books for their social relevance for contemporary young readers or for the way they may have a bad effect in terms of handing down racist, sexist or other undesirable stereotypes. Once again, there is a sharp distinction here between critical practice in the world of adult and children's literature. The days when social commentators like Henry Mayhew could denounce 'Trashy, wishy-washy cheap publications' for 'ruining' the deluded young women who read them are long gone (cited in Tucker, 1981, pp. 183–4). Anyone writing in the same tones about the possible effects upon any adults today of reading, say, the novels of Barbara Cartland would risk condemning themselves as both patronising and priggish. But where criticism of children's books is concerned, it is still common to find critics confident enough to assert that some books will almost certainly have a good effect upon the young while others almost certainly will not.

Because children are so clearly an adult responsibility, and because children's literature has always had as one of its aims the inculcation of good example, this tradition of concentrating particularly on moral and social judgements when reviewing children's books is a long one. Yet research in the last two decades has done much to undermine many of the reasons for continuing with this particular practice. Examination of short- or long-term reader responses has revealed that the effects of children's literature on young readers is in itself a highly problematic and often very subjective affair. Esteemed novels may leave some readers cold; lesser writing may, by contrast, be remembered later with great affection.

When such lesser writing comes in the form of comics or hastily written adventure stories, it has sometimes been described as illustrating a type of rich badness, exhibiting a coarse vigour often absent from more carefully considered children's fiction. But literary badness does not even have to be rich in order on occasion to be very effective with some young readers. Literature that is dull, derivative and second-rate in every conceivable way can still at times be recalled with love and gratitude. And where undesirable social stereotypes are an issue, however much some critics may condemn them for their possible bad effects upon readers in the mass, individual readers often seem relatively unaffected by them. In later life, socialists like George Orwell and Aneurin Bevan wrote nostalgically about the nationalistic, class-ridden comics of their youth (Tucker, 1981, p. 140). Many feminist writers today have emerged apparently unaffected by the strongly sexist fiction they once read and sometimes still admit to having enjoyed when young.

Different ways of assessing children's literature

This frequent lack of connection between literary cause and personal effect has begun to lead some critics away from assessing children's literature for any necessary influence it may have upon its readers. The present moral *laissez-faire* climate of the times has also helped in this process, given that issuing warnings about the possible effects of any literature on anyone is much less fashionable now than it once was. Even the Roman Catholic Church no longer takes its own Index of Prohibited Publications seriously. Children's critics in their turn are also becoming more careful about going public over their worst fears about certain types of reading.

This new lack of confidence shows itself in a number of other ways. It is also less common now to attempt to demarcate too precisely the type of reader a book is thought to be catering for. References to suggested age ranges still exist, but those confidently exclusive dedications of old now seem very dated ('To my youngest son Grenville Arthur and to all other good little boys', from Charles Kingsley's *The Water-Babies*; or 'To every little girl who has wished for an hour to be a little boy', from Beulah Marie Dix's *Merrylips*, first published in 1910.) As it is, we now know that the gender, age and social class of the intended reader may often turn out to be quite different from that imagined by the author and publisher. Grown-ups sometimes turn to comics while younger readers are wrestling with novels ostensibly aimed at adults. Within the readership of children's books, middle-class white children may possibly read more novels about the problems faced by inner-city black children than do the social group for which such stories are chiefly intended. In this new climate of uncertainty, it is quite touching to look back fifty years ago to the ideas of the Russian psychologist Nikolai Rubakin, who wrote that eventually all books would contain on their title pages a 'bibliopsychological' classification enabling each reader to choose a book corresponding exactly to his or her own psychological type (cited in Nell, 1988, p. 116). Such dreams are now so remote as to seem virtually impossible.

Children's literature and child development

It is not surprising therefore that today's critics tend to fall back increasingly on assessing literary values alone when reviewing children's literature, leaving ideas about any possible interaction between book and reader as largely unmapped territory. Yet it is still tempting to try to discover some psychological parallels to literary merit in the critical assessment of children's literature in terms of at least the *possible* developmental effect of such books upon the young. If a book is considered good to read, for example, can such merit also be described in terms of its potential for psychological growth in the young reader? After all, it does seem somewhat unlikely that literary merit as such exists totally independently from developmental ways of assessing how much or how little a book may have to offer a young audience still at a very impressionable age.

In seeking to answer this question it is always important to avoid making any *necessary* connection between a book's merits, literary or otherwise, and the effect it may then have upon some young readers. It is also essential to remember that less meritorious forms of writing can always have good effects should they happen to respond to their readers' particular needs at the time. But despite these caveats, if children's books of merit are looked at for their potential for psychological growth, I believe quite a good case can be made for bringing the literary critic and the developmental psychologist together in praise of particular authors, with each profession describing virtues which, when translated from literary to developmental terms or vice-versa, often amount to much the same thing.

The language of children's literature

Let's start with language itself and the needs of very young readers. Good writing for this age group from a literary point of view should be fresh, direct and rhythmic – easy to remember and a pleasure to listen to. Short, spare sentences are preferable to long, rambling structures, and a bright, lively vocabulary better than a dull repetitive one. Over now to the psychologists, who would surely agree with all these criteria from a developmental point of view, however much they habitually fail to follow such rules themselves when it comes to their own literary styles. For them, language acquisition is probably the most important feature in all development, as the ultimate tool which differentiates human beings from animals, enabling us to escape at an early age from domination by the here and now in favour of making sense of the present and planning for the future.

It follows that the early language children experience should be as attractive and interesting as possible in order for them to learn it quickly and easily, taking a natural pleasure in the process. Rhythmic structures, typically contained in nursery rhymes, television jingles or football chants, always prove especially easy for an infant to learn. What Beatrix Potter once described as 'Fine words' also have a fascination of their own simply because the sound of them is satisfying in itself at a time when the meaning of a word may be less important than the interesting noise it makes. Thus the way infants will happily learn certain archaic words and phrases drawn from nursery rhymes because they are fun to articulate rather than for their practical use. And regarding language as fun is of great significance for really positive individual attitudes towards language acquisition at any stage of life.

Dull, restricted or pretentious language of the type that is anathema to the literary critic also has no merit for the psychologist. Learning a number of synonyms early on in life (boat, ship; pig, swine) simply underlines for children the potential versatility of language as opposed to the idea that objects and words only exist in a strictly one-to-one relationship. Writers who constantly repeat themselves therefore restrict children's vocabulary as well as their own. Unnecessarily flowery language also lacks the hard, concrete base necessary at an early stage to link words clearly to whatever object or action they are setting out to describe. Circumlocutions, extended metaphors, elaborate subordinate clauses or heavily Latinate phrases may simply puzzle rather than enlighten a young reader.

Developing understanding

Once the reader has developed a reasonable vocabulary and therefore a way of conceptualising everyday experiences, the next developmental stage is to learn how to use this tool effectively in the never-ending task of escaping from egocentricity in favour of a world view that can take into account attitudes and knowledge other than one's own. This the child does principally through the medium of play and general conversation, during which time it inevitably becomes apparent that one's own particular way of thinking about things or doing something is not always shared by other people. For the Russian psychologist Vygotsky, whose views are increasingly influential in modern psychological theory, the full realisation that someone else on occasions may think differently from oneself is a most important step in human development. Even if the other person is wrong on any particular issue, the stimulus of having to take on another point of view can always enrich and extend those narrow, egocentric ways of computing the world with which we all start out in life.

Books too can play an important part in this process, and good books particularly so. By 'good', I mean those that succeed in going beyond mere story-telling towards sharing a particularly interesting or relevant individual vision of the world with the reader. By the end of a story of this type, readers may well feel that they have somehow advanced in their own understanding, not just of the book but of some of the rest of life as well. This is of course a very inadequate description of all 'good' literature, ignoring the difficulties posed by any proper critical assessment of different genres such as satire and light reading. But some critical shorthand is necessary here in order to advance my general argument, and henceforth I shall use 'good' to describe authors who have the ability to write readably about serious topics, and 'light' to describe authors who fail or possibly never even try to meet this challenge. In doing so, I am sensible of the enormous pleasures offered by such 'light' authors both to myself and to many other readers, and as such I am happy to recognise their essential part in the reading continuum, whatever seemingly harsh words I may say about them from now on in terms of the rest of this discussion.

One quality of good novelists is their skill in persuading readers that they are reading fiction that is also in many ways true to life. While light novelists may be content merely to reflect readers' wish-fulfilment fantasies or common social prejudices, the good novelist can push them instead towards taking another point of view that may previously have never occurred to them. So while light novelists may simply go along with a reader's lazy desire for happy endings, clear-cut distinctions between good and evil and other undemanding fare, skilled novelists may instead manage to get over some of the intractability and variousness of real life. While light novelists may be happy to offer stereotyped characterisations, with the lead characters always so fine and handsome and the villains regularly so deeply unattractive, good novelists may present a more complex view of human beings better in keeping with the realities of a reader's life either at that moment or still to come.

The potential developmental value of this type of fiction is clear. All readers approach a novel in a solitary state when reading silently and only semi-shared with others when hearing it read aloud, given that the story will still be absorbed in private. Essentially, therefore, the story acts as an invisible companion to the reader, travelling along with him or her from start to finish. Just as other children or adults can stimulate a child by commenting on everyday experiences or imaginings from a different point of view, so too can a novelist through the act of writing. Indeed, the intrinsic appeal of narrative is so strong that the particular way a novelist chooses to construct experience may often prove extra memorable for the reader. Conventional novelists here will hand on conventional ideas, very often confirming readers in their fundamental beliefs. Good novelists on the other hand often offer a quite original and therefore initially unpredictable way of seeing the world, both in what they say and in the particular style with which they say it. For readers ready to branch out intellectually and emotionally, this type of stimulus can be very powerful, especially if the novelist seems to have more in common with them than do many of the other non-literary voices surrounding them at the moment.

Intellectual development

Good literature can also be effective in giving shape and meaning to otherwise abstract ideas and concepts. Such ideas are often hard to understand or remember in themselves, but once presented in the guise of particular characters like Messrs Micawber or Pecksniff, then readers have a better chance of absorbing to what special characteristics 'Micawberesque' or 'Pecksniffian' actually refer. But these characters only become alive through the genius of Dickens, not because of the particular complex of human failings they represent. They will be remembered for their literary impact first and then after that for what they stand for. In the same way, abstract ideas such as compassion, tolerance, bigotry or egotism all become more memorable and immediate when represented by vital characters in a story rather than by abstract symbols in a general discussion.

Good novels also often touch on those larger questions surrounding all human existence. Images of hope and despair, birth and death, kindness and cruelty, joy and suffering, losing and gaining, are seldom far from the writings of good authors one way or another, just as they constantly crop up as major themes in fairy tales. While many readers may find it difficult to talk to others about some of these matters at a personal level, they may find it at times easier experiencing and discussing these ideas through an inner dialogue with the invisible author as the story proceeds. Finding an echo of one's most significant personal feelings in some stories has always been a key element in the appeal of fiction. The more limited the fiction, the narrower the range of feelings discussed and the more trite any final resolution offered in the text. Once again, good authors usually have so much more to offer by way of making some sense of the contradictions of everyday living, although how many readers will want to accompany them on this journey of understanding is always going to be another matter.

Imaginative play

Literature can also act as a form of imaginative play, especially where younger readers are concerned. Games often derive from it, with children playing out literary adventures drawn from anything between the Greek myths to the stories of Enid Blyton. For Vygotsky, such games are important in development, enabling children to experiment freely with different roles, different emotions and even with a different way of talking or thinking. This experimentation at an early age gives children scope for exploring their own potential as fully as possible, sometimes with important effects where their eventual ambitions for their own futures are concerned. Children themselves are of course adept at playing such games through their own volition. But an input from literature can enormously extend their range of play situations, with books taking on the role of an interesting friend full of new ideas for extra exciting imaginary games. Such games as well as being fun in themselves also teach children a certain amount about themselves and their capacity to act differently in different situations, albeit in the imagination.

Books also have much to teach about reality itself. When a novel describes a time, place or particular event unknown to readers, it is up to the veracity of such descriptions whether the audience comes away from them better informed or simply reacting to the author's own prejudices. Descriptions of geography, history and politics as depicted in novels can vary between a genuine desire to describe things as they are thought to be, and a range of sometimes farcical literary stereotypes. Once again, a good author will generally take any serious literary tasks set by them in their books seriously; light ones care less, often superimposing their own fixed views on whatever they are writing about. In addition, good writers make what they are describing come alive through the quality of their writing. Paul Scott's India, Graham Greene's Africa, Somerset Maugham's Malaya, Rosemary Sutcliff's Ancient Britain, all come across vividly as real places, startlingly different from details of ordinary living today. For readers who want to take the opportunity, such books transcend the here and now, replacing it with time-travel in the mind – the next best thing to real travel, and so much more accessible a journey for most readers at most stages of their lives.

Understanding personality

Another hall-mark of good writing is the life-like quality of the characters it describes. Not simply larger than life, emblematic types of character, but the quieter, often first person narrators like Jim Hawkins from *Treasure Island*, standing in so well for the ordinary reader suddenly faced by a quite extraordinary situation. Such characters are seldom consistently heroic, decisive or wise in their initial perceptions; it is usually only light novelists who create heroes who combine fearlessness with never ever being mistaken about anything. Some of the other characters they meet might not always seem very appealing to start with, but may improve with time and more understanding. In this way, part of the adventure undertaken in any good novel often consists of a purely internal journey from ignorance to eventual greater wisdom on the part of the main character and, should they wish to take the chance, by the reader as well. A light novel by contrast will generally concentrate mainly on external happenings, while a good novel will tend to link the chief events it describes with important psychological or attitudinal changes also taking place within the main characters at the same time.

Learning to better understand oneself and others is one of the tasks of childhood. To the extent that readers recognise some of their own behaviour in the books they read, so have they the chance to see how such behaviour seems in the light of other character's reactions in a story. A young bully, for example, could learn something about how he must appear to others by reading a novel like Robert Cormier's *The Chocolate War*. A young bigot may receive a similar jolt of recognition after reading a story where the main character suffers from such oppression rather than administers it.

Novels are also uniquely placed when it comes to closer understanding of the feelings and behaviours of others very different from oneself. Handicapped children, children from different ethnic backgrounds, children of different gender, class or physical shape – all have a chance in novels to speak up for themselves, so forcing the reader into realising something which always comes as a surprise, especially when we are young: that others may experience life very differently from the way we do. What exactly readers then choose to do with this knowledge is another matter. But once again, good writers can make those characters performing this type of educational function seem totally alive at the same time. Light novelists may instead simply go on repeating the very stereotypes when describing their characters that teach nothing beyond confirming already existing prejudices. Or, if such novelists do indeed want to show certain normally misunderstood characters in a better light, the temptation is often to describe them in impossibly idealistic terms, so carrying little conviction with readers trying to identify such characters with the real thing in everyday life.

The development of moral thinking

Part of growing up has always been associated with the development of moral thinking. Typically, children pass from early stages of believing in harsh, reciprocal justice to an eventually more balanced view, where motivation and other antecedent causes must also be borne in mind when assessing guilt in others. To the extent that nearly all fiction operates within a moral framework, with authors usually distinguishing between what they consider right or wrong attitudes and behaviour, then almost any book can harmonise or not with a reader's own feelings about everyday morality. Light novelists generally choose to deal with these matters more superficially. Good novelists will almost always see such matters in more complex terms. By showing the pros and cons inseparable from many moral choices, such authors can almost force readers into taking part in some sort of moral discussion on their own part.

The existence of such internal discussions can be very important in the general growth of moral thinking. Setting young people human dilemmas which allow no quick or easy moral solutions has been shown to be particularly effective in encouraging them to think in new and constructive ways. Psychological experiments confirming this finding have often consisted of getting young people to read brief paragraphs outlining dilemmas requiring a solution from their readers. After exercises such as these, young people often seem to have extended their powers of moral argument quite considerably from levels that existed before (see Tucker, 1981, p. 127).

Something like this psychological technique can also be conducted more memorably by a novelist who can create characters with whom readers strongly identify. If these characters then come to face particular dilemmas from time to time, reader reaction can be very involved indeed. Not all readers will want to take up such challenges, but for those really involved in a story the internal moral battles of Jean Valjean in *Les Miserables* or Raskolnikov in *Crime and Punishment* also become their own moral conundrums, to be resolved as they think fit whatever the final outcome in the novel itself. Children's literature rarely contains quite such titanic moral struggles as these, but good writers still set young readers tough moral tests which in essence can also evoke the same type of inner questioning and the need for some final, personal resolution over the main issue involved.

A sense of personal direction

The way that good books give shape and meaning not simply to other people, other places and other times but also to personal feelings and morality hints at their most important potential function of all. As it is, children by nature tend to be caught up in short-term considerations of their immediate environment.

But at some stage they will have the capacity to take a longer view of why exactly they are here and what they want to achieve. Such very personal matters are sometimes kept secret from others, especially those who are normally close, since in essence they can only be resolved by the individual concerned.

Clearly, books which themselves discuss such matters can be important in helping first to frame and then to suggest possible answers to these eternal questions. Such a service can be particularly significant for those children who never receive any other encouragement towards taking a longer view of things. The American psychologist Jerome Bruner (1975) has defined what he terms as the culture of poverty as an inability to believe that anything an individual can do will ever have any useful or permanent effect upon their lives. Within such a despairing philosophy, short-term aims are everything and long-term thinking something of an irrelevance. But as some autobiographical accounts of deprived childhoods have shown, fiction on occasion, has had the potential to act as a powerful counter-balance here (Tucker, 1981, pp. 177–9).

There are many reasons why this should be so. One of the hall-marks of a good novel has always been the way that the particular events described within it also play a larger, more symbolic role in the progress of the story in which they occur. In this sense, almost everything that happens can, by the story's conclusion, also amount to more than the mere sum its parts. Attaching significance to the whole of life in this manner is one way in which human existence can cease to seem a mere jumble of events. Instead, the novelist can, through his or her craft, transform it into something with more shape and therefore more meaning. Such insights are valuable for all of us, but especially for those who normally fail to find any particular sense of direction, either in their own lives or else in the perceived lives of others.

Many of the great myths that have always appealed to the human imagination also offer explanations to the young for why the world is as it is and why we do as we do. Jerome Bruner has described such myths as 'At once an external reality and the resonances of the internal vicissitudes of man.' (Bruner, 1962, p. 31) For him, 'Myth provides a ready-made means of externalising the human plight by embodying and representing it in storied plot and characters.' (p. 32) Novels too can share in this quality, with each depicted journey through life shown to have certain consequences, both positive and negative, for those characters choosing the particular path that they do.

Such consequential attributions may of course exist more in the mind of the novelist than in life itself. But giving shape to everyday choices also gives the reader a sense of understanding and even perhaps a sense of control so far at least as the perceived direction of his or her own life is concerned. Good novelists will usually take this responsibility seriously, standing back from the temptation to make grossly over-simplified connections between cause and effect in human affairs. Lighter novelists may suggest easier, more conventional patterns of human behaviour, based as much on what we wish from life as on what we know to be true. In both cases, readers are presented with what Bruner has described as 'A map of possible roles and of possible worlds' (Bruner, 1987, p. 91) and therefore with some sort of handle on experience, whether past, present, or even that which is contemplated for the future.

A sense of self

Bruner has also written that our sensitivity to narrative provides us with a major link between our own sense of self and our understanding and sense of others in the social world around us (Bruner, 1987, p. 94). For the reader in particular search of such meaning, fiction can therefore have much to offer, especially during late childhood and adolescence when questions about the precise nature of personal identity can seem so very important. In this way, books that take this particular task seriously at best serve the function of a bridge towards greater understanding, rather than a cul-de-sac leading readers up well-trodden fantasy paths going nowhere in particular.

In fact, in any act of reading the reader brings his or her own past experiences both of literature and of life to a book in order to make sense of it. A good book has the capacity to enlarge both experiences, so leaving readers with more to bring not just to their next reading experience but also to their feelings about life itself. But should a novelist hold superficial or distorted views of life, readers will be offered something in many ways of less value. Part of the merit of good writing, however, is its determination to wrestle with life as we know it rather than with comforting fantasies or with depressive delusions. That is why when reading a good book one so often has that feeling of encountering genuine experience, despite the way such raw existence has been dressed up and presented through the necessary artifices of fiction.

Principal readers

While readers of every age can turn to the best of fiction for support, insight, inspiration or whatever else they may be looking for, younger readers in particular are often most open to influences from what they read at a time in their own lives when their attitudes and impressions are at their most fluid. What, then, determines whether they are going to make the most of the books available to them? This is really another topic, but one which must at least be touched on here. It has been said, for example, that good books read us at the same time as we read them. In other words, fiction which has something new to offer in a voice that is not immediately familiar can initially pose a threat to all readers. Are we going to have the courage to take on this new point of view, thus possibly disturbing some of our own comfortably engrained ways of seeing things? And are we going to make the extra effort often needed in order to fill in any gaps within such novels from our own imaginations?

For good novelists often leave the reader with some imaginative reconstructions to perform on their own within a novel's main plot. This is in contrast to fiction of the spoon-feeding type, strong in established formulae of redundancy and repetition, and with few well-worn literary stones ever left unturned. Understandably, many readers are not equal or even interested in taking on any harder task than this. If they read good books at all, it may be for the bare minimum of their story alone. But for readers in search of something deeper than this, even the lightest of fiction can sometimes seem of the highest importance and relevance to them. Once presented with more serious fiction, such readers can usually find much more within it by virtue of an author's ultimate commitment to a personal vision of life that is both highly individual yet also universally significant at the same time.

What remains, therefore, is the greater *potential* of the good novel to have some of the personal effects I have described with those readers ready to seize the opportunity. To that extent, the argument for linking literary merit with psychological growth remains strong, providing no one ever tries to suggest that such connections are always going to happen in the case of each individual reader. But the aim of presenting all children with the best which has been written for them remains a sound one. What they then decide to do with this gift will depend on a host of other factors. The most that teachers and parents can ensure is that young readers should have ready access to the best in literature, and that such access, whether at home or in the classroom, should always be made available in the most effective and positive way possible.

the 'good book': non-narrative aspects

Alison Littlefair

Like me you will no doubt remember the early delight of reading and listening to stories. Perhaps you also remember the fascination of books which provided information. I seem to recollect that here my reading was restricted to the captions under the illustrations. Certainly, I came to know the information provided by those captions almost by heart. What I did not realise was that I was also becoming familiar with the expression of more formal writing.

We know that teaching children to read is not simply concerned with helping them to develop the ability to decode, but rather we teach children to read texts with understanding. However, we are not just helping our pupils to understand the meaning of a specific story or piece of information, we are, in fact, teaching our pupils how different kinds of meaning are commonly expressed within our culture.

The most common expression of meaning which young children meet is that of narrative. Children listen to narration in conversation, to stories that are read to them, and they watch and listen to narrative on television. Their understanding is carried along by the dynamics of narrative and thus most children become familiar with the form of narrative even before they learn to read. They come to know implicitly that a setting and characters will be introduced, they know that some kind of action will occur, that there will probably be a crisis of some kind and that, in their stories at least, there will usually be a happy ending. When young readers meet non-narrative texts, they meet quite different forms of meanings.

Common categories of books

We often differentiate books simply as being fiction and non-fiction. We refer to many non-fiction books as 'information' or 'reference' books. Such categorisation is really too simple for it is mainly based on the content of the books which masks the range of meanings and consequent linguistic forms of these books.

Recently we have seen a surge of non-narrative books produced for younger readers as publishers respond to the National Curriculum for Reading (DES, 1989a). These books are sometimes categorised as: books within a reading/language scheme, or 'trade books' which are sold to book shops, or 'resource books', or text books. Again these categories also overlook the range of reading experience which different non-narrative books afford young readers.

Limited reading debate

Despite all the debate about the initial teaching and learning of reading, little attention seems to be paid to how children are to be assisted to become competent independent readers of a variety of texts. We seem to assume that as children progress through the primary school and middle school, they transfer their ability to read narrative into competent reading of non-narrative, upon which much of their further education and capacity to deal with adult life will depend.

Research (Chapman, 1987; Littlefair, 1991) suggests that this confidence is misplaced and that it is only the minority of young readers who adequately transfer their ability to read narrative to a competence to read a range of non-narrative. Her Majesty's Inspectorate for England and Wales (DES, 1991b, p. 16) state: 'Firmer foundations must be laid to ensure the widespread and effective development of reading beyond the initial stages.'

The National Curriculum for Reading for England and Wales (DES, 1989a) draws attention to the value of teaching important research skills such as skimming and scanning, and use of a list of chapters and index. However, there is a vital aspect of the teaching and learning of reading which is hardly mentioned – that of sustained reading of chunks of non-narrative texts.

Linguistic insights

Reading is not quite such a receptive language process as is sometimes supposed. As we read we construct our understanding of the meaning of the text. As we do this we are influenced by our own relevant past experience and our awareness of the way in which writers construct meaning. We have implicit knowledge of a range of text forms but our ability to express this understanding is perhaps more limited. Perhaps we lack 'an adequate language in which to discuss features'. The SEAC Report (1991, p. 20) certainly suggests this reason for the preference of secondary school readers to look only at the content of the text and not at linguistic expression.

There has been extensive study of language as it is used and of the implication of this work for education. This kind of linguistic thought has been developed by Michael Halliday and other systemic linguists. This research enables us to understand more about the varieties of language we all use as we write or speak in different situations for different purposes, and audiences.

Language and culture

Halliday (1978) has indicated the relationship of language and culture for as we speak or write we express cultural meanings.

Some seventy years ago the anthropologist Bronislaw Malinowski (1922) studied the Trobriand Islanders in the South Seas. The later inability of his colleagues to appreciate the implications of his translations of the islanders' conversations illuminated for him the need to explain the social activities which were going on at the time.

We live in a western society which has evolved as a result of people undertaking social activities in ways which have become common place but nonetheless organised. We continually alter those patterns of activity as our social behaviour and perceptions change. Studies have been made (Hasan, 1989; Ventola, 1987) of how we organise spoken language within specific activities such as shopping or making an appointment with the doctor's receptionist. In other words, we organise our meanings in certain patterns.

A group of Halliday's colleagues have termed all of these social processes as 'genres'. Genres used simply to describe literary forms of writing but these linguists suggest that the meaning of every communication is organised and therefore can be termed a genre. They describe their definition of genres like this:

> Genres are referred to as social processes *because members of a culture interact with each to achieve them: as* goal oriented *because they have to get things done; and as* staged *because it usually takes more than one step for participants to achieve their goals.*
>
> (Martin *et al.*, 1987, p. 59)

As we write we similarly take part in a social process or genre. We organise our written meanings in ways which have evolved through constant need to communicate for different purposes. These ways are recognised and if this were not the case there would be no understanding!

We know through experience how to organise a letter to a bank manager, a shopping list or an explanation of how to cook a special dish. As soon as we have a purpose for communication we usually know how to organise it. Unless we are being deliberately provocative we will follow the accepted way of expressing that purpose. Of course our communication will not be formulaic but rather it will be our own expression of that form of meaning.

Writers' purposes and genres of books

We have seen that as soon as we have a writing purpose, we usually have an idea of the genre form we will choose. We might say that purpose and genre are almost synonymous. Authors of non-narrative books write for a range of purposes which they express in a range of genre forms. Thus we can categorise the genres of books on the basis of writers' purposes rather than on the basis of the content of books (Littlefair, 1991).

Books used in school can be categorised into a *literary* genre where the author's purpose is to narrate, to express personal response; an *expository* genre where the author's purpose is to inform, explain, describe, persuade, argue; a *procedural* genre where the author's purpose is to give instructions, to list the stages of a process; and a *reference* genre where the author's purpose is to list explanatory condensed information about certain topics.

Of course, each major genre category includes sub-genres each of which has a characteristic arrangement of meaning. In the literary genre, examples of sub-genres are fairy stories, short stories, poetry, plays, essays etc. In the expository genre, examples of sub-genres are subject text books which explain and describe, newspaper leaders etc. In the procedural genre, examples of sub-genres are reading and language activity books, mathematics books etc. In the reference genre, examples of sub-genres are dictionaries, encyclopaediae etc.

It is important to recognise that genres are not waterproof. For example, descriptions may be written within a story, many explanatory texts include some activities, and reference books often include explanatory writing.

We have already seen that different genres of books are organised in ways which we recognise. A characteristic organisation of a story is that of setting, events, complication, resolution. Many expository texts have an initial introductory general statement about the subject, followed by more detailed descriptions of relevant aspects logically arranged in paragraphs. A procedural text often has a list of items which are necessary for an activity followed by the steps of that activity stated in order. A reference text has items of information organised in a logical manner with a brief description of each item.

Organisation of text or writer's purpose

I have argued that social purpose determines the way in which we organise writing. Kinneavy *et al.*, (1976) take another perspective by looking at the 'modes of discourse' as abstract concepts. They point out that there has been interest in methods of composition since Greek and Roman times.

Kinneavy *et al.*, describe the modes of discourse as narration, classification, description and evaluation. They see these modes as determining the organisation of writing and are concerned with how we can recognise one mode from another. Their answer is not based on a linguistic perspective but rather on the view of reality which each mode gives. They explain, 'What discourses are about is the province of what are called the modes of discourse' (p. 1) and their framework attempts to show how texts 'represent realities': static (description and classification) and dynamic (narrative and evaluation i.e. forward and retrospective time sequences). They see 'exposition' as an imprecise term which has had several meanings: it has been used as the 'opposite' of literary or creative writing; it has been used along with narration and description to define a group of modes; it has been used as a category which included classification and evaluation.

Here is the difference between a linguistic approach and a more philosophical approach. The genre categories described in this chapter are taken from the study of the relationship between the purposes of authors of books used in school and the linguistic form they select to express that purpose. Therefore my use of 'expository genre' refers closely to the recent definition of 'exposition': 'an explanation or commentary' (Fowler and Fowler, 1990). However, a linguistic description of genres is not complete without looking at the choice of language within the genre form.

Writers' choice of language

Some writers will experiment with linguistic expression and then we recognise literary innovation or experiment. Usually, however, writers' choice of language is constrained by the situation they are in. For example, we readily recognise that the language of a formal report is quite different from the language of conversation at a family party. A writer or speaker is always in a certain situation which is composed of a topic or area of interest, how that is being discussed and who is taking part in the language exchange.

Halliday (1989) describes these three features of any communicative situation as follows: the general area of concern as the *field of discourse*; the medium of language and its internal organisation as the *mode of discourse*; and the degree of familiarity between participants as the *tenor of discourse*. For instance, in writing this chapter I am writing about non-narrative books which is the field of discourse. I am using written language which is organised in a logical sequence which is the mode of discourse. There is some formality because I am writing for a professional audience which is personally unknown to me. This is the tenor of discourse.

The three aspects of field, mode and tenor interact. In other words no factor is superior to the others. It is the interaction of the *field, mode* and *tenor* which produces a *register of language* which is expressed through a choice of appropriate vocabulary and grammar. It has to be noted that as I write this chapter I am constantly making a conscious choice of what I hope is appropriate vocabulary and grammar. Were I taking part in a general conversation my choice of vocabulary and grammar would be far more spontaneous.

Genre and register

Some linguists use 'genre' and 'register' as synonymous terms. However, as teachers and not linguists, we will probably find it clearer to consider genre and register as fulfilling complementary, although different functions. In other words, a writer choses a genre which is suitable for his or her purpose. The genre form relates to the cultural form of expressing meaning. Genre can be considered as the framework of a written or spoken communication. The writer expresses the details of the communication in a register of language which is inevitably constrained by the immediate situation. Figure 9.1 shows this relationship (see overleaf).

Knowledge about genre and register gives us linguistic tools to look at the range of books for young readers. We can look for the choices of vocabulary and grammar which authors make as they write non-narrative. We can judge how far a non-narrative book for younger readers mirrors these choices and can therefore be considered to be 'authentic' non-narrative text.

Features of registers in expository books

Perhaps the most important non-narrative text in school is expository for here is the complex language of exploration and description, of persuasion and argument. It is this register of language which presents the greatest challenge to readers and which is ultimately of the greatest importance for their development as readers and as competent language users.

When pupils read explanation and description they have to understand a text which is arranged quite differently from narrative. As children read, their interest is not carried along by the dynamics of a chronologically ordered story, for the organisation within the non-narrative text is likely to be non-chronological. This could be based on a logical arrangement of information which might involve the notion of problem and solution; of compare and contrast; and of cause and effect (Perera, 1984; Horowitz, 1985). We can see facts arranged in the following passage in a way which explains the reason why mountain sheep and goats have special hooves:

> *Animals such as mountain sheep and goats have special hooves. These are hard and sharp and grip the rock almost like pincers. Their hooves*

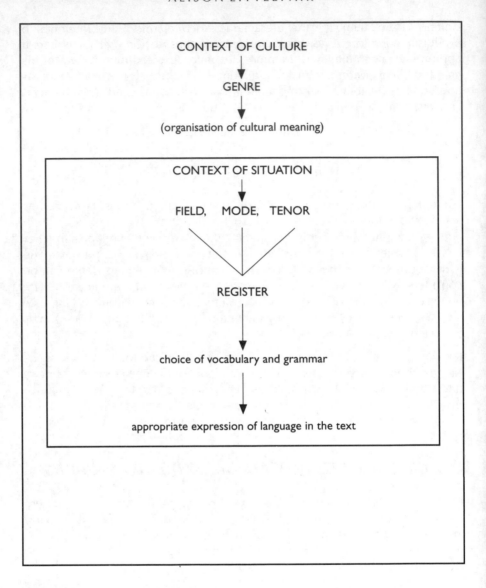

Figure 9.1 Genre and register

> *help mountain sheep and goats to climb steep rocks without slipping
> and falling.*
>
> (*The Young Geographer Investigates Mountains*, p. 17)*

The grammar used by writers of more advanced expository texts is complex.
The way in which different parts of a text are linked may be difficult to follow.

*NB full details of all books mentioned are given in Appendix 1.

Indeed, many subject texts are characterised by distinctive methods of linguistic cohesion. A common grammatical construction used by writers to achieve greater objectivity in more advanced explanations is that of the passive voice as in the following sentence: 'The fabled wealth of Troy was probably collected as toll money from ships using the Dardanelles' (*The Legend of Odysseus*, p. 45).

Longer sentences are yet another characteristic of expository texts. Further, these sentences often have complex introductions so that readers must retain a sense of the meaning of the introduction until the main information of the sentence is given and then understand the whole statement. Look at this sentence, for example: 'When Schliemann, the discoverer of Troy first visited the site in 1868 it was far different' (*The Legend of Odysseus*, p. 45).

Longer sentences of expository text contain a much larger number of 'content' words than narrative text. A content word is one with meaning beyond its grammatical function. For example, look at the amount of content in this sentence [author's emphasis]: '*Volcanoes occur* where the *earth's crust* is *weak*' (*The Young Geographer Investigates Mountains*, p. 8). Readers have therefore to manage quite large chunks of information. Another way of saying this is that the meaning is 'packed'. As a result, as texts become more subject oriented the content words become more technical and the 'packed' meaning increases.

But we should not think that readers who experience difficulty in coping with this kind of writing are simply having difficulty with unfamiliar vocabulary. Jeanne Chall *et al.*, (1990) describe studies of the reading development of children of 'low economic status'. They note that children who read with meaning in Grade 3 began to slip in Grade 4. The lack of a wide vocabulary seems to be a contributory factor but so is the lack of awareness of different linguistic structures.

As authors write about knowledge, particularly within subject areas, they introduce ideas and 'concepts'. The formality of language is increased in order to express this thinking. For example:

> There are problems of conservation on all coasts whether they are especially attractive or not. Some of these problems are caused by conflicts between groups of people who want different things.

> (*Finding Out About The Coast*, p. 44)

We may wonder whether we should confront our young readers with this kind of reading challenge. Indeed, there has been a tendency for teachers to try to help struggling readers by simplifying, even by rewriting more advanced expository text. This strategy has been termed 'the curse of the vernacular' (Marland, 1991).

Margaret Donaldson (1989) describes such language as 'the language of systematic thought' and has alerted us to its importance. This language is very different from the language of popular story books; it is also quite different from the spoken language of many children, particularly those coming from less literate homes. This language is more distant, it is not spontaneous. It is the language of official documents, of business communications, indeed, it is the prestigious language of our society.

Many readers who are able to read simply structured text probably require further help so that they can read complex written expression:

> They need now to enlarge their understanding of the many ways in which words can be handled with skill on the printed page – handled to achieve economy, or elegance, or emphasis, or surprise, or cohesion between sentences, or logical clarity in a sustained argument, to name only a few of the aims that concern an author.

(Donaldson, 1989, p. 29)

Of course, we do not anticipate very young readers meeting all the complexities of this genre of writing but we should be aware of the kind of future reading tasks which will be given to these readers.

Selecting a 'good book'

Opinions vary as to how to simplify expository text for younger readers. There is the problem that simplified language can lose much of the original meaning. When writers reconstruct knowledge for young children they sometimes mix the more impersonal language of reality with personal and imaginative language. Of course, children learn by relating new knowledge to their existing concepts but this does not mean that the introduction of scientific ideas, for instance, should be couched in the language of narrative or of conversation.

Unsworth (1990) notes the importance of introducing young readers to the characteristic discourse of different subject areas. Children are interested in both imaginary and factual interpretations of the world and there is little reason to think that children are unable to read appropriately simplified explanatory text.

Of course, some children will select non-narrative books which they find of particular interest. And it is also important that we make a deliberate choice of non-narrative books. Just as children begin to read simple stories they should also begin to read simple non-narrative books and gradually progress to more complex texts. This means that we should look for books which include something of the form and choice of language of more advanced texts. Look at the careful construction of this extract from an explanatory booklet:

Making a Wildtrack programme
You are now going to learn how one special programme was made. It

was one of a series of nature programmes called Wildtrack. *Wildtrack goes out in the afternoon, and it is a live programme. It is introduced by two well-known presenters, Sue Ingle and Michael Jordan. Wildtrack comes from a studio, but it also has stories about wildlife that have been filmed in the countryside. Because it has many different items, and up-to-date information about interesting events, it is called a magazine programme. There are many magazine programmes on television, and they are all made in much the same way.*

Planning the programme
Planning the programme has to start in good time. A few weeks before the programme is going to be broadcast, the two presenters, Mike and Sue, have a meeting with the people who made the programme. There are six of them, and they are called the production team.

(*Making a TV programme*, p. 8)

Clearly the previous text is good preparation for a more demanding objec-tively written text (such as the one which follows which is valuable reading for more experienced readers):

The Voyages of Odysseus

The Greek View
The Illiad *and* The Odyssey *were sacred books to most Greeks. Yet the wanderings of Odysseus were a subject of heated argument even in those days.*

The earlier Greeks believed that the places mentioned were to be found in the western Mediterranean. This area was little known even though Mycenaen ships had traded along the coasts of Italy and Sicily.

Beyond Gibralter
Later, as Greek traders opened up the western Mediterranean, establish-ing colonies on the coast of Spain, people began to look beyond the Straits of Gibralter for Odysseus' wonderland. But many now concluded that the search was hopeless and dismissed the whole story as pure fiction.

(*The Legend of Odysseus*, p. 60)

There are publications which signal one genre from another. The last extract is set out clearly from narrative sections of the book so that a change of writer's purpose and language is apparent to the reader. Another publisher uses different coloured paper to distinguish the explanatory and procedural genres within a book.

Features of registers in procedural writing

It may be a reflection of the difficulty of writing explanatory and descriptive text for younger pupils that a large number of non-narrative books are written in the procedural genre. The complexities of grammar can be avoided by listing information or by writing instructions.

None the less, these books are important for they contain information which is organised in a distinctive way. The reader is addressed more directly as the instructions become commands. Simple instructions often relate more personally to the reader by the use of 'you' in their instructions:

How to blow up a balloon

What you need
- *a balloon*
- *a piece of string*
- *a person to blow up the balloon*

Steps
1   First you have to pick up the balloon and put the opening to your mouth.

(*Exploring Procedures About Magic*, p. 25)

There is a greater complication in more advanced texts which may introduce explanations to complement procedures or instructions, e.g.

Make a compass

Equipment: *A large needle, a small piece of cork or polystyrene, a magnet, a saucer of water.*

First you need to turn the needle into a magnet; this is called **magnetising** *the needle. To do this, stroke one pole of the magnet gently along the whole length of the needle in the same direction 20 times.*

(*Electricity and Magnets*, p. 32)

Children may need some assistance as they 'unravel' the varying meanings which can be involved in this form of text. In this way we prepare pupils to read and write highly organised instructions in science books.

Features of registers in reference books

When children read reference books such as an encyclopedia they meet features of both procedural and expository language. So although many books in this genre are attractively produced we should not overlook the fact that they may demand very flexible reading skills. Our judgement of the suitability of these books for young readers should be based again on the clarity of the information.

The arrangement of the listed information is procedural. It may be alphabetical or it may be to do with the area of interest. The language used in the explanations may well display complex characteristics of the expository genre. If space is limited there may be further reading difficulties as the language of explanations is abbreviated. The following extract seems appropriate for a first encyclopedia:

Cheetah
The cheetah is a member of the cat family. Cheetahs have very long legs. They are the fastest land animals. They can run at up to 112 kilometres per hour. In India people used to train cheetahs to hunt other animals. Now there are not many cheetahs left in India. Most cheetahs live in Africa. Cheetahs hunt in pairs at sunrise and sunset when it is cooler.

(*The Macmillan First Encyclopedia*)

An integrated approach

When we initially teach children to read we are greatly assisted by their general familiarity with a story form. When we introduce young readers to non-narrative books we usually do not have this advantage. In other words we must create contexts in which non-narrative can be experienced by our pupils.

Perhaps the clearest way to familiarise children with the construction of non-narrative text is for them to write and discuss their own information texts. Together with children, we can construct simple descriptive reports and instructions. We can discuss new knowledge with young children and we can become more conscious of the way in which we, as teachers, use language in the discussions. In this way we can gradually introduce more impersonal phrases and less familiar vocabulary.

Gradually, we can introduce more involved writing of procedures and explanations. This is not the expression of personal response but the language of knowledge. Thus we will help children to construct the chronological organisation of instructions. On the other hand we may help them to note the logical arrangement of simple descriptive reports. Considerable work (Martin and Rothery, 1981; 1986) has been done with Australian children which suggests that even young children respond well to this kind of teacher intervention.

We have already noted that conceptualisation features in later expository texts. If pupils are to develop as competent readers and writers of description and explanation they may well need us to model, to suggest and to innovate language by conferencing and class discussion of non-narrative expression. The Schools Examination and Assessment Council Report (1991, p. 19) states:

They should be given opportunities to 'reshape' information into a form different from its source and always for a communicative purpose. They should be encouraged to consider the appropriateness of the choice of any given format.

Balancing the reading curriculum

Our success in continuing to teach pupils to read a range of texts depends not only on our choice of books themselves but also on our ability to devise a way of monitoring the genres of books they read in school. We have seen that we can identify the main genre of a book by looking at the overall purpose of the writer. If we categorise the books that we provide for our pupils we can compare the number of books in each genre.

A review organised in this way of genres of books read by pupils revealed that children in different schools were reading varying 'balances' of book genres (Littlefair, 1991). The same was true of two classes of similar age in the same school. There was a noticeable lack of expository books read by these primary school children but an even smaller number was noted by those pupils after their arrival in the secondary school. In contrast, both primary and secondary school pupils were reading a large number of books in the procedural genre. This suggests that we must be aware just how often we give pupils the opportunity to read different non-narrative genres and, in particular, extended expository text. Otherwise it may well be that the 'retreat from print' in the secondary school noted by Lunzer and Gardner (1979) still continues.

If pupils are to become competent readers of non-narrative, able to discover information and reconstruct it for their own purposes, they require a sense of the overall forms of these genres and of the language which is commonly used to write about knowledge. Most readers require some direction if they are to develop this awareness. The effectiveness of the direction we give to them is not only one of helping them to extract information from non-narrative texts but also one which gives emphasis to reading and experiencing a well-selected range of books.

Appendix 1   **NON-NARRATIVE BOOKS MENTIONED**

Bentley, J. and **Charlton, B.** (1985) *Finding Out About The Coast.* London: Batsford Academic and Educational.
Beynon, M. 'Making a TV Programme' in **Reid, J.** and **Donaldson, M.** (eds), *R and D.* London: Macmillan Education.

Cash, T. and **Taylor, B.** (1989) *Electricity and Magnets.* London: Kingfisher Books.

Christie, F.; Gray, P.; Gray, B.; Macken, M.; Martin, J. and **Rothery, J.** (1990) *Exploring Procedures About Magic.* Sydney: Harcourt Brace Jovanovitch.

Connolly, P. (1986) *The Legend of Odysseus.* Oxford: Oxford University

Jennings, T. (1986) *The Young Geographer Investigates Mountains.* Oxford: Oxford University Press.

Turner, D. (1988) *The Macmillan First Encyclopedia.* London: Macmillan.

teaching literacy and children with special needs

Keith Gaines

Introduction

Enthusiasts for the various approaches and cults which have characterised the teaching of reading rarely acknowledge that the evidence of teachers' experience and of a substantial body of research is that many children learn to read adequately, and some learn to read well, whatever scheme, course, programme, or set of experiences is used with them. Of course, if all children learned to read, there would be far less discussion of approaches or methods. It is the problem of children who fail to learn to read that provides the focus for the debate on how we teach literacy. For many teachers, and for most parents, special needs in literacy is synonymous with lack of progress in literacy.

Many of the definitions of special needs in literacy are essentially circular. An assertion that 'This child is failing to learn to read because he has special educational needs' is easily transposed to become 'This child has special educational needs because he is failing to learn to read.' This kind of circular definition is not uncommon even in attempts to assess more precisely the reasons for a child's failure. It may be stated that a child cannot read because he is dyslexic; it may equally be stated that a child is dyslexic because he cannot read. Before I disappear up my own analysis, I will consider, in relation to children with special educational needs:

- the nature of 'special needs';
- the debate on teaching reading;
- the nature of reading research;
- effective educational practice;

and try to resolve this circular dilemma.

The nature of 'special needs' ('I have dysharmonia. You can't sing.')

Broadly speaking, there are two groups of 'children with special educational needs':

1   Children who have a deficit, disability or sensory impairment, specific to an individual child, which may affect the child's ability to benefit from normal educational experiences. Such disabilities are often the result of illness, injury or complications at birth and may frequently be observed and assessed before a child starts school, although, of course, disabling injury or illness can occur at any time. Typically, a child in this group might be described as being blind, deaf, or mentally or physically impaired (although the neologism 'challenged' seems to be creeping in). Children with a deficit or disability can be found in every social class.

2   Children who fail to make expected progress and whose failure is not immediately attributable to any specific deficit, disability or handicap. Such failure to make progress is rarely assessed before a child starts school. Typically, a child in this group might be described as 'less able' or 'a low attainer'. Such children who perform poorly in school are found overwhelmingly in lower socio-economic groups.

These two categories can be further simplified as:

1   Children who have difficulties in and out of school.

2   Children who have difficulties mainly in school.

A child's special needs cannot exist in a social or cultural vacuum. There is a natural sympathy for children perceived to have a deficit or disability which is clearly 'not their fault', whereas other children can often be perceived disapprovingly as contributing to their own misfortune. Teachers should (and do) recognise that many 'special needs' are social class based, hence the almost traditional joke that 'Wayne is illiterate, but Peregrine is dyslexic'. In Britain, this cheap jibe can now be levelled at government policy; the decision that up to 5 per cent of marks will be deducted for poor spelling in examinations (even exams intended to test science and maths) was rapidly qualified by assurances that 'dyslexic' pupils will not be disadvantaged. So the child who has not been adequately taught how to spell will be punished; the child whose parents have been able to obtain the required exemption certificate will not, although both children may be equally blameless in their poor spelling.

The 1981 Education Act established a new set of assessment procedures and funding mechanisms for pupils with special educational needs. Over the past ten years, there has indeed been an increase in funding for pupils with defined special needs. However, since special education budgets are rarely generous and always cash-limited, this increase has mainly been funded by diverting resources from pupils whose performance is similar but not attributable to a socially acceptable 'cause'. You can test the mechanism of this process, and the reality and strength of social attitudes to special educational needs, by collecting money in the street for 'hyperkinetic and hyperactive children' – compare the receipts of your efforts with a similar collection for 'loud and aggressive teenage boys'!

Much practice in special needs literacy teaching, both for 'specific' needs and for general retardation has been based on a tradition of assessment and 'diagnosis' of a learning disability and a consequent delivery, or 'prescription', of a structured corrective programme. This construction of a deliberately unbalanced literacy curriculum was associated with a pseudo-medical educational philosophy which sought to isolate the child and his disability from the whole range of his skills, his background and his social and educational experiences. To see why this should be so, we need to consider the broad nature of the debate on how children learn to read and how we teach them.

Teaching reading (the great non-debate)

The alleged 'debate' on how to teach reading has rarely been a debate at all. One might wonder what has changed since 1967 when Jeanne Chall, noting that educational researchers had devoted more time and effort to the study of reading than to any other school subject, pointed out that researchers' claims and conclusions were usually designed to 'buttress a strongly held view about a method or practice that was already in use or that was a reaction to one in use' (Chall, 1967, p. 18). Characteristic of the recent 'debate' in England has been a growing assertion that children learn to read naturally, just as they learn to talk, despite the absence of any valid theoretical model or observational evidence for this claim. (The assumption that reading is a 'natural' process, rather than a human invention, itself reveals an imprecise grasp of language, for reading is about as 'natural' as a vegetarian hedgehog-flavour pot noodle.) Strident propaganda for 'real books' and 'an apprenticeship approach' has, predictably, produced an equally irrational 'back-to-basics' backlash, with traditionalists calling for phonetics (and this from the Secretary of State!), structure and a return to that mythical golden age when all children learned to read, write, spell, count, respect their elders, get a short haircut and still have change from a shilling.

Although there are many methods, schemes and materials for reading instruction, there are essentially two approaches towards teaching children to read. Chall (1967) used the terms 'meaning emphasis' and 'code emphasis'.

The first approach, often referred to as a 'top-down' approach, holds that children need to approach learning to read with a knowledge and experience of the nature and uses of print, and with experience of stories and books. Children therefore start with books (usually stories) and gradually work down to the skills of word recognition and word building. Within this approach an important consideration, it is argued, is the literary quality of these earliest texts. The second approach, often called a 'bottom-up' approach, emphasises the concept of reading as a set of code-breaking skills and holds that children should begin with letters (or sounds or whole words), progress to phrases and sentences and gradually work their way up to the point at which they can read whole books. In most British schools today these two traditions can be seen in sensible co-existence.

The 'code emphasis' or 'bottom-up' approach has been the dominant tradition in English reading teaching for at least 500 years, although there have always been attempts to introduce children to reading through mean-ingful texts. To many reading teachers, much of the debate between proponents of meaning-based approaches and code-based approaches will have seemed sterile and irrelevant, as the value of effective and interesting texts is often self-evident, especially with children with reading difficulties. The effect of an inappropriate text is highlighted in the following dialogue, passed on to me by a Sheffield teacher:

Miss   (*an enthusiastic and skilled teacher*): 'Now then Wayne, do you think that nasty Mr Fox will get baby bunny, or will baby bunny reach his burrow in time?'

Wayne   (*an unenthusiastic and unskilled reader*): 'Miss, I couldn't give a f*** if nasty Mr Fox gets baby rabbit. This book is f***ing boring.'

Being an experienced special needs teacher, Miss was not struck dumb (temporarily orally challenged) by this criticism, but, after a gentle reprimand (so she said) sought out some reading material for Wayne with a more appropriate meaning content.

Probably the longest surviving system of reading instruction using a meaning-based approach is in New Zealand, where it has been common practice for the past thirty years. It is interesting to note that in terms of books read and magazines purchased (indicators of literacy used by UNESCO and other agencies) New Zealand can lay claim to be the most literate country in the world (McNaughton, 1987). New Zealanders themselves dispute the reason for their high literacy. Some claim that a meaning-based approach is the cause; others argue that there is little else to do in New Zealand but read; some point to a classless (or overwhelmingly middle-class) society, and others to the fact that, until recently, the pubs were shut on Sundays.

It is rarely possible in literacy research and teaching to show clear and unequivocal evidence of cause and effect, but this has not prevented the adoption in other countries (and now in Britain) of the Reading Recovery scheme, originated in New Zealand by Marie Clay of Auckland University (Clay, 1979). Reading Recovery is designed to help the weakest readers, after a year in school, to catch up with their average classmates. The programme involves intensive teacher training in literacy teaching, individual or very small group teaching of children withdrawn from normal lessons, and teaching which is based on a detailed analysis of the child's abilities, interests and skills in literacy. The success of a pilot scheme using teachers trained by Surrey LEA has been widely and enthusiastically reported. The estimated cost per pupil of £1000 has been less widely reported. Hardly reported at all were the substantial reductions in other areas of Surrey's provision for special educational needs and literacy which funded the pilot scheme, another example of the drift from funding the general to funding the specific.

The question, 'Will Reading Recovery work?' is hardly worth asking. Politically, now that £3,000,000 of government money has been invested in setting up the programme in targetted urban areas, it has to be seen to work, or at least, not to fail to work. The pragmatist (and every infant teacher I have discussed this with) could argue that, with £1000 per pupil and individual tuition, almost any child will make substantial progress, regardless of the approach, the materials or the method of instruction. Peering into my crystal ball, I see a number of reports over the next two years which will show that, for most pupils, Reading Recovery is a great success. A few pupils will make disappointing progress, but they will be shown to have had initially undetected intellectual, behavioural, emotional or social problems. As the funding for pilot projects ends, all schools will be exhorted to follow the basic principles of the Reading Recovery 'approach' as far as they can, for resources will not be available for the extension of funding to the whole population of failing readers. A cynic might suspect that the whole initiative owes more to the attraction of the words 'reading recovery' as a snappy political slogan than to the quality and complexity of Clay's important contribution to interventionist literacy strategies.

The nature of reading research (1001 reasons for illiteracy)

Just as the debate about how children learn to read is, in reality, a debate about how children fail to learn to read, so much of the body of reading research is not about what makes children into good readers but what might prevent children becoming good readers. For researchers there would seem to be essentially two kinds of reading failure:

[1] An interesting failure with a definable cause which is often remediable – for example, perceptual deficiencies (auditory/visual/ kinaesthetic); cognitive-processing difficulties (memory/phonological and visual processing); and, with any combination of these, dyslexia.

This interesting failure is almost always viewed as being within the individual child, and not the result of social pressures or environment.

2   A less interesting failure with social and cultural causes, affecting vast numbers of children, and which, from sociological research and reading surveys, does not appear to be readily remediable.

It is not surprising that the majority of reading research is concerned with the first pathological or individual kind of failure rather than the second epidemiological or group failure; for not only may individual reading failure be an intrinsically interesting study, it is a great deal easier to research the failings of two or twenty children than to research the failings of five hundred or five thousand. Research into this first kind of failure, which would include specific reading disabilities, almost invariably starts from an assumption that learning to read is a code emphasis (or 'bottom-up') approach, wherein deficiencies in code-breaking skills or sub-skills of reading must, by definition of 'specific', lie within the child.

Regrettably, much of the body of older psychological research into the supposed correlates of reading difficulties can appear to teachers to be of doubtful relevance or problematical when applied to children in school. I once tried to apply the findings of a collection of research papers, about the relationship between cerebral dominance and reading retardation, to a group of pupils in an infant class. Having ascertained for each child which eye was dominant (i.e. which one they tended to use when only one was required) I asked them to cover their non-dominant eye with one hand (Bannatyne, 1971) and their left ear with the other (Thomatis, 1967). I then asked them to read to me *The Big Red Lorry* (Gay Way Readers) with the left side of their brains (Chasty, 1979). According to the research, this should have produced a significant improvement in their accuracy and fluency. It didn't. As the Goodmans once observed, 'young readers . . . do complex things for which we may be unprepared; and, not having studied the latest theories, they do not always produce confirming evidence' (Goodman and Goodman, 1977, p. 333).

There are serious dangers in assuming that a cognitive deficit (i.e. a particular mental skill that the child is weak at) may be responsible for reading failure. In most books used at one time or another as standard texts on literacy, one can find a list of factors involved in learning to read (e.g. Haffner and Jolly, 1982; Ball, 1977; Moyle, 1976). Such lists rarely, if ever, indicated any order or scale of importance of the alleged sub-skills of reading, but they invariably included a range of visual perception skills. In terms of what we normally understand by skills of visual perception, children who are born blind ('visually challenged') are non-starters, yet many blind children learn to read in a way which satisfies most definitions of literacy. Similarly, many deaf ('auditorily challenged') children learn to read despite an absence of the auditory discrimination skills which some authors maintain are essential for literacy acquisition. To the best of my knowledge, there is no cognitive or perceptual deficit and no medical condition, except death ('mortally challenged'), which absolutely guarantees that a child will not learn to read. Indeed, it is a proud boast of many colleagues experienced in assessing learning difficulties that, given ten minutes with any child who has no problems at all with reading, they will be able to find at least one valid reason why that child should be illiterate.

Perhaps the greatest danger with such approaches when planning to meet special needs is that the discovery of a cognitive deficit such as 'short-term auditory memory' may lead to the abandonment of teaching appropriate to the gross skill of reading in favour of teaching assumed to be appropriate to the identified deficit. In other words, the teacher may stop teaching reading and start teaching to improve 'short-term auditory memory'. Such specific teaching may not transfer to, or enhance, a child's literacy skills. Should the deficiency prove persistent or intractable, it can even become a justification of a child's lack of progress. Many children who are 'slow to get off the ground', may well be made even slower by the provision of pre-reading exercises or perceptual skill programmes rather than experiences such as hearing stories, seeing someone read, or learning phonic skills in a meaningful context, which might be more appropriate to their cognitive development in helping them to appreciate an overall purpose in reading.

In one of the most cautionary studies in this field Ellis and Large (1987, pp. 14–15) noted that:

> If you look for associates of general reading ability in a fairly heterogeneous population then just about any ability will correlate to a significant degree ... if we pick a random subset of a small number of cognitive abilities and test whether people who are good at these are also good at an important, ecologically valid, gross cognitive ability such as reading, then we find, should we run a sufficient number of subjects, that they are.

In other words, people who are good at one thing tend to be good at other things, and children who are poor readers tend to be poor at lots of skills which are often assumed to be related to reading, but what, if anything, is causal? We are back to the circular definition again. Is the child poor at reading because his/her visual memory is poor or is his/her visual memory poor because the child is poor at reading? Virtually all the educational research into dyslexia shows how dyslexics are deficient in this or that subskill, but in my own observations of children identified as dyslexic almost the only common factor is that dyslexic children do not read much and have not read much. Do children who read little become dyslexic? Even I, as a 'dyslexic sceptic' might find this latter contention a bit hard to swallow were I not aware of a number of children assessed as dyslexic and even severely dyslexic who, having been persuaded to read, and given a balance of reading experience and skill training, largely overcame their dyslexic reading problems.

The teaching of dyslexic children throughout Britain appears to be characterised, despite the alleged variety of types of dyslexics, by a suspiciously homogeneous diet of highly structured and decontextualised training in decoding skills. Perhaps the teaching of dyslexics provides one of the clearest instances of the circular process which permeates special needs: a child is assessed as 'dyslexic' – they are then taught as a 'dyslexic', by a 'dyslexic' method – they progress slowly through the drills and exercises (as 'dyslexics' are expected to) – as they rely more and more on rigid decoding strategies, they find the extraction of meaning more difficult. In other words they become even more dyslexic, justifying both the original diagnosis and the subsequent treatment. Educational research provides overwhelming data on the assessment and the nature of dyslexia – overwhelming in its quantity, if not its validity – but there is still surprisingly little discussion on the effectiveness or otherwise of different educational experiences on dyslexics. Dyslexia might prove to be a less intractable condition if it were treated with a wide and balanced literacy curriculum, rather than a bland and rigorous set of skill-training drills.

After more than twenty years of 'special needs' teaching, I still see little evidence that dyslexics are significantly different from the majority of pupils whom schools consider as having special needs; i.e. children who, in general, eventually learn to read but not fluently or widely. The difference between these hesitant readers and their literate peers may well be that for good readers the organisational processes of both decoding the print and deriving meaning from the text have become fully automatic. Many 'slow' readers in junior and even in high schools are not particularly deficient in decoding or 'phonic' skills, neither may they be deficient in their ability to recognise whole words, nor may their general comprehension skills be inadequate to cope with the meaning of the texts they are stumbling over. The essence of their slowness may often lie in the speed at which they organise their strategies. And yet they may not be children who seem generally slow in their cognitive processing. Perhaps the slow reader is not merely processing information at a substantially slower rate than his literate peers, but is processing a great deal more information consciously, because for the slow reader many of the lower or more elementary processes of reading have not become automatic. The slow reader is not unlike the learner driver, in that he may know all of the correct strategies, rules and procedures, but, in continuing to perform all of them consciously, he is unable to integrate them into what for the proficient reader, or driver, may seem to be a single coherent activity. Proficiency comes, of course, with meaningful practice.

In considering the various levels of processes involved in the development of fluent reading skills, LaBerge and Samuels (1974) pointed out that the earliest processes have to become fully efficient and automatic before more complex processes can be mastered. It may not be specific skills which poor readers lack, but rather an appreciation of the whole nature of reading, or indeed the purposes of reading. However, like pupils with a 'specific' difficulty, pupils with generally poor reading skills may also face a reading curriculum which becomes increasingly narrow and skill-based.

The researcher may seek to control variables such as sex, social class, linguistic background and gross ability (IQ) in the pursuit of a pure uncontaminated cognitive skill or process. This procedure becomes questionable, even counter-productive, when applied to a gross skill like reading, since the effects of controlled variables, and even more the effects of uncontrolled and unobserved variables, are frequently of greater significance for the individual child learning to read than the possible existence of a cognitive deficit or developmental delay.

Children's success in learning to read is influenced by their socio-economic and cultural background. The transmission of the attitudes and skills of literacy was, for example, a significant factor which the Israeli psychologist, Reuven Feuerstein, identified in his comparisons of the abilities and attributes of different groups of immigrants to Israel, specifically in the contrast between Morrocan and Yemenite Jews. The low (initial) academic performance of the Morrocan children was:

> ... in stark contrast with the experience of the Yemenites ... The children had the same rights and duties as the adults as regards the prayers: they gathered together around the Torah praying together and were accorded real status. This had a tremendous impact on the children, all of whom were literate between the ages of three and four years.
>
> (Sharron, 1987, p. 20)

A complementary effect is reported by Schieffelin and Cochran-Smith (1984) in their study of Kaluli children attending boarding school in Papua New Guinea, run by evangelical Christian missionaries who wished to enable the Kaluli to translate and to read the Bible. The authors noted that in the village to which the children returned at weekends, most village people did not think of literacy as something relevant to their lives. Presumably to the dismay of the missionaries the young members of this non-literate culture remained, for the most part, non-literate. It appears that the Kaluli were not hostile to literacy, but rather that they continued to view the materials, the practice, the instruction, indeed the processes and purposes of literacy as largely irrelevant to their lives. The attitudes of the Kaluli may not be too far removed from the attitudes of some children in our schools. The earnest faith of the missionaries may not be too far removed from the earnest faith of those who see reading salvation as the achievement of literacy through the experience of a wealth of literature, or, to be even-handed, those who regard the self-flagellation of a multi-sensory, step-by-step, skill-based approach as the true path.

To return to a more pragmatic plane, the process which Feuerstein describes as 'the mediation of meaning' (Sharron, 1987) would seem to be substantially different from either the process of skill training or the mere provision of experience. The attachment of meaning or significance to a cultural activity such as reading is likely to be of at least as great a significance for pupils with special educational needs, as it was to the Yemenite children.

The future for schools
(Coming round full circle?)

The past ten years in Britain have seen a growing expectation that all teachers will become aware of special needs and that all schools will become more able to provide for pupils with special needs. Furthermore, the role of central literacy support services has been changing (and diminishing) from a traditional model involving teaching groups of pupils withdrawn from the class to a model involving a support teacher working within the class and 'targetting' support to children (DES, 1989b). The effectiveness of this support is uncertain but parental perception of the effectiveness of this support is predictable:

> It will be hard to convince the parents of pupils with specific learning difficulties that their child is likely to benefit from changes in resource allocation that reduce the time available for individual and small group instruction . . . The current absence of empirical evidence of the efficacy of such changed practices on children's attainments does not engender confidence in any disinterested observer. Observers of the scene whose children do have specific learning difficulties are far from disinterested. They will almost certainly continue to seek highly specialized and very expensive support for their child paid for from the public purse.

(Pumfrey and Reason, 1991, p. 142)

It seems likely that funding for special needs in mainstream schools will increasingly be spent on providing for children's 'specific' needs, outside the mainstream curriculum and indeed outside the mainstream classroom. Even Baroness Warnock, whose committee's report led to the 1981 Act, is now reported to favour a return to a system of fitting children into pre-determined categories which cover educational disabilities (Pyke, 1992, p. 5). Since these 'categories' would attract special funding, it looks increasingly unlikely that additional funding will be available for children whose literacy skills cannot be categorised, but are simply poor. The Reading Recovery programme, bearing, it seems, more than a superficial similarity to models of intervention which were current (and often successful) twenty years ago, will undoubtedly prove popular with parents whose children are included. However, unless there is a major change in government spending priorities and mechanisms, Reading Recovery and any provision made for 'specific' literacy difficulties, will never reach more than a small proportion of children with reading difficulties. Teachers will need to consider the practices and materials which will help them to develop literacy teaching as the support (or pressure, depending on your viewpoint) from external authorities, agencies and advisers declines.

Studies (e.g. Tizard, 1982; Wells, 1985; McNaughton, 1987) suggest strongly that children learn to read within a social context in which reading is perceived as a valid activity. Learning to read is about acquiring skills within a social context and a meaningful context. For children with special needs it is often a context for reading and the activity of reading that has been neglected. There are hopeful signs. The spread of active parental involvement, though not a panacea for reading problems, is encouraging. The institution of National Curriculum assessment may lead to better and earlier identification of special needs and the quality of published materials for special needs has greatly improved since the days of the cheaply printed 'remedial workbook'. We may still be a long way from resolving the profound disagreements as to the origins of a whole range of specific and general reading difficulties, but whether we are considering the child assessed as a severe visual dyslexic, or a child assessed as lacking any literacy experience, there are strategies, techniques and teaching programmes which have been shown to have considerable effectiveness.

The key to raising pupils' attainments in literacy is the quality of their learning experiences. There is a terrible danger that we look too hard at the deficits of pupils with special educational needs. We need to look at what is being learned, but we need much more to look at how learning is taking place. There is little point in monitoring precisely a child's reading vocabulary, if that vocabulary is drawn from a series of drills which bear no relationship to the purposes and functions of meaningful print. There is little point in sharing beautiful books with a child if the child has no conception of the relationship between print and meaning. We need to look at the context within which learning to read is taking place.

Five years ago, the reading debate was almost drowned by the extremist cries of 'real books' enthusiasts proclaiming the death of reading schemes. The irrelevance of reading schemes was the only point on which they agreed with 'phonics' extremists, whose highly structured skills programmes sometimes appeared to exclude reading books altogether. Fortunately for their pupils, all but a handful of schools resisted the pressure to throw out their schemes. The reading scheme at its best can provide a coherent structure within which the reader develops word-recognition and decoding skills. It can provide fiction and non-fiction every bit as lively and appealing as many of the books which are held to be 'real'. Most importantly, it can provide the reader with a secure but developing context of characters, locations and language which is carried over from book to book.

Of course it is easy for critics to quote forty-year-old examples of meaningless prose of the 'Run, dog, run. Look, look, look,' variety. It is easy (although unjustified) for critics to blame reading schemes for poor teaching practice.

Nevertheless, together with the expertise of teachers, reading schemes have for many years represented a balanced reading programme. Schemes, just like 'real books' and phonic programmes, become outdated, but reading scheme publishers are commercial organisations (just like the publishers of 'real books' and phonic schemes) and are under the intense pressure of the market place to produce the kinds of materials which teachers want, and therefore buy. It is a fine ideal, but unrealistic, to expect every teacher to become informed, well read and expert in the teaching of reading. To expect all teachers to become expert in teaching literacy to pupils with special needs is simply pie in the sky. If there is a solution to the circular dilemma I have discussed above, it lies not in the examination in more and more detail of the ways in which children fail to learn to read, but in the investigation of the quality of the learning experiences and environments which enable children to learn to read. The best reading schemes embody a combination of the expertise and experience of reading researchers, reading teachers, children's authors and children's illustrators. As schools face the challenge of teaching children to read within the educational pressures of a National Curriculum, delegated funding, and a market-place philosophy, the 1990s could well prove to be the decade when reading schemes, far from dying out, will prove themselves to be the most effective vehicle for the provision of a balanced literacy curriculum.

writing

composing and writing*

Carl Bereiter and Marlene Scardamalia

Writing as both natural and problematic

Writing – by which we mean the composing of texts intended to be read by people not present – is a promising domain within which to study the relationship between easy and difficult cognitive functions. On the one hand, writing is a skill traditionally viewed as difficult to acquire, and one that is developed to immensely higher levels in some people than in others. Thus it is a suitable domain for the study of expertise. On the other hand, it is based on linguistic capabilities that are shared by all normal members of the species. People with only the rudiments of literacy can, if sufficiently motivated, redirect their oral language abilities into producing a written text. Indeed, children lacking even the most rudimentary alphabetism can nevertheless produce written characters that have some linguistic efficacy (Vygotsky, 1978).

There is, indeed, an interesting bifurcation in the literature between treatments of writing as a difficult task, mastered only with great effort, and treatments of it as a natural consequence of language development, needing only a healthy environment in which to flourish. Convincing facts are provided to support both views. On the one hand we have evidences of poor writing abilities, even among relatively favoured university students (Lyons, 1976) and professional people (Odell, 1980). On the other hand we have numerous reports of children taking readily to literary creation when they have yet scarcely learned to handle a pencil (Graves, 1983). While children's writing is unquestionably recognisable as coming from children, it often shows the kind of expressiveness and flair that we associate with literary talent.

One could perhaps dismiss such contradictory findings as due to the application of different standards of quality. It may, in short, be easy to write

---

*This chapter has been taken from the book *The Psychology of Written Composition* by Carl Bereiter and Marlene Scardamalia (1987), published by Lawrence Erlbaum Assocates.

poorly and difficult to write well. But that is a half truth which obscures virtually everything that is interesting about writing competence.

The view of writing that emerges from our research is more complex than either the 'it's hard' or the 'it's easy' view or any compromise that might be struck between them. We propose that there are two basically different models of composing that people may follow. It is possible to write well or poorly following either model. One model makes writing a fairly natural task. The task has its difficulties, but the model handles these in ways that make maximum use of already existing cognitive structures and that minimise the extent of novel problems that must be solved. The other model makes writing a task that keeps growing in complexity to match the expanding competence of the writer. Thus, as skill increases, old difficulties tend to be replaced by new ones of a higher order. Why would anyone choose the more complex model? Well, in the first place it seems that not very many people do, and it is probably never used to the exclusion of the simpler model. But for those who do use it, the more difficult model provides both the promise of higher levels of literary quality and, which is perhaps more important for most people, the opportunity to gain vastly greater cognitive benefits from the process of writing itself.

One way of writing appears to be explainable within a 'psychology of the natural.' It makes maximum use of natural human endowments of language competence and of skills learned through ordinary social experience, but it is also limited by them. This way of writing we shall call *knowledge telling*. The other way of writing seems to require a 'psychology of the problematic' for its explanation. It involves going beyond normal linguistic endowments in order to enable the individual to accomplish alone what is normally accomplished only through social interaction – namely, the reprocessing of knowledge. Accordingly, we shall call this model of writing *knowledge transforming.*

A two-model description may fit many other domains in addition to writing. Everday thinking, which is easy and natural, seems to follow a different model from formal reasoning, which is more problematic (Bartlett, 1958). Similar contrasts may be drawn between casual reading and critical reading, between talking and oratory, between the singing people do when they light-heartedly burst into song and the intensely concentrated effort of the vocal artist.

In each case the contrast is between a naturally acquired ability, common to almost everyone, and a more studied ability involving skills that not everyone acquires. The more studied ability is not a matter of doing the same thing but doing it better. There are good talkers and bad orators, and most of us would prefer listening to the former. And there are surely people whose formal reasoning is a less reliable guide to wise action than some other people's everyday thought. What distinguishes the more studied abilities is that they involve deliberate, strategic control over parts of the process that are unattended to in the more naturally developed ability. That is why different models are required to describe these processes.

Such deliberate control of normally unmonitored activity exacts a price in mental effort and it opens up possibilities of error, but it also opens up possibilities of expertise that go far beyond what people are able to do with their naturally acquired abilities. In the case of writing, this means going beyond the ordinary ability to put one's thoughts and knowledge into writing. It means, among other things, being able to shape a piece of writing to achieve intended effects and to reorganise one's knowledge in the process. The main focus of this chapter is on the development of these and other higher-level controls over the process of composition.

From conversation to knowledge telling to knowledge transforming

Although children are often already proficient users of oral language at the time they begin schooling, it is usually some years before they can produce language in writing with anything like the proficiency they have in speech. Longitudinal studies by Loban (1976) suggest that the catch-up point typically comes around the age of twelve. The most immediate obstacle, of course, is the written code itself. But that is far from being the only obstacle. These less obvious problems have to do with generating the content of discourse rather than with generating written language. Generating content is seldom a problem in oral discourse because of the numerous kinds of support provided by conversational partners. Without this conversational support, children encounter problems in thinking of what to say, in staying on topic, in producing an intelligible whole, and in making choices appropriate to an audience not immediately present.

In order to solve the problems of generating content without inputs from conversational partners, beginning writers must discover alternative sources of cues for retrieving content from memory. Once discourse has started, text already produced can provide cues for retrieval of related content. But they are not enough to ensure coherent discourse, except perhaps of the stream-of-consciousness variety. Two other sources of cues are the topic, often conveyed by an assignment, and the discourse schema. The latter consists of knowledge of a selected literary form (such as narrative or argument), which specifies the kinds of elements to be included in the discourse and something about their arrangement. Cues from these two additional sources should tend to elicit content that sticks to a topic and that meets the requirements of a discourse type. In essence, the knowledge-telling model is a model of how discourse production can go on, using only these sources of cues for content retrieval–topic, discourse schema, and text already produced.

The main features of the knowledge-telling model are diagrammed in Figure 11.1. The diagram indicates a composing process that begins with a writing assignment. It could also begin with a self-chosen writing project, however, so long as there is some mental representation of the task that can be analysed into identifiers of topic and genre or discourse type. The task might, for instance, be to write an essay on whether boys and girls should play on the same sports teams. Depending on the sophistication of the writer, the topic identifiers extracted from this assignment might be *boys*, *girls*, and *sports* or *amateur sports* and *sexual equality*. According to the model, these topic identifiers serve as cues that automatically prime associated concepts through a process of spreading activation (Anderson, 1983). This process does not ensure that the information retrieved will be relevant, but there is a built-in tendency toward topical relevance. As Anderson explains, 'spreading activa-

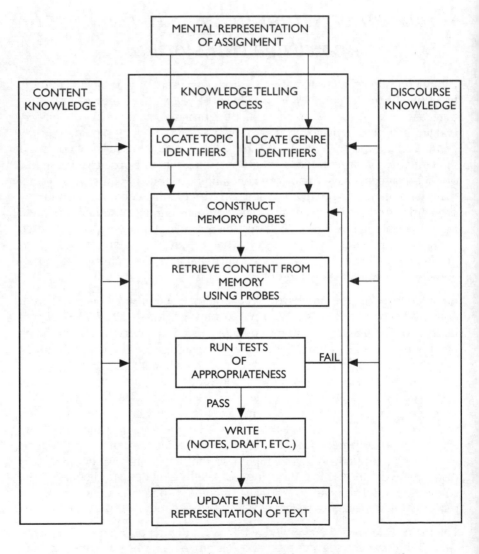

Figure 11.1 Structure of the knowledge-telling model

tion identifies and favours the processing of information most related to the immediate context (or sources of activation)' (Anderson, 1983, p. 86). Naturally, the appropriateness of the information retrieved will depend on the cues extracted and on the availability of information in memory. For instance, one would expect that the cues, *amateur sports* and *sexual equality*, would have a greater likelihood of eliciting information fitting the intent of the assignment than would the cues, *boys*, *girls*, and *sports*, provided the writer had knowledge stored in memory related to those cues. In either case, however, the retrieval is assumed to take place automatically through the spread of activation, without the writer having to monitor or plan for coherence.

Cues related to discourse type are assumed to function in much the same way. The assignment to write an essay on whether boys and girls should play on the same sports teams is likely to suggest that what is called for is an argument or *opinion essay*. Again, the cues actually extracted will depend on the sophistication of the writer. Some immature writers may have an opinion-essay schema that contains only two elements – *statement of belief* and *reason*. Others may have more complex schemas that provide for multiple reasons, anticipation of counterarguments, and so on. In any case, it is assumed that these discourse elements function as cues for retrieval of content from memory, operating in combination with topical cues to increase the likelihood that what is retrieved will not only be relevant to the topic but also appropriate to the structure of the composition. Thus, the cues, *boys*, *girls*, *sports*, and *statement of belief* would be very likely to produce retrieval of the idea that boys and girls should or should not play on the same sports teams, an appropriate idea on which to base the opening sentence of the essay.

According to the model shown in Figure 11.1, an item of content, once retrieved, is subjected to tests of appropriateness. These could be minimal tests of whether the item 'sounds right' in relation to the assignment and to text already produced or they could be more involved tests of interest, persuasive power, appropriateness to the literary genre, and so on. If the item passes the tests it is entered into notes or text and a next cycle of content generation begins. Suppose, for instance, that the first sentence produced in our example is 'I think boys and girls should be allowed to play on the same sports teams, but not for hockey or football.' The next cycle of content generation might make use of the same topical cues as before, plus the new cues, *hockey* and *football*, and the discourse schema cue might be changed to *reason*. A likely result, therefore, would be retrieval of a reason why boys and girls should not play hockey or football together. Content generation and writing would proceed in this way until the composition was completed.

This way of generating text content was described for us by a twelve-year-old student as follows:

> *I have a whole bunch of ideas and write down until my supply of ideas is exhausted. Then I might try to think of more ideas up to the point*

when you can't get any more ideas that are worth putting down on paper and then I would end it.

Knowledge telling provides a natural and efficient solution to the problems immature writers face in generating text content without external support. The solution is efficient enough that, given any reasonable specification of topic and genre, the writer can get started in a matter of seconds and speedily produce an essay that will be on topic and that will conform to the type of text called for. The solution is natural because it makes use of readily available knowledge – thus it is favourable to report of personal experience – and it relies on already existing discourse-production skills in making use of external cues and cues generated from language production itself. It preserves the straight-ahead form of oral language production and requires no significantly greater amount of planning or goal-setting than does ordinary conversation. Hence it should be little wonder if such an approach to writing were to be common among elementary school students and to be retained on into university and career.

Knowledge telling versus knowledge transforming

In the preceding discussion of the knowledge-telling model, it was allowed that there could be large differences in outcome depending on the writer's knowledge of the topic of discourse and on the writer's sophistication in the literary genre. In addition, of course, quality of the written product will vary depending on language abilities, such as diction and syntactic fluency, that are not dealt with in the knowledge-telling model. With all this allowance for individual differences and for improvement through learning, it is not obvious that a second model is required to account for the different ways writers go about generating text context.

Consider, however, the following description by Aldous Huxley of this composing process:

> *Generally, I write everything many times over. All my thoughts are second thoughts. And I correct each page a great deal, or rewrite it several times as I go along. . . . Things come to me in driblets, and when the driblets come I have to work hard to make them into something coherent.*
>
> (Cited in *Writers at Work*, 2nd series, 1963, p. 197)

The process described here does not sound like merely a more sophisticated or elaborate version of the process sixth-graders describe of writing down thoughts that they already have in their minds. The process Huxley describes is one in which the thoughts come into existence through the composing process itself, beginning as inchoate entities ('driblets') and gradually, by dint of much rethinking and restating, taking the form of fully developed thoughts. This is the process that we shall call 'knowledge transforming.' It is a process that cannot be accounted for by the knowledge-telling model and that seems to require a differently structured model.

This reworking or transforming of knowledge has been described in a variety of ways by professional writers (Lowenthal, 1980; Murray, 1978; Odell, 1980). But is it, then, a process found only in exceptionally talented people who have made writing their life's work? No. Evidence of a knowledge-transforming approach to writing can be found even among people who have no particular talent for or commitment to writing, some of whom would even be judged to be bad writers by literary standards.

Where are writers who use knowledge-transforming strategies to be found? We find them among talented young students, undergraduate and graduate students in psychology, education, and English, but they could probably be found among people at advanced levels in any intellectual discipline. These are people who, like Huxley, actively rework their thoughts. While they may not have Huxley's skill in expressing those thoughts, they are used to considering whether the text they have written says what they want it to say and whether they themselves believe what the text says. In the process, they are likely to consider not only changes in the text but also changes in what they want to say. Thus it is that writing can play a role in the development of their knowledge.

To account for this interaction between text processing and knowledge processing, it is necessary to have a model of considerably greater complexity than the model of knowledge telling. Such a model is sketched in Figure 11.2. It will be noted that the knowledge-telling process, as depicted in Figure 11.1, is still there, but it is now embedded in a problem-solving process involving two different kinds of problem spaces. In the content space, problems of belief and knowledge are worked out. In the rhetorical space, problems of achieving goals of the composition are dealt with. Connections between the two problem spaces indicate output from one space serving as input to the other. For instance, a writer might be working in the rhetorical space on a problem of clarity and might arrive at the decision that she needs to define the concept of *responsibility* that she is building her argument around. This is a content problem, however, and so one might imagine a message going from the rhetorical problem space to the content problem space, saying 'What do I really mean by *responsibility*?' Work on this problem within the content space might lead to determining that responsibility is not really the central issue after all but that the issue is, let us say, *competence to judge*. This decision, transferred to the rhetorical space, might initiate work on problems of modifying the text already written so as to accommodate the change in central issue. This work might give rise to further, content problems, which might lead to further changes in the writer's beliefs, and so on until a text is finally created that successfully embodies the writer's latest thinking on the subject.

It is this kind of interaction between problem spaces that we argue is the basis for reflective thought in writing. Writing is not always problematic, of course, and often we write things that have been so thoroughly thought out and rehearsed on other occasions that there is no need to reflect on them. Some writers, furthermore, may intentionally suppress problem-solving operations until a first draft is completed. In all of these cases, knowledge telling might function much as we described it in the preceding section. In this way, knowledge telling remains one of the capabilities of the knowledge-transforming model. But the distinctive capabilities of the knowledge-

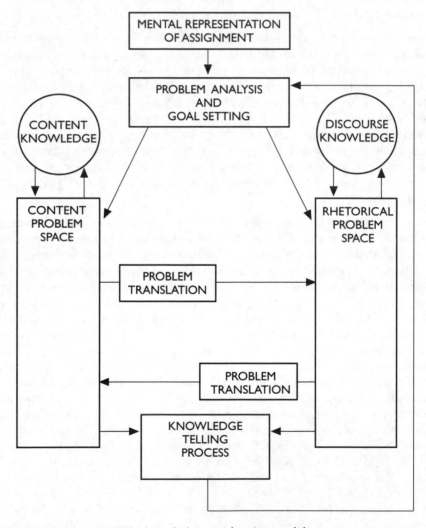

Figure 11.2 Structure of the knowledge-transforming model

transforming model lie in formulating and solving problems and doing so in ways that allow a two-way interaction between continuously developing knowledge and continuously developing text.

What can be shown is that some people exhibit very little evidence of goal-directed planning in writing. The job of the knowledge-telling model in this context is to explain how it would be possible to produce a normal-appearing composition without any more planning than such writers exhibit. Similarly, the knowledge-transforming model is not intended to assert anything about the cognitive behaviour of an identifiable group of expert writers. Its explanatory job is to show (a) how the process of writing can lead to growth in knowledge, as many expert writers claim it does, and (b) how writing could be such hard work for some people, even though they are highly skilled at it.

Nevertheless, there is an issue of psychological reality to be addressed. We want to be able to say that there are processes going on in the minds of real people of which the knowledge-telling and knowledge-transforming models are idealised descriptions. Furthermore, we want to be able to say that psychological reality requires both models, one to provide an idealised description of what is common to the processes of many immature and inexpert writers (although the processes are by no means absent in expert writers) and one to provide an idealised description of what is distinctive about the composing processes of more expert or thoughtful writers.

It may not be obvious what virtue there is in idealised models as opposed to careful descriptions of real people doing real things. The virtue lies in the possibility of making scientifically or educationally worthwhile generalisations. Naturalistic descriptions leave one with the options of either not generalising at all or else generalising by averaging over cases. Neither option is at all satisfactory. Each individual case presents innumerable unique, idiosyncratic or incidental details. Even if the case is chosen as representative, there is bound to be much about it that is not representative and which anyone would be foolish to generalise. As a result, investigators who use naturalistic case methods (e.g. Graves, 1983) almost always end up formulating idealised descriptions, albeit informally. That is, they try to state essential truths, which would have to be qualified in order to fit any actual case. If one is going to go in for such ideal generalisations, there is obvious value in doing it formally, by creating models or theoretical propositions, so as to get a better hold on inconsistencies, gaps, and implications that need to be tested.

The other way to generalise is empirically, by extracting some kind of average from the individual cases. It does not matter whether the averaging is done quantitatively or whether it is done impressionistically, through statements of the 'What we usually find. . . .' type. There remains a fundamental obstacle, which was stated most succinctly by Newell (1974): We must not average over methods. We can determine the average amount of time writers devote to one activity and another. We can determine the average number of thinking-aloud protocol statements of one type and another. But there is no way that these results can add up to a description of something that can be called 'the average writing process'. If different writers are going about the task differently, the averaged results will not only fail to reveal these differences but will probably also fail to reveal whatever underlying similarities these methods may have.

Seemingly the only way to make worthwhile generalisations about a process is to formulate an idealised model of the process and then investigate its validity. This means seeing how well it fits with known facts and testing its implications on new kinds of data. Also, when one is interested in a model's usefulness, it means testing its practical implications. These are the matters that will concern us in the remainder of this chapter.

Our initial focus will be on the knowledge-telling model. It is clearly the more controversial of the two models. If the knowledge-transforming model, with its dual problem spaces for dealing with content and rhetorical problems, were proposed as a general model for all written composition, there would probably not be much argument. Differences in writing skill would be accounted for by differences in how the various subprocesses are carried out or by differences in amount of problem-solving activity. We take it, therefore, as a nontrivial matter to show that there is reason to suggest a radically simpler model, the model of knowledge telling, to account for the composing behaviour of many writers.

Accordingly, we shall first turn to reviewing the knowledge-telling model and the evidence relating to its psychological reality; and secondly, we will turn to educational implications. On this account, the most important implication arises from the fact that the knowledge-transforming model is not simply an elaboration of the knowledge-telling model. Rather, it is a different kind of model – essentially a problem-solving as opposed to a task-execution model – which incorporates the simpler model as a subroutine. This implies that helping students move from a knowledge-telling to a knowledge-transforming approach to writing is not a simple matter of promoting growth and elaboration of skills. It is a matter of bringing writing under the control of a problem-solving executive that does not initially control it. What this implies for educational strategies is the subject of the final section of this chapter.

Origin of the knowledge-telling model

The knowledge-telling model grew out of the effort to make sense of a growing body of facts about novices' composing. Regardless of how the model itself fares, the body of facts still needs to be explained. Consequently it seems worthwhile to review the thinking that led up to the model, of what we thought needed explaining and of how we came to explain it the way we did.

One starts out looking at the writing process from one's own perspective, which in our case is that of adults who experience much of their most strenuous wrestling with the complexity of ideas and the limitations of their own capacities while trying to put thoughts into writing. Thinking-aloud protocols have borne out the notion that for people in our walk of life writing is a form of very complex, ill-defined problem solving (Flower and Hayes, 1980a, 1980b). If one thinks of children and novices as engaged in basically the same kind of problem solving, but less well equipped to cope with its demands, then one expects to find the composing process continually breaking down or on the verge of doing so for such people. But obviously that is not the way it is. To us, a task such as writing the present chapter is close to overwhelming because of the abundance of information that needs to be considered, the variety of sometimes incompatible goals we would like to achieve, and behind all that, the spectral legions of questions not yet answered or even fully formed, the doubts, the inklings, the yearnings after something not yet identified. But as far as we have been able to ascertain, such problems are side-stepped by novices. As we have seen repeatedly, when young writers do have problems composing, these tend to be problems of finding too little rather than problems of finding too much to say.

Now if one persists in the adult perspective, one starts immediately to form a proposition that begins, 'The reason young writers have trouble finding enough to say is. . . .' Almost invariably, this line of thought seems to lead to identifying situational determinants of children's differences from us – the artificial nature of school tasks, the lack of audience, etc. Such a line of thought may lead to significant conclusions about how to improve educational conditions, but it advances us nowhere in understanding how immature writers do what they do.

We chose to take a more positive approach, by looking at what the children we have studied are able to do in writing and trying to explain how it is possible for them to do so. We first looked at completely unassisted writing, an assigned topic, no preparation, no time or length specifications. The one thing that seemed to be achieved in every case (at least by children of age ten and up) was local coherence, a meaningful connection of the sentence to the topic or something preceding (McCutchen and Perfetti, 1982). Initial efforts to account for such an achievement gave rise to the idea of associative writing (Bereiter, 1980). The idea was that by processes much like those involved in free association, the topic would give rise to a first utterance, something in the first utterance would provide a cue for a second, and so on.

Although there are examples of immature writing that appear to be explainable by a purely associative model, it quickly became apparent that such a model was too simple to do justice to all that beginning writers can do. Associative writing could not, for instance, account for children producing well-formed stories, something which even primary-grade children appear able to do (Stein and Trabasso, 1982). Furthermore, even the least developed compositions exhibit an appropriateness to the genre – in this case the opinion essay. Something beyond topical associations had to be guiding the

165

children to give opinions and reasons rather than, say, fragments of autobiography.

Granting that children have some kind of knowledge of literary forms, the problem then becomes to explain how this knowledge is brought into use in writing. One way could be by deliberate planning, within constraints imposed by genre requirements. But although such planning could be observed in the protocols of mature writers, it has not been found with young children. Deliberate planning also seemed unlikely because of its heavy information processing load, caused by having to hold constraints in mind while searching for content to meet them. To be realistic, a model of immature composing would have to show a way that knowledge of literary forms could function without a high processing load.

The key idea for meeting this requirement was the idea that knowledge of literary forms could function as a source of prompts for retrieving content from memory. To get an idea of how this might work, imagine that you are a twelve-year-old who has got stuck while composing an essay on why students should learn foreign languages. Suppose that from somewhere (from the outer world or some vagary of memory) comes the suggestion, *world peace.* Immediately this brings forth an idea connecting foreign languages with world peace, and you are off and running again. That is the kind of association based on simple topics that was assumed to form part of the composing process. But suppose that instead the suggestion was *reason on the other side.* This suggestion might also bring forth an idea, which would set you off on stating and responding to some argument against studying foreign languages. The prompt in this case is of a more abstract kind, but it seems to work in much the same way as a topical prompt.

The basic structure of the knowledge-telling model, depends on the processes of retrieving content from memory on the basis of topical and genre cues. With these as the processes that drive composition, it is possible to account for children's ability to generate coherent and well-formed texts without attributing to them the resource-demanding planning or problem-solving processes that make writing difficult even for highly skilled writers. To be more precise, however, these processes account for children's ability to produce texts that *tend* to be coherent and well formed. Retrieval cues cannot be expected to work perfectly. Consequently, there will be a probability of generating content that strays from the topic or is inappropriate to the genre. To account for the level of coherence we have typically found in children's compositions, it seemed necessary to hypothesize a testing function applied to retrieved content that rejects content which happens not to match the topical and structural probes. With the addition of this testing function to the cuing functions, we have essentially the knowledge-telling model as shown in Figure 11.1.

Validity of the knowledge-telling model

Let us briefly review evidence that supports the knowledge-telling model:

1 Texts written by inexpert writers tend to have characteristics derivable from the knowledge-telling model

(a) *Topical coherence* According to the model, topical coherence is achieved by the use of topical cues drawn from the assignment and from already-generated text. This should result in texts that tend to stick to their simple topics but that do not necessarily conform to the requirements of an elaborated topic. For instance, a text on the topic of whether television is a good or bad influence on children would be expected to deal with television watching and children, but would not necessarily address the issue of television's influence. In keeping with this expectation, McCutchen and Perfetti (1982) found that in fourth-grade texts the simple topic was usually the only reference for given (as opposed to new) information, so that sentences were coherent with the topic but not with each other, as they would be in a more carefully planned treatment of an issue.

(b) *Well-formedness* The model presupposes that the writer has a structural discourse schema, which can also serve as a source of cues for retrieving content from memory. This should tend to result in texts that are well formed in the sense of conforming to the structural requirements of literary forms. Such texts would not necessarily be successful in fulfilling the functions of the literary form, however, because that would often require problem-solving capabilities not available in knowledge telling. A written argument, for instance, might meet the requirements of stating a position and supporting reasons, but fail to develop a convincing line of argument. This, in fact, proved to be the modal type of persuasive essay produced by both thirteen-year-olds and seventeen-year-olds in the National Assessment of Educational Progress (1980a; 1980b) evaluations of persuasive writing. Similarly, in narrative writing, almost a third of the stories produced by seventeen-year-olds were judged to fall short of developing a plot, even though they conformed to the basic structural requirements of narrative (National Assessment of Educational Progress, 1980a, p. 14). The basic structural requirements of narrative, in fact, appear to be met by most children by the second year of school (Rentel and King, 1983).

(c) *Weak adaptation of content to audience* Although the knowledge-telling model provides means for generation of text content appropriate to topic and to text type, it does not provide means for finding and organising content with the reader's needs in mind. (Note that the model does not imply anything one way or another about writers' ability to adapt language to an intended audience.) Flower (1979) has identified a pervasive kind of student writing that is distinguished by the very weaknesses implied by the knowledge-telling model. 'Writer-based prose,' as Flower calls it, presents content that is salient in the mind of the writer but not necessarily sufficient or relevant for the reader. The arrangement of this content tends to reflect its chronology in the experience of the writer and therefore is often not in an order suitable to gain the interest or comprehension of the reader.

2 Self-reports of immature writers are consistent with the model

Interview statements by elementary school students indicated that they saw writing as primarily a matter of recalling what they knew about a topic and writing down either all their ideas or the best of those they had retrieved. Although self-reports of cognitive processes are not convincing evidence in their own right, when combined with other evidence they contribute to confidence in the psychological reality of the model.

3 Thinking-aloud protocols of immature writers show little evidence of goal setting, planning, and problem solving, except at a local level

This finding, accords with the lack of provision for such operations in the knowledge-telling model. Absence of protocol evidence is not conclusive, since it could mean that immature writers carry on processes covertly that are more overt in mature writers. The objection is not very compelling, however, because skill acquisition normally works in the opposite way presupposed by this objection – that is, procedures become more automatic (and therefore less reportable) in the later stages of skill development (Anderson, 1982). Consequently, protocol evidence cannot be dismissed.

4 Start-up times of immature writers are unrelated to time and length constraints

This finding argues against any composing process that involves a great deal more deliberation than is hypothesised by the knowledge-telling model. Correspondingly, the fact that more mature writers do vary their start-up times according to the amount of writing time available and the amount to be written suggests a process involving more planning.

5 Novice revising behaviour is consistent with a knowledge-telling way of generating content

One of the strongest points of the model is that it makes students' avoidance of revision, and their tendency to confine revision to cosmetic language changes, predictable from the way they write rather than treating them as additional phenomena in need of special explanation (and special treatment). Whereas the knowledge-transforming writer can use text already produced as a basis for problem identification and clarification of goals to be achieved through revision, to the knowledge teller existing text serves mainly as a source of cues for retrieval of additional content – so that, at best, revision is likely to consist of adding content rather than replacing or overhauling it. Revision can be fostered in young writers, but results demonstrating knowledge-transforming operations are virtually nonexistent.

6 Immature reading comprehension follows procedures similar to knowledge telling

There is evidence pointing to a comprehension strategy that, like knowledge telling, focuses on topic identifiers and functions without construction of high-level syntheses of content. This parallelism lends support to the knowledge-telling model, because, as van Dijk and Kintsch (1983, p. 262) remark, 'It seems highly implausible that language users would not have recourse to the same or similar levels, units, categories, rules, or strategies in both the productive and the receptive processing of discourse.'

7 Good writing through knowledge telling

If the knowledge-telling model is to apply to writers ranging from elementary-school students to a sizable portion of the university undergraduate population it must obviously be compatible with a wide range of differences in the quality of performance. Many differences in writing quality can, of course, be attributed to differences in language skills, vocabulary, and so on, which are not directly related to the process by which content is generated. In addition, differences in the quality of written compositions can be attributed to differences in the two knowledge stores that form part of the knowledge-telling model: content knowledge and discourse knowledge. The older students' advantage in content knowledge to be drawn on in writing is obvious; it is also reasonable to assume that older students have more elaborate knowledge of discourse forms and conventions, which within the knowledge-telling model can serve to prompt more richly structured compositions. Another way in which experience may contribute to performance without altering the basic model, however, is by providing a more elaborate set of tests to be applied to content retrieved from memory. Some very immature writers may apply no tests at all, writing down whatever is retrieved via the topical and structural prompts. More sophisticated students may test not only for appropriateness to topic and text function but also for criteria such as clarity, plausibility, and interest.

Finally, the quality of texts produced by the knowledge-telling process may be enhanced by incorporating the process into a more sophisticated composing routine. Whereas the untutored elementary-school student may set the process in motion immediately upon receiving an assignment, and use it to generate an essentially finished version of the text, a more sophisticated knowledge-teller might begin by carrying out some form of prewriting exercise designed to generate high-quality content (Odell, 1974), and then instead of generating text directly, might use the knowledge-telling process to generate notes, which could later be culled, arranged, and added.

With all of these refinements to knowledge-telling, one might ask whether it any longer makes sense to think of it as the same model as that which applies to the beginning writer. By the time it has incorporated tests of clarity, interest, and the like, and taken on prewriting, culling, and organising procedures, has not knowledge telling evolved into a higher form? Has not the novice begun to write like an expert?

The answer to this question is purely analytic, since we are talking about the properties of models, not about the empirical data of writing behaviour. From an analytic or design standpoint, it does not matter how many tests are added or what activities are tacked on before or after. The essential design features of the knowledge-telling model are that it generates content by topical and structural prompts, without strategic formulation of goals, subgoals, search criteria, and other components of problem solving. So long as these essential features remain, the composing process retains its knowledge-telling character and remains fundamentally distinct from the expert process previously described and characterised as knowledge transforming. With enough elaboration and supplementation, it is quite conceivable that the knowledge-telling process could produce texts of a quality difficult to distinguish from the products of a knowledge-transforming process. Even then, however, differences in the underlying mental operations could result in differences in what the writer gets out of the writing process.

Educational implications

Traditionally, the teaching of writing has been a thankless task. For the writing instructor it has meant long, long hours of marking and commenting on student compositions, with little reason for confidence that this effort would have any positive effect. Starting around 1970, however, there have been waves of innovation and reform that have raised hopes for a brighter future in writing instruction. Some of the earliest and most successful innovations have involved changes in what is taught. These included transformational sentence-combining exercises designed to increase syntactic fluency (O'Hare, 1973) and 'new rhetoric,' which features methods of exploring and developing ideas before writing (Young et al., 1970). More recent developments, however, have had to do with changing the nature of the school writing experience itself. These include encouraging children to start writing before they have learned to read, inventing their own spellings (Clay, 1975), encouraging large amounts of free writing, with children sharing their productions with one another, and the teacher playing a largely supporting role (Crowhurst, 1979; Graves, 1983), and the use of computers for word processing and for communication among writers (Quinsaat et al., 1983). These recent innovations all share the aim of making writing a more worthwhile and intrinsically satisfying activity for students.

These innovations all took shape before there was any substantial research on the composing process. Knowledge of underlying cognitive processes should be valuable, however, in developing these innovations beyond their initial stages. At present, for instance, many educators are looking to computers to produce a breakthrough in the teaching of writing. This hope seems to be supported mainly by the dramatic motivational effects of word processors on young writers, and this alone may make them a worthwhile educational investment. But there is so far no indication that using a word processor causes students and pupils to adopt more sophisticated composing strategies. There is much talk in computer circles about developing more interactive software that will in some fashion teach children to write better. Micro-computers do in fact show promise as a way of providing procedural support for more complex composing strategies and for directing attention to parti-cular aspects of the composing task (Woodruff *et al.*, 1982). But the design of such software puts heavy demands on one's understanding of the cognitive processes that the system impinges on. Some current software, for instance, merely provides utilities for taking notes, generating outlines, and the like. This can hardly be expected to have much impact on students and pupils who see no virtue in planning in the first place and whose composing strategies create no need for it. In fact, there is evidence that having a computer interact with students and pupils while they write can be disruptive to thought rather than facilitative (Woodruff *et al.*, 1981). It seems that any really sophsticated piece of educational software in writing would have to be a virtual embodi-ment of a sophisticated theory of the writing process. The same, however, could probably be said of sophsticated versions of any of the currently popular approaches to writing improvement. Improvements in instructional methods can go some distance on the basis of bright ideas and enthusiasm, but further progress is likely to depend on basic understanding of the cognitive processes involved.

Knowledge transforming as an instructional goal

The main educational implications of the present research, however, are not at the level of contributions to instructional know-how. They are at the level of altering what are seen as the principal goals and problems of instruction. What began as a focus on writing abilities *per se* turned increasingly into a view of writing as a way of processing and developing knowledge. Coordinate with this change in research focus has been a shift toward seeing the central problem of writing instruction as that of altering the way students and pupils operate on their knowledge when they write. In short, the problem is that of shifting students and pupils from knowledge telling to knowledge transforming.

Such a view of the goal of writing instruction is not out of keeping with current thought among language arts educators. There is much talk about 'writing as a tool of thought,' about 'language as a way of knowing,' and about 'writing as a process of discovery.' Where the present research has import, therefore, is not in suggesting what writing may be good for. It is in suggesting what the problems may be in enabling students to achieve these cognitive benefits of writing.

The 'meaningful task'

The popular view seems to be that writing is inherently conducive to personal knowledge. The contribution that a particular writing experience makes to the writer's knowledge development is seen as depending on contextual factors. An arbitrarily assigned topic, with an error-hunting teacher as the sole audience, may do little for the writer, whereas a topic the writer cares about and an audience responsive to what the writer has to say are the essential ingredients for a profitable experience. Hence the over-riding concern of the teacher becomes that of making writing a meaningful experience for the students (Graves, 1978; Muller, 1967). The argument is extremely persuasive, and so there is little wonder that this 'let them write' position occupies the high ground in any debate over pedagogy. There is hardly a point one can get hold of to disagree with. Yet there is a weak side to the position, and it is revealed in the phrase, 'making writing a meaningful experience for the students.' We must remind ourselves that mature writers are able to make writing tasks meaningful for themselves and *that this is part of their competence.* We must ask what this ability consists of, how it is acquired, and what effect different educational practices may have on its development.

Making a writing task meaningful for oneself is a matter of constructing a goal representation that takes account of external requirements (such as those imposed by a school assignment) but also includes goals of personal significance to oneself (Scardamalia and Bereiter, 1982). A goal that almost any writing task lends itself to is reinterpreting or reorganising some part of one's knowledge. That seems to be what phrases such as 'writing as a tool of thought' and 'writing as a process of discovery' refer to. What our research on composing processes indicates, however, is that purposeful pursuit of such knowledge goals requires a knowledge-transforming executive structure.

Knowledge telling, which involves stating what has previously existed in some less articulated form, is certain to have some knowledge-transforming effect – at times possibly even a major effect. The point is, however, that its effect depends on the topic and how it happens to connect to the writer's knowledge. It depends on the prescribed or chosen literary form. And it depends on transitory states of feeling and concern, on what the young writer has been thinking or learning recently, and so on. That, according to our analysis, is why students and pupils are so dependent on the teacher to provide a 'meaningful context' for writing.

All of us are affected by context, of course. But the knowledge-transforming model provides resources for action that is not bound to context. It provides means for deliberately formulating and pursuing personally meaningful goals in writing, for recognising and overcoming problems, and for assessing and revising choices made at a variety of levels. If it is acknowleged that young writers must develop these cognitive resources, then it must be asked whether the best environment for writing is one in which things are continually made meaningful by others.

The larger instructional problem

We believe that knowledge-telling is but one manifestation of a more general educational failing. It is the failure of education to promote intentional cognition (Bereiter and Scardamalia, 1983). Intentional cognition may be briefly defined as the setting and deliberate pursuit of cognitive goals – goals to learn, to solve, to understand, to define, and so on. People do a great deal of learning, solving, understanding, etc., both in school and outside. But very little of it is intentional. Most of it is either spontaneous, evoked by things that capture their interest, or else it is incidental to achieving some more worldly goal, such as making the garden grow or getting a satisfactory mark on an assignment. The schools may be faulted for failing to promote the spontaneous, the incidental, and the emotionally guided as well, but that is not the point at issue here. It is failure on the intentional side that leaves students enchained by circumstance.

What we have called the knowledge-transforming model could be called a model of intentional writing. It involves the setting of goals to be achieved through the composing process and the purposeful pursuit of those goals. The knowledge-telling model lacks this intentional component, and thus represents a composing process that depends on evoked memories and emotions and on external assistance for its direction. Similarly, in reading we can identify an intentional kind of process that sets goals of discovering the gist of a text and actively monitors attainment of those goals, and we can identify a more passive kind of reading that responds to the immediate saliency and plausibility of text elements and depends on external assistance to convert text propositions into knowledge.

Contemporary school practices of all kinds seem to encourage the more passive kind of cognition. One set of school practices favours passivity by continually telling students what to do. The opposing set of practices favours passivity by encouraging students and pupils to follow their spontaneous interests and impulses. Largely absent, scarcely even contemplated, are school practices that encourage students and pupils to assume responsibility for what becomes of their minds.

Symptoms of a lack of intentional cognition are to be found in the undeveloped thought content of student and pupil writing. They are equally to be seen in pupils' and students' difficulties in learning from texts. Pearson and Gallagher (1983) report that it is common for elementary school teachers to restate the content of every text passage for students and pupils, on the assumption that many will have failed to grasp it. The failure of many adolescents to perform at a formal level on Piagetian tasks (Lawson and Renner, 1974) may also be taken as symptomatic, in so far as formal thought involves deliberate operations on one's knowledge. Recent evidence of the persistence of prescientific schemata in students and pupils who have studied physics (McCloskey *et al.*, 1980) further bespeaks a failure of students and pupils to revise their existing cognitive structures in light of new information.

All of these findings can, of course, be interpreted in less damning ways, and it is not our intention to claim that the schools are failing utterly or even that there has been a decline. A much less contentious claim will suffice: namely, that there is room for improvement. But it is not improvement through doing better what the schools already do. It is improvement through rising to a higher level of educational objectives than are currently being pursued.

These higher-level objectives all involve imparting to the students those kinds of competence that have previously been reserved to the teacher. It has been the teacher who is expected to know what is worth learning and how it relates to what was learned previously. It has been the teacher's job to establish links between current activities and the student's and pupil's needs and interests. It has been the teacher's job to recognise the spark of originality in the student's or pupil's work and fan it into a flame. It has been the teacher's job to ask the probing question, to reveal the unexamined premise.

Writing, especially expository writing, offers an opportunity for students or pupils to work actively and independently with their own knowledge. They can clarify meanings, find inconsistencies, discover implications, and establish connections between previously isolated fragments of knowledge. In order to do this, however, they need to function according to a knowledge-transforming rather than a knowledge-telling model.

From what we know so far, it appears that for students or pupils to develop a knowledge-transforming model of composing is itself a major intellectual achievement. It is an achievement that seems likely to require more than simply a rich diet of relatively unrestricted writing experience. We would suggest the following as additional elements that ought to be present in writing instruction:

1 Students or pupils (and teachers) need to be made aware of the full extent of the composing process. They should understand that most of it does not involve putting words on paper but consists of setting goals, formulating problems, evaluating decisions, and planning in the light of prior goals and decisions. It needs to be constantly clear to students or pupils that they should be working toward independence in managing the whole process.

2 The thinking that goes on in composition needs to be modelled by the teacher, who can thereby show the problem-solving and planning processes that students and pupils are often unaware of. The ability to model these processes needs also to be conveyed to the students, however, so that they can benefit from observing and discussing each other's mental efforts.

3 Acquiring higher levels of competence should be a clear goal in the minds of the students or pupils and not only in the mind of the teacher. One way of bringing issues of competence to the forefront in a constructive way is to involve students in investigations of their own strategies and knowledge. Ideally, students and pupils should see it as their responsibility to help each other develop their knowledge.

4 Although students need a supportive and congenial environment, they also need to experience the struggles that are part of the knowledge-transforming process in writing. This means pursuing challenging goals and not always writing what is most prominent in mind or what is easiest to do well.

5 The use of procedural facilitation – simplified routines and external supports – can help students through the initial stages of acquiring more complex executive processes. Students and pupils need to share in an understanding of the purpose, however, and to understand as much as possible about the nature and function of the process they are trying to acquire. Without such understanding, students are likely to adopt only superficial aspects of the complex process.

Writing is, of course, not the only medium for fostering the development of intentional cognition. Reading comprehension, especially insofar as it involves revising one's knowledge on the basis of what is read, is another area in which more active strategies need to be fostered. There are, in fact, promising instructional approaches to reading comprehension strategies that are highly congruent with the five principles suggested above (e.g., Bereiter and Bird, 1985; Palincsar and Brown, 1984). Pilot studies suggest that computer programming is also a medium in which strategies for more purposeful control of cognition might be taught. Finally, there is the growing body of evidence that science students accumulate new knowledge without revising the naive beliefs that they entertained before instruction (McCloskey et al., 1980). Helping students and pupils to develop independent knowledge-transforming skills in science and other subject matters is a problem that has scarcely been approached. But if students or pupils can develop powerful knowledge-transforming skills in writing, this should help them to become more active builders of their own knowledge in all domains.

the teaching of spelling

Margaret Peters

The balancing of perspectives in the teaching of spelling has long reflected ideological conflicts in education, and though the emphasis within each perspective has narrowed with our knowledge of psycholinguistics, the controversy has remained and still centres ultimately in the classroom. The two perspectives have dominated both spelling research and the teaching of spelling for the last century. In the early days it was between those who saw the learning of spelling as incidental, and those who thought the teaching of spelling should be systematic. It was, in effect, a debate as to whether spelling is 'caught' or 'taught'. In support of 'incidental' learning it was assumed that merely by reading a child learns to spell! Those who supported 'systematic' teaching mainly concerned themselves with list-making and list-learning, paying much attention to the rules of spelling.

The different perspectives have remained, but in the last decade or two the incidental school has assumed a developmental stance, happily countenancing inventive spelling and the inevitable emphasis on auditory input, while the systematic school has taken the visual route to spelling.

Incidental/systematic perspectives

As early as 1897, when the teaching of spelling was a universal practice, the possibilities of its being 'caught' were beginning to be considered. J. M. Rice, in that year, wrote an article called, 'The futility of the spelling grind', and this was followed up by, for example, O. P. Cornman (1902) criticising the systematic teaching of spelling and suggesting, with statistical evidence, that spelling could be approached through other activities such as written work and reading. Though the possibility of spelling being caught rather than taught was challenged soon after by John Wallin (1910), with further statistical evidence in favour of the taught rather than caught school, the controversy had to come to stay, simmering in America, but not boiling until the second quarter of the century with Grace Fernald, who, in *Remedial Techniques in the Basic School Subjects* (1943, p. 206) emphasised that 'the most satisfactory spelling vocabulary is that supplied by the child himself' in the course of his own expression. George Kyte (1948) supported this view with reservations, advocating the withdrawal of good spellers from formal spelling lessons. Even they, he said, would need to be regularly tested, to ensure that they maintained their competence.

Meanwhile in 1941, in England, Stanley Nisbet pointed out that children are likely to 'catch' only one new word out of every twenty-five they read. With older people who are unsophisticated readers, this may also be true, but, with serious, slower, more focused readers such as students, the gain in spelling ability from mere reading could be expected to be greater, particularly in more technical words that may be new to the student, who might pick up the spelling from the significant etymology of the word. Some years before this, Luther C. Gilbert (1935) had found that college students' spelling certainly improved as they read, the extent of the improvement depending on the type of reading and the reader's purpose. Words that had been recently brought to their attention were caught more effectively than words encountered more remotely, and good spellers learned more words than poor spellers.

It is clear then, that the more competent the reader, the greater the resource for spelling reference. As David Mackay et al., (1979, p. 131) point out, 'It is likely that fluent readers have an internalised model of the orthography, although they are unlikely to be able to say what this model looks like.' But this is not to say that the model provides a sufficient condition for spelling competence. The model may be internalised, without the strategies for utilising this being exploited. So good reading ability is not enough to ensure good spelling. The role of incidental learning had become respectable.

Incidental learning is indirect learning, wrote Gertrude Hildreth (1956, p. 33), '. . . which takes place when the learner's attention is centred not in improving the skill in question, but on some other objective . . .' and she qualified this a moment later with: 'Teachers should not think of incidental learning and integrated teaching as excluding systematic, well organised drill. Rather from the child's attempts to write will come evidence of his need for systematic word study.' So not only may spelling be caught, but the need to learn to spell also. Incidental and systematic teaching are thus mutually supportive and interactive.

The old incidental/systematic controversy, of interest educationally, but now outmoded, generated later spelling research. The controversy which has succeeded ideologically, is between those who favour a phonological route into spelling, and those who favour a visual route. The incidental school took a developmental approach, through a child's reading, but little attention was paid to children's writing. Spelling was a bonus, not a requisite. Children usually learned to read via a well-structured phonic system which duly provided the basis for phonological spelling. This has been effective, at least in the early years of school, though this approach has frequently been found to be counter-productive with children who have failed to learn to read and write at an early age. Lynette Bradley and Peter Bryant (1985) emphasise the value of phonic training upon spelling.

From my own research it was clear that nine-year-old children who had been taught on a purely phonic basis were better spellers than children taught to read entirely by the pure 'look and say' method or by the initial teaching alphabet (ITA) in that in their spelling they made fewer transpositions, and fewer substitutions of vowels. Also when a major substitution was made by children taught to read by a pure phonic system it was more often a plausible phonic alternative (Peters, 1970).

The systematic school concerned itself from the beginning with the visual approach, and this was indeed the precursor of the visual route to spelling. In the light of teachers' growing awareness of the 'visual' nature of spelling, and in the context of psycholinguistic studies since the late 1960s, spelling has been seen in terms of the serial probability of letter sequences.

Spelling strategies

List learning

To return to 'systematic' teaching of spelling, this has concerned itself mainly with the compiling and teaching of lists; lists of words which are often remote from and irrelevant to a child's world and what he or she wants to write about. As Grace Fernald (1943, p. 210) wrote: 'Formal word lists will always fail to supply the particular word a person should learn at a particular time.'

If the teaching of spelling depends on fulfilling the felt need of a child to spell a word, there must be a safe resource from which children can obtain the word they want to write, and an efficient and economical strategy by which they can learn that word when it has been provided. So lists of words are valuable only if they are derived from words asked for by the child.

Rule learning

Again, those who support the systematic approach have paid much attention to teaching spelling through rules. But it is now generally agreed that using spelling rules in school is unproductive since the rules frequently include concepts not yet acquired developmentally and are unreliable since rules ignore exceptions, are often misleading and are not exploited outside the rule-learning situation, that is in the child's 'free writing'. John Sloboda (1980) doubts if the achievement of good spellers does indeed stem from rules.

Factors in spelling

The visual factor

The most important factor in the teaching of spelling is now considered to be the visual factor (Simon, 1976). It is common practice for adults to practise visual checking, i.e. to write down possible spellings for a word when in doubt, to 'see if it looks right', and the success of this practice is demonstrated by Yvette Tenney (1980). Such visual checking depends on our extensive experience of the serial probability of letters within words. For it is what James Beers (1980, p. 43) looking at spelling developmentally within a cognitive framework speaks of as 'being continually exposed to written words and their similar letter combinations with different pronunciations' that brings about awareness of stability in the visual presentation of spellings. We accept that a word we have written is probably correct if it conforms to a close approxima-tion to English, i.e. if there are precedents for such spelling in our own language, for spelling is language-specific. We know the serial probabilities of letters in our first language better than we know the serial probabilities of letters in an unknown or unfamiliar language.

In the teaching of spelling, therefore, it is important to make children aware of high-frequency letter-strings and words already in their own vocabulary in which these letter-strings occur. For spelling, a system of systems, has been defined as 'a kind of grammar for letter sequences that generates permissible combinations without regard to sound' (Gibson *et al.*, 1962).

If spelling is dependent upon a 'kind of looking' (which is not at all the same as acuity of vision) it depends on looking with 'interest, intent and intention to reproduce a word' (Peters, 1985) and the reproduction is obviously in writing. Fred Schonell (1942, p. 277) emphasised that in learning to spell a word the 'visual, auditory and articulatory elements must be *firmly cemented in writing*' and this indicates the importance of the well-formed legible hand-writing for which Rosemary Sassoon argues in the next chapter. In my own research with nearly 1000 children (Peters, 1970) swift and well-formed handwriting was one of the three most correlated factors for success in spelling; the other factors being verbal ability and visual perception of word form.

Imagery

Another teaching strategy employed with various refinements is teaching by imagery. John Sloboda demonstrates that though visual imagery seems unlikely to be at the root of good spellers' success, it is task-dependent and supports other strategies. Thus, Grace Fernald (1943) exploits imagery in the child's finger tracing of a word by concurrent tactile, visual, articulatory and auditory means. Such a strategy directs the child's attention to letter sequen-ces and word structure, which is obviously crucial to the teaching of spelling.

Furthermore, in order to exploit the visuo-motor nature of the spelling skill it is important to teach children to look carefully at words and to write them without copying, for it is this strategy that helps the child to generalise from common letter sequences to new and previously unknown spellings.

Generalisation

Eleanor Gibson and Harry Levin (1975) consider that learning to generalise must be something a child learns on his or her own. But learning to generalise can be built into the strategy for learning as teachers point out to children, and encourage them to note and explore the occurrence of letter-strings in different words.

Such familiarity with letter-strings comes from reading. It is as Uta Frith (1980a, p. 505) says 'by looking at written or printed words carefully – that is their letter-by-letter sequences – we gain incidental knowledge of the orthographic peculiarities of the different underlying systems.' It is this looking carefully at the structure of a word that makes for successful generalisation, and this is what makes a good speller. 'Creative' and 'inventive' spelling, at the pre-spelling stage exploits and eventually cultivates children's knowledge of letter-strings (Chomsky, 1970). It is from studies of such 'invented' spellings (a more positive alternative to the traditional concept of spelling errors) that Leslie Henderson (1980) demonstrates the systematic, though gradual development of children's knowledge of word structure; how they move away from the idea that pronunciation is the major control in English spelling. And it is looking carefully at letter-by-letter sequences that can be exploited successfully in computer-assisted learning, if, in learning-to-spell programmes, the child, having typed a word incorrectly, is instructed to look carefully before retyping without copying.

Word structure without regard to sound

Unlike 'phonics for reading', learning to spell depends on looking carefully at words containing the same letter sequences without regard to sound. For example, in phonics for reading we would teach 'bone' with words like 'stone', 'alone', 'throne' etc. but in spelling this would be extended to include words like 'one', 'done', 'none' and 'gone'. For it is by using word groupings of this nature that children are given the opportunity of associating an unknown word with one they already know, e.g. 'shoulder' is a relatively easy word to write if associated with 'should'.

Lexical spelling

What also makes for good spelling is the use of subtle regularities at a deeper linguistic level. Carol Chomsky (1970) has shown that uncertainty about a spelling can be resolved by relating words lexically, thus 'medicine' can be related to 'medical'; 'sign' to 'signal'; 'national' to 'nation' but this only helps in certain specific lexical relationships and is not infallible (Marsh *et al.*, 1980; Simon and Simon, 1973).

These are the kind of strategies a teacher would follow, from a systematic perspective, a perspective which has come to be seen in the wider context of children writing.

Product within the process

Until the 1970s teachers had been concerned with what the child wrote, with the product, and with what could be seen and analysed. The trend in research on children's writing that followed has been seen to focus on the process of writing, rather than on what children actually write (Stahl, 1980). As research into children's writing has become less 'text based' and more 'writer based', spelling has come to be seen very much as a support system to composing and writing. When children are writing there are so many things to be dealt with at the same time that to pay conscious attention to all of these would be 'to overload the information process and capacity' (Scardamalia, 1980). For Marlene Scardamalia, spelling is only one of a number of supportive aspects of writing which must clearly be automatic if children are to be free to attend to other aspects related to content, in other words if children are to be free to write without being overloaded, without circumlocuting, and with contextual precision.

The 'process' in the classroom

It was during the last decade, with the publication of the work of Donald Graves (1983), that consideration of the process really began to take over. Teachers watched children writing, and listened to them as they talked their way through what they were writing. This uninterrupted discussion about their writing with individual children came to be known as 'conferencing' and it led to the now widely used practice in schools of drafting and redrafting, with the teacher, other adults or other children in the class, paying attention, not only to meaning and clarity, but also to expressions of feeling on the part of the child.

One caveat teachers might make here is that, in addition to meaning and clarity, they might be asking also about expressions of *feeling* on the part of the child. 'Cognitive clarity' is not the only objective in the discussions with the teacher, sometimes referred to as 'conferencing'.

Secretary or author?

Redrafting and reflection on what has been written will be helped by the teacher's clear understanding of the difference between what Donald Graves refers to as the 'authorial' and the 'secretarial' aspects of writing. Children can be encouraged to concentrate on either composing or on the spelling and presentation of their work for others to read. It is only at the final draft that children and teachers will be particularly concerned with surface features of spelling and punctuation.

It is important to remember that the secretarial aspect should not be allowed to predominate over the authorial aspect. With the increasing acceptance of drafting and redrafting in writing in school, teachers have come to accept children's early drafts unmoved by the appearance, the spelling, or the punctuation. For teachers view the skills of spelling and handwriting as surface skills, the province of the final draft. Writing for a public audience is seen to require more care to be taken with the finished product than writing for oneself as an aid to memory. In other words, work that is to be published in a class book, or to be displayed, demands the correct spelling that may not have been present in early drafts.

In the 1980s teachers began to focus much more on the context of what was being written, on the circumstances in which the product had arisen, in terms of motivation, and on the importance of audience. There was a concern with content, context and sharing in the Cox Report. Teachers were encouraged to help children to respond more to the content of what was written whilst developing an awareness of their audience and the purpose of their writing. This was reflecting the changing nature of the view of writing which is exemplified in the National Curriculum for England and Wales (DES, 1990).

Developmental spelling

The National Curriculum also reflected what had become central to interest in children's writing. As children were observed actually writing, they were seen to be passing through clear developmental stages (Gentry, 1981). They are seen to pass from the point when they look as if they are writing intentionally but with very rudimentary letter formation, and with no knowledge of letter-sound correspondence, so letters are written according to their sound. Such knowledge arises gradually and intermittently, as the child learns how to form letters and call them by their names. Indeed young children often offer a letter to stand for a word. This is the semi-phonetic stage.

By the phonetic stage there is awareness of letter-sound correspondence and with this knowledge, letters are written according to their sound, and children seem to be developing particular spellings for certain details of phonetic form. This is the time of 'inventive spelling' and it is a very important watershed in learning to spell.

It is here that there is clear evidence of phonological awareness (see Chapter 6). This is the ability to analyse and manipulate the sounds of spoken words, split them up into smaller units of sounds, and say what they are. It is a growing awareness of the spelling system, necessary but not sufficient for good spelling.

How do young children acquire phonological awareness? It is acquired through exposure to a literate environment, where, for example, the parent or teacher reads the same book and says the same rhymes and plays the same word games to the child repeatedly, and runs a finger from left to right while reading, or where children see other children writing and saying the word as they write. This is the time when inventive spelling is at its height.

We may be somewhat mystified by some of a child's spelling at this time, for it is the time when a child writes words which as adults, because of our sophisticated phonological knowledge, we may no longer be able to recognise. For example, a child writes 'poukyorparn' for 'porcupine' and we do not recognise it since we do not notice that the 'ore' in porcupine is more like 'pouk' than 'pork', and the 'ine' is more like 'arn' than 'ine'. Our reading of invented spellings can be uncomfortably inefficient!

Such children are developing their phonological knowledge efficiently, sometimes, as in the case of 'porcupine' above, excessively, and as yet without real spelling knowledge. They are developmentally at the phonetic stage.

Teacher intervention in spelling

This is where the need arises for intervention in the form of spelling teaching. There is indeed a danger that children may remain at this stage of being over-reliant on auditory input, and it is important to intervene with spelling teaching at this point. It is essential between the developmental stage known as phonetic, where the child is matching letters and sounds, and the following stage, often termed 'transitional'. Here the child is moving on from sound to visual appearance, putting vowels into 'words' and applying a rudimentary knowledge of spelling patterns.

Children at the transitional or morphemic stage are applying knowledge of spelling patterns, or letter-strings, that is to say units of language smaller than words. They are moving into the developmental stage of correctness. For them words look like English, and they are able to proof read their own writing. Now they can say 'It doesn't look right', for their visual knowledge is secure.

There is clearly a difference between phonological knowledge and spelling knowledge. Phonological knowledge, as has already been stated, is a necessary but not sufficient condition for spelling ability (Bradley and Bryant, 1985). Poor spellers are those who have not internalised the spelling system as part of their phonological knowledge (Ehri, 1989). With developing phonological awareness comes the need for intervention in the form of spelling teaching.

Spelling routes: phonological or visual?

Now at this point children can either change their strategies or develop them. It is a controversial point and it highlights the difference in perspective of those who favour the visual as opposed to the phonological route.

It should be remembered that by the phonological route children can produce spellings only for regular words. By the visual route, correct spelling derives from knowledge specific to the word, but spelling knowledge is not limited to these words since, by analogy, that is by generalisation, spelling knowledge can be infinite.

Though some studies show that phonological strategies continue to play a crucial role in many aspects of children's school life, there is a strong case to be made for accepting the visual strategy as the chief factor in helping children to spell. There is much evidence and one only needs to ask 'How do we behave when we don't know how to spell a word?' The answer is universally: 'Write it down to see if it looks right.'

We know when a word looks right because it conforms to our coding system of which letters can occur together in English. It is similar to the situation when we are asked to reproduce visually-presented nonsense words.

The spelling of nonsense words

How we spell nonsense words, or non-words has long been of interest in spelling research. An early and seminal study was carried out by Michael Wallach (1963) who, investigating the coding system by which children learn to spell, presented good and poor spellers with briefly exposed flash cards (i.e. by visual presentation), and asked them to write what they saw. Some words were random strings of six letters. Some were groups of letters with a close approximation to English. What was revealed was that for random words there was very little difference between good and poor spellers, but good spellers were found to recognise nonsense words resembling English much more readily than poor spellers. The good spellers had learned the coding system based on the probabilities of letters occurring in certain sequences in English.

Ability in reproducing nonsense words, though not necessarily of specific diagnostic value, has been used with visual presentation in, for example, Denis Vincent and Jenny Claydon's *Diagnostic Spelling Test* (1982) and seems to be a good predictor of future literacy. This is what was to be expected from the Wallach research. Research using nonsense words with oral as well as visual presentation occurs again and again, for it is a clean vehicle for spelling research.

Using real words, Usha Goswami and Peter Bryant (1990) demonstrated the important role of such analogies in learning to spell. Analogies occur phonologically, but they are limited to sound-symbol contingency. Analogies presented visually are limitless. Nevertheless phonological analogies are not to be ignored. Such learning is a pre-requisite for spelling knowledge.

All this is far removed from the child writing, where the child is spelling within the context of what he or she is writing, when spelling is at the point of the pen, and when the child is dependent on the intervening teacher, who, having moved the child on from phonological dependence, intervenes with visual generalisations.

Spelling intervention

There is no reason why young children should not be taught words by multi-sensory methods. After all, Grace Fernald was highly successful at this. She was one of the first to teach children to write before they learned to read, and her multi-sensory approach by finger-tracing, articulating and pronouncing, with immediate auditory feedback of the word as it sounds, is unbeaten in its success with failing children. In my own work, I have had no failures in teaching dyslexic children to write and read in this way. We are thinking, here, also of children who have not received welcome acceptance of their writing in the early developmental stages, from scribble writing onwards, who have not received acceptance of what they write, irrespective of how they write it. These are children to whom spelling remains a mystery, who are not free to write.

By the time the child has reached the transitional stage, visual intervention is essential. Children must be taught, if they have not already learned it, the 'Look, Cover, Write, Check' routine. But here again, there is uncertainty. Some, for example, Peter Bryant and Lynette Bradley (1985) in their 'Simultaneous Oral Spelling approach for backward readers', advocate saying the names of the letters within the routine. For most children, it is probably not necessary to spell out letter names for by this time most children should already know them. In addition, the saying of the letter names causes distraction from the word being written and avoids the possibility of generalisation, that is to say, making analogies with known words. For example, the child learns 'today' and says it as it sounds while writing it. She/he then has a resource for writing 'tomorrow' or 'together'.

But for some children, still unfamiliar with letter names, it is useful to say the names of the letters. Intervention should occur when phonological knowledge is secure.

Besides giving a strategy for learning a word the child needs, there must be an opportunity provided for learning every word the child has 'asked for' and for testing by the teacher or by a child of similar spelling ability. Obviously the teaching of common letter-strings, of words within words, and of words within the children's own names with children in groups or in the class as a whole, is a central part of spelling intervention.

Clearly we do not want 'correct spelling' merely for reasons of status, educational or social, nor is it entirely in the cause of communication or even courtesy. There is, however, one overriding case for our concern with correctness and it is this that is the justification for (and implicit in) all that is said about spelling in the National Curriculum. It is that spelling ability frees children to write what they want to write. It is only when children have spelling literally at their fingertips that they are free to write without backward glances to see if a word looks right, and without circumlocuting and offering a less precise synonym or phrase.

Of course, children only resort to uneasy circumlocution and backward glances if parents and teachers are, or have been, so pedantic as to demand correct spelling at all costs on all occasions. Where teachers wield the red pencil, children will inevitably be wary of writing adventurously.

Children who write freely and confidently at an early age will inevitably invent spellings which deviate from conventional spelling. According to the Cox Report 'invented spellings often demonstrate logical consistency; this grasp of regularity should be recognised as an initial achievement and children should be helped to be confident in attempting to spell words for themselves without undue dependence on the teacher' (DES, 1989a para. 17.11). This we expect and accept; for if we do not accept and welcome what a child writes, irrespective of how he or she writes it, the child will develop a self-image as a poor speller which is almost impossible to banish in later years.

Emphases and perspectives

Any emphasis upon spelling in the early years must therefore be sensitive, indirect and subtle. Attention to essentials, such as looking carefully at word structure, should occur incidentally; it should not intrude upon occasions when young children are writing freely. If they ask for a word, however, this should immediately be given by the teacher for them to reproduce without copying; they are thus expected to look with the intention of remembering what they have asked for. But such help should all be given in a low key, with no tension; the interaction should reflect the confident awareness by both teacher and child that a correct spelling can be learned when the child requires it. Competent spellers are confident spellers who will write adventurously, at ease in their control of the medium.

Whatever the perspectives in research, it would seem that teachers, aware of the need for confidence and competence in spelling as a support system, and guided by the clear demands of the National Curriculum, balance for themselves the perspectives of the child as author and secretary.

Such children are, and know they are, authors, writing for a specific audience, and served by secretarial skills that are not only habitual but secure for all time.

handwriting

Rosemary Sassoon

Handwriting has been the forgotten facet of literacy for the past few decades. Certain educational planners fell into the trap of believing that teaching handwriting was repressive and would stilt young children's attempts at creative writing. They preached with tempting 'logic' that if children were allowed to play with letters then somehow they would eventually be able to pick up the complex skill by themselves. Many of our children therefore have not been taught how to write; but nonetheless later on they are blamed for being unable to do so at an acceptable level. Criticism of their written work, and dismay at the visible display of failure confronting them each day, discourages many children from writing more than a minimum. In addition it can foster a distaste for writing that may last a lifetime. In the end our children have been deprived of that very skill that would enable them to be creative.

This neglect of a vital area of education has persisted for so long that today's teachers have often not been taught adequate strategies for handwriting themselves at school. To make matters worse they were seldom taught how to teach handwriting during their training. Furthermore the movement towards developmental approaches to writing in the last decade positively discouraged any systematic early teaching of the correct movement of letters. While welcoming the imaginative ideas promoted, for instance, by the National Writing Project (National Curriculum Council, 1988), it was difficult to approve of their attitudes to the very skill that would enable children to express their ideas in a written form later on. By encouraging play with letters after school entry, the automating of incorrect movement of letters became a stumbling block. Handwriting is a motor skill so movement faults once automated become increasingly difficult to overcome. Too many of our teenagers now have writing problems as a result of this muddled thinking.

Planning for the future

We now need to plan for the future. Handwriting is not static, it has developed throughout the centuries to meet both educational and social needs. We do not want to go back to the restrictive techniques of the past, nor to exactly the same letterforms, because the priorities for handwriting have altered as well as writing implements. Today our pupils need to write at speed as well as legibly, and children are encouraged to be creative in their written work as soon as possible. This means that there is little time for teaching the basics before handwriting needs to be used, so it is vital that any system for teaching young children really works. Above all everyone involved in teaching young children to write – teachers, therapists and parents – needs to understand what handwriting is, how it works and what any problems may indicate. Handwriting is a complex matter involving the whole body, not only the eyes and the hands. It combines and reflects performance in several cognitive functions. It is an interdisciplinary subject and those who plan for our children's future should have a knowledge of letterforms and psychology and a certain amount of physiology as well as education. Of all these subjects it is the letterform aspect that is perhaps the least understood.

Handwriting and the National Curriculum

Those who look to the National Curriculum document for England and Wales for guidance find goals to achieve and not particularly difficult ones either. As in other subjects, the document does not lay down details for the teaching of handwriting, and personally I think that is a good idea. The one trap that we need to avoid is that of prescribing a national model – a concept that has bedevilled so many other countries. They change models periodically still pursuing the idea that a magic one will solve all their problems. Where there is a concept that a particular slant proportion or designed detail of letter is the only correct way to write then the important aspects of writing are ignored while the copying aspects are exaggerated. When this is enshrined in a national model and curriculum children are judged not on their ability to write fast and efficiently.but on their capacity to adhere to an arbitrarily chosen model. More seriously, those for whom any particular style is not natural may be held back from automating their handwriting by consciously struggling to keep to a slant or proportion that does not work well for them. Many countries are finding that the more strictly models are adhered to and the longer they are kept in use in primary or elementary schools, the more trouble pupils seem to have with their handwriting in their secondary schools. They seem more likely to revert to separate letters when needing to write at speed. This can be explained very simply by the fact that children when allowed or even encouraged to experiment with personal simplifications and personal joins, find the many efficient but legible shortcuts that lead to a fast handwriting. It was with dismay therefore that I read an article that was given prominence in the national press. It stated; 'The Government should issue a standard handwriting model to accompany the National Curriculum'. Only then, the writer mistakenly argues 'will teachers be able to assess pupils fairly'. To the contrary, what we need are good teaching methods and informed teachers who can carry them out.

Terminology and the National Curriculum

Where the National Curriculum documents caused confusion was not over the lack of a prescribed model, but in the use of particular terminology. It would have been more helpful if the first two attainment targets talked about the 'movement' of letters instead of 'orientation'. Of course, letters need to be correctly orientated, i.e. to be facing in the right direction, but the point of entry and direction of stroke that together make up the movement of letters would deal with this. If the word 'movement' or even the less explicit term 'formation' had been used, it would have emphasised the importance of this vital aspect of early training.

In the draft proposals some slightly controversial terms crept in, and seem to have left an indelible impression on some people, despite having been omitted from the final document. Level 3 referred to 'cursive style', level 4 to 'more fluent cursive style' and worst of all level 5 to 'both print and cursive styles'. The simple terms 'separate letters' and 'joined letters' would have been much better as well as more accurate. British teachers relate to the term 'joined-up' which is now used for the level 3 attainment target. It now reads: 'Begin to produce clear and legible joined-up writing'.

To me the words cursive and joined-up mean the same and I have used them both quite happily together in the past. The term 'cursive' however, seems to suggest something different to some people. They see it as more joined than joined-up, perhaps looped as well. Some people are going further and saying that this means that we should revert to versions of copperplate-based commercial cursives that went out of use in this country in the 1920s. To further justify these models, those promoting them are saying that the French teach 'cursive' from the start. This is adding inaccuracy to misinterpretation. For many years it has been said, maybe half jokingly, that in the first term of school in every classroom in France all the children on any particular day will be learning exactly the same letter. French children have been taught for decades to learn their separate letters in this way, a whole page of one letter at a time, written on squared paper. Their separate letters have entry as well as exit strokes and maybe that is where the mistake arose. The French are finding that their secondary students are increasingly reverting to print because the continuous cursive that is the result of these letterforms disintegrates at speed. The whole matter of their national model has been under consideration for several years by a multi-disciplinary committee. Meanwhile Du Pasquier-

Grall (1990) describes in some detail how the majority of French children actually learn to write

'Les lettres sont tracées une à une au début (âge 6–7 ans).'

It is not advisable to compare national models without detailed knowledge about actual teaching methods within another country. The wording of the National Curriculum should not be distorted and such misleading statements must be countered. They must not be allowed to be used to justify commercially lucrative, but not necessarily appropriate, handwriting models and to impose them on our children.

Understanding handwriting

So what is handwriting? Handwriting is the graphic counterpart of speech, wrote Diringer (1962). Most people would agree that it is a form of communication but beyond that handwriting could also be described in several different ways including:

– a taught skill with a conventional set of rules;
– a motor skill;
– the visible trace of a hand movement;
– a reflection of the writer on paper.

However we describe it, handwriting is something that we as adults do automatically and in doing so tend to forget the many intermediate learning stages. Informed teachers are vital if our children are to be equipped with the handwriting that they need for the various tasks that confront them in education and beyond. Where handwriting has been given a priority in the school curriculum in recent years, the emphasis has usually been on providing a model and hoping that copying it will somehow teach the child to write. However it is the method, and the teacher that are more important than any particular model. An extension of each of the descriptions of handwriting mentioned above should widen the understanding of the task of writing, and raise awareness of its complexity.

Handwriting is a taught skill

It is not instinctive or in any way natural to write the letters of the alphabet. The rules that govern our writing system are conventions applicable to our culture alone and each of them needs to be taught in such a way that children are aware of them from their first writing lessons. Any of these rules if misunderstood can become a stumbling block for the writer in years to come. They are:

The direction of writing. This is from left to right and from top to bottom.
The movement of letters. The strokes that make up individual letters should commence at a conventional point and be written in the correct direction.

Height differentials. Letters are of different heights and this contributes to the ultimate legibility of writing.

There are two sets of letters, capital letters and small letters. These each have their appropriate uses.

Spacing. Words and letters both require adequate spacing.

Handwriting is a motor skill

The act of writing is governed by the motor memory, or as Montessori referred to it in her teaching during the first half of the century 'the muscle memory'. This means that once the coordinated action of the muscles that is needed to produce the written trace of a letter is automated, it is difficult to alter. This alone is a forceful argument for the insistence on teaching the correct movement of basic letters to young children as soon as they are in a learning situation. It also provides the reason why so many of those educated in the years when a dismissive attitude to teaching handwriting held sway, have found it so difficult to alter the visual approximations of letters that they taught themselves. To acquire an adequate handwriting much less a fluent joined hand, requires the correct movement of basic letters. The implications for the early teaching of handwriting are also clear. A systematic method of movement training will be the best way of stocking the motor memory.

Handwriting is the visible trace of a hand movement

How we write in terms of writing posture is as important as what we write in terms of letters, and inevitably affects those letters. Handwriting posture includes not only how we sit but the hand position, and the penhold as well as the paper position which affects all the other factors. The necessity for teaching good postural strategies from the start is based on the argument that posture automates in the same way as any other feature of handwriting. How to sit may be a fairly straightforward matter given appropriate furniture, and paper position is also straightforward given enough working space for both left-handers and right-handers to have the paper to the side of their writing hand. Penhold, however, is much more complex. Writing masters as long ago as the fifteenth century accepted the relationship between the pen, the hand and the resulting letterforms. As pens developed and altered so did the prescriptions for penhold. In recent years there has been a great change in writing implements. With no preliminary research, modern pens, that work best at different elevations to traditional fountain pens or pencils, have come into general use. Penhold research was reported in Sassoon *et al.,* (1986). The findings showed that unconventional penholds were faster than conventional ones. This has led to the conclusion that maybe we need to reassess the conventional attitude to penhold, taking into account alternative penholds that might work better with modern pens.

Over and above the individual details of penhold that would affect personal letterforms, the individuality of handwriting is explained in various ways. Montessori (1967, p. 203) said 'Even though we use the same alphabet the motions that we use are so individual that each one has his own particular style of handwriting and there are thus as many styles of writing as there are of men.' This refers to the way we use our bodies and explains the difference between individuals. If we carry this argument further, to relate it to teaching policies, it reflects on the issue of expecting children to copy models that require all children to perform the same action to produce the identical trace.

Handwriting is a reflection of the writer on paper

Handwriting is the result of personal action, so it is a visible and permanent record of the writer's condition at the time of writing. In that way it is a useful diagnostic tool. In addition to variations between writers, handwriting will differ within an individual's efforts. It will differ according to the demands of different tasks, perhaps also affected by pupils' attitude to a particular subject or even to a particular teacher. Writing will mirror the writer's general development, in particular the ups and downs of teenagers. It will reflect variations in health, tiredness and above all tension. A certain amount of tension may be a necessary stimulus to learning but excess and detrimental tension can arise at any time from a wide variety of causes, some quite out of the control of the teacher. The result of physical and mental tension is transmitted via the hand to the paper. Too much tension can interrupt the taking in or putting out of any information, and can so disrupt even a competent handwriting to make it almost unrecognisable. As handwriting interacts with other cognitive functions, a problem with one will reflect through the written trace. What initially appears to be a handwriting problem may actually be indicating worry about spelling. Graphologists might go further. Saudek (1932) suggested that 'It [children's handwriting] even offers possibilities absent from maturer specimens. From the latter we are able to observe what a person is. From a child's handwriting, on the other hand, can often be seen what he or she is likely to become.'

Putting all the factors together

Handwriting is more often judged from the viewpoint of the reader than that of the writer. From this short introduction to the subject alone it becomes clear that we must alter our attitudes to fit in with the altered requirements of handwriting and its usage. If we accept that the letters are the result of practical factors such as penhold and posture as well as different kinds of pens, then we need to be more flexible in our attitude to the results, and more informed in our treatment. Whether teaching or correcting handwriting it will be necessary to understand this inextricable involvement between the hand that writes and the letters that are the result. It may no longer be appropriate to dictate exactly what is right or wrong about several matters including penhold, or the appearance of handwriting. Now that a crowded curriculum leaves less time for the teaching of skills, it will be more important than ever to separate those matters that need to be taught and taught thoroughly, from those that can be, and may be better left to develop on their own.

Teaching the early stages of handwriting

This section sets out to balance the issues involved in teaching but not necessarily to deal with the details. Such details are to be found in Sassoon (1990b) and elsewhere. The focus is on the initial stages and the changes of priorities that need to occur during the children's development. We need a system that is progressive but flexible enough to be adapted for all levels of children. At school entry there are likely to be some who may already be able to write their names and more, but others who may have barely used a pencil. There will be some with bad habits already automated, and others who have been pressed by over eager parents and are already wary of writing. The first lessons are the most important. What is learned then may affect the writer for many years to come. The teacher's attitude to the subject is also important; and if this is bored or dismissive of the task this will quickly be picked up by the children and will be reflected in their written work for a long time to come. If on the other hand it is an imaginative positive approach then children will react in the same way and the lessons can become satisfying and even creative. At the pre-writing stage and when beginning with letters, it is important to include all three modes of learning; through the eyes, through the ears and by touch. The importance of kinaesthetic awareness is now widely acknowledged, the need for visual comparison is really a matter of commonsense, but the importance of teaching letters by an oral description of the movement is less obvious. Techniques that involve all three modes will not be wasted on the competent, and are essential for the few children who may have problems in one area or another.

Teaching techniques

Little and often

Teachers who have planned daily short pre-writing and writing sessions relate that soon they become so popular that there are complaints from the children if they have to be omitted. Maybe we have forgotten how satisfying such small repetitive tasks can be. But to be satisfying for everyone, the standards, within a systematic method, must be flexible to allow the least capable to attain satisfaction as well as the more competent. How teachers deal with children of such varying levels must be left to individuals, but whatever method is used a certain amount of one-to-one supervision is vital for all children when in the early stages of skill training. This ensures that no movement problems go unobserved, and that practical matters such as pencil hold can have individual attention. This may sound time-consuming; however, once teachers are aware of all the issues, and realise their importance, then they will find it much easier to recognise and deal with such matters in an informed way.

The importance of one-to-one supervision

When the implications of motor training are considered then certain recommended techniques need to be scrutinised. Most handwriting manuals promote pattern work for fluency, and often tracking or tracing as well. However, none of these three is of much help when unsupervised. They may even be harmful. Young children may start at the right-hand side of a row of pattern and go 'backwards' quite happily if left alone. They may start in the middle of a word or manage some magnificently unconventional movement within a letter which once approved of and repeated can remain as a more intractable problem thereafter. Again the role of the teacher is all-important. Exercises will be needed to illustrate height differentials, spacing and mirror image, as well as direction. It may be left to the teacher to invent exercises to deal with these points at a level appropriate to any particular group. Such exercises can be tactile, visual or oral, but preferably all three.

Teaching the movement of letters

The movement of letters can be dealt with in logical sequences. Alphabetical order is not appropriate and can be left until a later stage. The twenty-six small letters of the alphabet divide themselves into families that are made up of similar strokes. They are best taught, compared, assimilated, and practised together.

iltuyj   hnmr bpk   cadgqoe   vwxz sf

Early sessions should also include the comparison between capital letters and small letters, and exercises in name writing. The letters in children's names are interesting because they are the ones that are usually the earliest to be learned, praised and repeated. If the wrong movement has been automated then these will be the letters needing most attention.

Letterforms for handwriting

Letterforms are a personal matter, and those who design models often produce a version of their own handwriting, the theory being that it has worked for them so should be good for everyone else. But we are not all the same. We have different aspirations, characteristics, tastes, talents and, above all, different bodies that influence how we view and produce letters. Letterforms should be viewed in an unemotional and practical way. We must not look backwards. The models that influenced the writing of one generation may not be suitable for the requirements and writing implements of the next.

The starting point for designing a model should be the relationship between the hand, and the letter formed by the trace of the hand movement. Marion Richardson said in 1935 (p. 3) of her simplified cursive: '. . . it employs only the easy movements of the hand and arm such as are used in primitive forms of decoration and childish scribble.' In addition, the first letters must promote the right pressures and movement between letters that will lead to an easy transition into joined writing. The best way of ensuring this is to include exit strokes on those letters that terminate at the baseline, a concept which Marion Richardson appreciated, but many designers in the intervening years ignored. The idea that the straight letters of print script are best is a misconception, and unfortunately a widely held one. Statements such as that by William Gray (1956) influenced handwriting worldwide for several decades. He said, 'Because of its proved advantages, all countries which use Roman letters but which have not yet adopted the use of print script during the first two years, should seriously consider the wisdom of doing so.' That statement was based on a false premise. Those straight letters taught the hand an abrupt movement with maximum pressure on the baseline. The movement of the hand between letters must also be taken into account, and here again print script fails. Exit strokes promote adequate spacing between all letters.

Some people have very strong views on the slant and proportion of letters, and insist that all pupils conform precisely to a chosen model. Others realise that both slant and proportion are related to hand position and penhold, so that many children may be unable to conform. At the early stages there are many aspects more important than uniformity, but exposure to a variety of good models at a later stage might benefit children who could then choose one nearest to their personal style. There are acceptable alternatives to certain letters even within the models taught in the United Kingdom, which raises the question, should children be confined to one, or be exposed to several and allowed to choose at a certain stage? At a deeper level we need to understand the value of personal variations, not to deplore them.

Balancing commercial schemes with a school's own ideas

This is an issue that needs to be seen in the light of the situation in the United Kingdom today. There are risks involved in both ways and they need to be explained. Many schools have become disillusioned with commercial schemes which provide standard letterforms and exercises. Pupils have not learned to write through their use, and this is not altogether surprising. Either a 'copy the model' technique or the use of standard exercises in a class with children at various levels of attainment is unlikely to be adequate. The temptation to leave sheets or a copybook to do the job of teaching handwriting is the real risk of depending on a commercial handwriting scheme.

Photocopiable sheets take away choice from both teacher and pupil. Without choice the real lessons of handwriting often get missed. Copybooks worked well when there was plenty of time to teach the basics of handwriting, and the teachers were knowledgeable, but today the model is often the only part of the scheme to be valued and can become a crutch for the under-confident teacher, to the detriment of the pupils. To be fair to the writers of handwriting schemes, some of the fault lies in the fact that few copies of the teachers' manuals are bought. Frequently the copybooks are all that is available in the classroom.

A school-made policy has the advantage of being the result of discussion between the staff to evolve something to fit their exact needs. The discussion of the various choices will in itself have led to a more informed attitude to handwriting which should pervade the school over the whole age range. Perhaps the main disadvantage lies in the letterforms. It could be argued that the letters that result from home-made schemes will lack expertise and polish. I have found in my own research, however, that many teachers have difficulty reproducing designed models and their own representations of whatever model is used are likely to be influenced by their personal handwriting (Sassoon, 1991). In turn, the children will be influenced as much by the teacher's writing that they see on the blackboard each day. If nothing else, this is an argument for more training for teachers in blackboard-writing techniques.

Tools and materials

A 'writer-orientated approach' has been recommended towards letters. Now this approach can be extended to the tools and materials that will also affect how the pupils learns to write. When dealing with the practical issues of handwriting, some points are fundamental, while others may best be dealt with by surveying the preferences of children within a particular group. It is, for example, the school's responsibility to ensure that there is appropriate furniture to suit the needs of those who may be much taller or shorter than average. This can usually be arranged between classes with a minimum of inconvenience throughout a school. Adequate desk or table space will be needed to allow both right- and left-handers to position their paper where it best suits them. Pens and pencils, however, are more a matter of personal choice. What suits one child at any particular age may not suit the next. A choice of pencils of different shapes and sizes as well as different points is desirable in all classrooms. A quick survey of the preference of five-year-olds will soon inform a teacher that the old directive of fat pencils for small hands to write with is just another misconception.

The use of lines should also be considered in a flexible way. Some teachers dislike their use at all in infant classes, while others want tramlines used at all times. There are two issues at stake here. Some tasks at school entry may be better undertaken on plain paper, but in others, such as the difficult discrimination between the different heights of letters, a baseline at least would help young children. The teacher could also demonstrate this particular lesson using coloured lines on the blackboard. But tramlines, whether two or four, introduce another influence on the writer. If only one size of ruled lines are available, then pressure is being put onto a whole group to write at the same size. Size, like so much of handwriting, is a personal matter and within reason should not be dictated. Even though teachers might wish to alter the size of a particular pupil's handwriting it would be wise to bear in mind that small handwriting is often an indication of tension, whereas over-large handwriting may signal that the child has difficulty producing complex movements in a small space. In neither case will the imposition of uniform lines help them.

Joining-up

So many handwriting issues are argued along inflexible or illogical lines. Joining-up is no exception. There are some experts who believe that children should learn separate letters only and never be allowed to join for the first two years at school. Such children will be chastised if their letters join at speed and are held back however competent and eager they are. Those who have been restricted to neat print for two years are expected to be able to alter overnight to exit strokes and joins. Not surprisingly, it is often the best printers who have most difficulties in joining. There are others who proclaim that children should join from the start, ignoring the belief that the movement of basic letters must be well taught and confirmed before joins are practicable, and that some children in today's crowded classes may not be ready to join all their letters at the age of five.

The more balanced argument is that children are taught letters with exit strokes from the start, with correct movement of letters being stressed. They should then be encouraged to 'join' as soon as they are able. The exit strokes will promote spontaneous joins along the baseline, while joins, crossbar joins and reverse joins can then be taught slightly later.

We write today with our hand resting on the table and only very relaxed writers can produce more than half a dozen letters without needing to reposition the hand. It is therefore misleading to teach children to join every letter all the time. Handwriting is a mixture of the movements that are visible on paper because the pen is on the paper, and those between separate letters that leave no trace because they occur when the pen is lifted. A penlift in the middle of a long word may be essential to the hand and will cause little delay in writing when the movement is efficient. Joining three or four letters at a time, particularly those that occur most often in our language makes good sense, but making children join every letter all the time means that they will be disadvantaged when wanting to write comfortably and efficiently at speed.

Those who say that it is easy to develop penlifts later on would be wise to study the problems of mature writers in countries whose national models still impose continuous cursive. Perhaps the only way of assessing the effects of any particular model, joined or unjoined, is to seek a representative group of school-leavers who have been taught a particular model and to hear their views on how it has met their needs.

Basic joins are only the first stage, it is the personalising of joins that permit handwriting to mature and speed up. Teachers need to understand the complex movements of personal joins. Children can then be helped to understand that some short cuts are helpful, while others may go too far and affect the legibility of their handwriting.

Speed, legibility, uniformity and creativity

Each generation has its own style of handwriting marked by changes in fashion, and attitudes. We no longer live in the gentle world that was reflected in the graceful letters of 150 years ago. We cannot expect our pupils to employ such forms in the world where speed and competition mark their lives. Skills have been given a low priority in recent years, so pupils are often ill-equipped with the discrimination and training to tackle such a specific task, much less to refine it. The aggression and even desperation that marks so many of the lives of our older pupils also leaves its impression on this generation's handwriting. We may deplore this, but we must try to accept and understand it. Above all we must not confuse distaste for a particular style of writing with illegibility.

The quality of letterforms will of necessity be affected by speed. It has already been said how important it is to recognise suitability of level of writing to the task. While not wishing to condone poor handwriting, too high an expectation of the quality of handwriting required can so inhibit certain students so that they risk failing their examinations because they write too slowly. It is often said that everyone has their own optimum writing speed. We may be asking too much of our hands to write at the speed required in some examination tasks. Excessive speed may destroy good handwriting, and damage the writer as well.

Fast handwriting needs planning from the start with efficient letterforms taught at school entry, and efficient joins as soon as possible. Attitudes need to alter so that there is respect for fast letters, and for different levels of writing for different tasks. Understanding that some tools may restrict speed will also help. Junior school children (aged seven to eleven) can profit from light-hearted speed tests, so that by the time they reach secondary school they may have a reserve of speed to use when required. Writing is for communicating, therefore it must be legible, but if we accept that our education system is geared to encouraging creativity in most areas of written work, then we must also expect individuality to show through in handwriting.

Consistency within personal writing may be desirable but not uniformity within the whole group. In years gone by, uniformity may have been achieved through intensive training, but times have changed. Writers are best served today by the consistency that comes from letterforms that suit their preferences and their hands. In this way personal handwriting automates fastest and becomes the tool for effortless recording of facts or creative thought. We must learn to value the variations for what they mean, not only to the writers' efficiency but as an expression of their own creativity. These are the realities of handwriting. Neither speed nor quality can or should be subject to norms.

Handwriting in the curriculum

The timing of the teaching of handwriting and the way it is assimilated into other subjects is important. The early stages of the skill of handwriting need to be taught carefully and systematically, preferably before the rush of ideas that make the formation of letters not only a restriction on the recording of ideas but a more difficult task to assimilate with the conflicting demands of spelling. There is less need today for constant practise in the formal exercise sense of the word. Once the basic movement and principals of the writing system are internalised, then any corrections can take place within the daily written work. This can be done gently and imaginatively by an informed teacher who should know what is essential to correct and what will refine as the child's own system develops. Handwriting lessons need not be sterile times of copying useless phrases where any problems get more deeply ingrained because of unsupervised repetition. The lessons can be linked both to the way the hand and body learn best – rhythmically within our writing and language system. Letters taught in families can be used almost from the first day in simple words comprising the letters in each family. The different heights of letters can be practised or corrected in words that include such letters. Once all the letters are learned they can then be practised in the strings of letters that are most commonly used in our language. When learning to join up letters, the automation of common letter strings may well assist with spelling. By internalising the movement of such letter sequences, future spelling difficulties may be avoided. Such exercises, preferably involving a certain element of repetition, can with the help of imaginative teaching, involve children in exploring our language while learning the basics of handwriting. It is not suggested here to link the learning of letters to phonics because handwriting might then be subsumed to reading and spelling.

Handwriting problems

However good a handwriting policy, some children will end up with problems at some time of their lives. These may occur at the beginning of school life where children may have a delay in the development of the very specific skills required for perceiving or producing the delicate and definite marks that we call letters. This slight deficiency bears no relation to the intelligence of a child, and must not be treated as such. It is a challenge to the teacher to find the best way to encourage such capabilities to develop without the loss of confidence that so often accompanies a delay in motor skills. Some children may have problems at the joining stage, even when their separate letters move correctly. Left-handers who can produce neat separate letters may have problems with the continuous left-to-right flow of cursive. Others who have had the need for neatness drummed into them, may not be able to relax enough to risk the slight deterioration in quality that is the result of learning to join. Speeding up is a problem for those with postural and penhold difficulties, while for others idiosyncratic teenage letters become habitual and in their turn affect the movement of the hand.

Handwriting problems are seldom the child's fault. Problems are likely to be caused by inadequate or inappropriate teaching, a physical or developmental problem that requires special attention, or the intervention of excess tension from any number of possible causes in the child's home or school environment. It is not possible to discuss the details of diagnosis and remediation here. All that there is space for is to introduce the idea that detection of handwriting problems should not be confined to special needs. Classroom teachers can start by observing and, if possible, tabulating details of difficulties of children under their care. Once the function of writing is viewed more the writer's angle than only from the reader's, the way forward becomes clearer.

Writing by hand and the use of keyboards

A keyboard should never be offered in such a way that writers' confidence in their ultimate ability to write is destroyed. As computers are increasingly used in the classroom, questions inevitably arise about their use to supplant handwriting. It is important once again to keep a sense of balance, even when planning the needs of severely handicapped children. Needs within school must be balanced against the needs that are likely to arise later in life. Handwriting is a vital skill; those who are unable to fill in a form or to produce a consistent signature are 'non-persons' in society. They are likely to be dependent on relatives or friends to deal with their business for the rest of their lives. This may sound extreme, but it is worrying to hear how unheedingly children with relatively minor problems are given a word-processor and told that they can forget about handwriting. Even severely handicapped pupils can, with encouragement, produce quite adequate letters suitable for some tasks. It is often a matter of expectation and allowing keyboard and personal writing lessons to go together.

On the other hand, children with a motor delay (or even ordinary five- or six-year-olds) deserve to see their stories produced and printed out in a professional way sometimes. Children of any age who have a tremor that impedes the adequate production of legible handwriting would profit from the use of a word processor for much of their written work. When it comes to secondary school, most pupils might profit at times from the benefit to clarity and organisation that keyboards provide. It should not be forgotten that to acquire the necessary speed is time-consuming in itself. Keyboards should not be allowed to supplant the personal skill, but used in circumstances when they support pupils' own handwriting. When such relief is provided, poor writers may relax and in doing so actually improve their own written trace.

Summary

Much of what has been discussed in this chapter may be new to many people who thought handwriting was a matter of learning to follow a model and of copying standard exercises from time to time in the classroom. The ideas may even sound threatening to over-stretched teachers who could interpret them as just one more burden. However, if the subject is understood, taught with a systematic method at the right time and in the right way, then it will be a saving to all concerned in both time and money. The benefits to the potentially problem-free children will be obvious, and special needs teachers will be freed from the quantity of children whose handwriting problems have been induced by the previously inadequate provision for the subject. They will have time to deal more thoroughly with the small percentage of children for whom, unfortunately, handwriting may always pose a certain problem.

balancing perspectives

beginning to read: an overview

Marilyn Jager Adams

The most fundamental and important issues in the field of reading education are those of how children learn to read and write and how best to help them. Moreover, these issues are nowhere more important than in the initial stages of literacy instruction. Every child enters school expecting to learn to read. Those who make reasonable progress are well on their way to a successful school career. Those who do not, experience disappointment in school and in themselves as students, even in their very introduction to the system. Understandably, children who have struggled in vain with reading soon decide that they neither like nor want to read (Juel, 1988). But without reading, what is their future – academic or otherwise?

Today, more than ever before, we need to understand the knowledge and processes involved in learning to read and the methods, manner, and progression through which their development may best be fostered. Levels of literacy that were held, even recently, to be satisfactory will be marginal by the year 2000 (Commission on Reading, National Academy of Education, 1985). But even as the social and economic values of literacy are multiplying, so too is the evidence that many children are not adequately learning to read beyond a basic level (Chall, 1983). Moreover, the dropout and illiteracy statistics are especially marked among those very children who depend most of all on schooling for their formal literacy education.

Yet, the effectiveness of literacy instruction cannot be expected to improve measurably until our understanding of what it must entail improves significantly: what do our students and pupils need to learn in service of reading and writing? With what knowledge and expectations do different children approach the challenge of learning? How can we modify our classrooms so as to reach *all* of them most effectively and engagingly? How can we enable teachers to understand and build on their students' and pupils knowledge and expectations so as to lead them to become reflective and self-improving readers and writers?

In recent years, progress in the domain of beginning reading and writing instruction has been stymied by the heat of the debate in the United States of

America over phonics versus whole language. Indeed, so paralysing and divisive had this debate become that, in 1986, the United States Congress passed a law requiring an evaluation of the alternatives. That task fell to me.

To produce the report (Adams, 1990), I spent a year reviewing not just the literature on the merits and demerits of phonics instruction per se but also theory and empirical research related to the nature of reading and its acquisition and mastery. I reviewed the history of the debate, the literature on the relative effectiveness of different instructional approaches, the theory and research on the knowledge and processes involved in skilful reading, and the various literatures relevant to reading acquisition.

Making this task still trickier was the fact that the relevant information and arguments are scattered across so many fields. The relevant research literature divides itself not only across the fields of education, psychology, and linguistics, but also the fields of computer science and anthropology. Within each of these fields, moreover, it is divided again and across scores of subdisciplines. Inasmuch as each of these subdisciplines is supported by its own separate sets of journals and books, each has accrued its own per-spective on the issues – along with its own relatively distinct terminology and knowledge base.

Within education, for example, there exist essentially separate literatures on classroom research and practice, on preschool literacy development, on special education and disabilities, on educational psychology, on policy research, and on large-scale statistical modelling and meta-analyses. Within psychology, the relevant literatures include not just those focused rather directly on reading and its acquisition, but also those on cognitive develop-ment, on language and text comprehension, on visual perception and pattern recognition, on eye movements, on the dynamics and limitations of attention and memory, and on the nature of thinking and learning. Within computer science, the work on machine learning, artificial intelligence, and computer modelling has provided important means of expanding and testing our theories about learning and the structure of knowledge. At the same time, the linguistics literature provides key insights into the orthography, phonology, syntax, and semantics of English while the anthropological literature offers ethnographic studies of home literacy support and practice as they vary across different cultures and neighbourhoods.

Although this cross-disciplinary dispersion of the literature made my task more difficult, I think it also made it far more worthwhile. Clearly it was past time to bring the pieces together. More than that, however, the overlap was there: key issues had been recognised again and again, both within and across the different fields. Within fields, as researchers scrutinised, chal-lenged, and reassessed each others' hypotheses and findings, they gradually peeled away mistaken notions even while gradually defining, affirming, and refining their successors. Across fields, meanwhile, research has not only given us independent validations of this work, but more: approaching the sues from different perspectives and through different methods of inquiry, e various literatures tended, not merely to replicate, but also to complement and extend each other in invaluable ways.

In all, the work synthesised in my report stands as awesome testimony to the progress these fields have made towards understanding the knowledge and processes involved in reading and learning to read – so much more complex and powerful than any armchair vision. Bit by bit, by testing theories and observations through the sometimes slow and assiduously self-critical cycles of science, we have collectively learned a great deal. I stress this point because there is now developing in the United States a wholesale rejection of the value of using or attending to the results of the scientific method. Do not let this movement overtake you. Qualitative and quantitative research are productive only in complement. Where the former gives us values and direction, the latter protects us from letting the strengths of our beliefs blind us to their limitations.

In many ways, the debate over phonics versus whole language can be seen as a dramatic reflection of these very tensions. Grown from qualitative observations of learners and learning, the whole language movement is an impassioned assertion that there is far more to literacy than phonics. Through such activities as read-alouds, big-book sharing, language experience, and creative writing, an effort has been made to invite active exploration and appreciation of its many dimensions. It is a reaction to routines evolved to mindlessness, and a movement to replace them with activities that will usefully develop and enrich. It is a reaction to overly controlled stories in children's reading books, and a movement to provide text that is worth reading and learning to read. It is a reaction to compartmentalisation of instruction, and a movement towards integration across the curriculum. Most of all, perhaps, the whole language movement is an unflagging effort to remind us that effective instruction depends on meeting and responding to children's individual needs by building on their strengths, interests, and confidences.

In fact, the value of most of the whole language initiatives are increasingly endorsed through research. But there are exceptions. Most troublesome among these are the notions that the spellings of words are minimally relevant to reading and to the challenge of learning to read. As initially put forth by Frank Smith in his seminal book, *Understanding Reading* (1971), these hypotheses were received with enormous excitement, and not just by teachers. Indeed, researchers eagerly flocked to the laboratory to affirm and extend Smith's ideas. But that is not how it worked out. Over the twenty years since publication of Smith's book, science has over and over, firmly and indisputably, refuted both of these hypotheses. In the course, however, it has also significantly advanced our understanding of the knowledge and processes involved in language and reading. (See Adams, 1991, for an overview of this saga.)

Most of all, learning to read is not natural (see especially Liberman and

Liberman, 1990). Rather, it depends critically on certain insights and observations that, among many if not most children, are not forthcoming without some special guidance. In particular, to read with fluency and comprehension children must develop a functional understanding of the alphabetic basis of English print along with working knowledge of its spellings.

Skilful reading, moreover, is scarcely a 'psycholinguistic guessing game', as Goodman (1967) termed it. Instead, for skilful adult readers, meaningful text – regardless of its ease or difficulty – is read through what is essentially a left to right, line by line, word by word process. Furthermore, skilful readers visually process virtually every individual letter of every word they read, tending strongly to translate print to speech as they go. True, skilful readers neither look nor feel like that's what they do when reading. Yet, that is only because they recognise the words so quickly and easily that their conscious, reflective attention is all the while focused on monitoring and extending the meaning of the text (see Adams, 1990, Section 3).

More specifically, research indicates that the skilful reader's remarkable ability to recognise printed words derives from a deep and ready knowledge of their composite sequences of letters along with the connections of those spellings to speech and to meaning. Even as the print on the page activates this knowledge, by its very structure, it serves reciprocally to organise, recognise, and give base meaning to the print. Indeed, provided that this knowledge is reasonably well developed, word recognition proceeds all but automatically – and that is very important because active, thoughtful attention is limited. Where readers must instead struggle with the words, they necessarily lose track of meaning.

Because, in the end, the words on the page are authors' principal means of conveying their message, it will not do for readers to ignore them. Nor will guessing suffice: even skilful adults are unable to guess correctly more than 25 per cent of the time (Gough *et al.*, 1981); besides that, the process of guessing itself requires time and effort that can only be found at the expense of the normal processes of comprehension. In fact, contextual cues contribute significantly to the speed and accuracy of word recognition only for those whose word identification skills are poor; meanwhile, poor word identification skills are strongly coupled with poor reading comprehension (for a more recent view of these issues, see Vellutino, 1991).

Because visual knowledge of words consists, at core, of knowledge of the ordered identities of their component letters, its growth depends on solid visual familiarity with the letters of the alphabet. To the extent that a child's attention is focused on the identity of any single letter, it cannot be usefully distributed across the sequence as a whole. Worse still, to the extent that any letter cannot be recognised, it obstructs learning of the sequence as a whole. For children who, on entering the classroom, do not yet have a comfortable familiarity with the letters of the alphabet, finding ways to help them is of first order importance.

Even so, knowledge of letters is of little value unless the child knows and is interested in their use: Correctly perceived and interpreted, print conveys information. In keeping with this, children's concepts about print are also strong predictors of the ease with which they will learn to read. Before formal instruction is begun, children should possess a broad, general appreciation of the nature of print. They should be aware of how text is formatted; that its basic meaningful units are specific speakable words; and that its words are comprised of letters. Of equal importance, they should have a solid sense of its various functions – to entertain, inform, communicate, record – and the potential value of each such function to their own selves.

All such awarenesses are powerfully fostered by reading aloud to children, by engaging them regularly and interactively in the enjoyment and exploration of print. As it happens, in homes where book-sharing with preschool children occurs with any appreciable frequency, it tends to occur with great regularity – and significant impact. An hour a day cumulates to more than 2000 total hours of lap-time reading across the preschool years. Moreover, this is 2000 hours of very special print exploration – one to one, face in the book, and with all the love, attention, and discussion that comes alongside. Yet, ethnographic studies show that many children have barely even seen a book before entering school. To learn to read, a child must learn first what it means to read and that he or she would like to be able to do so. Our classrooms, from preschool on up, must be designed with this in mind.

Although the ultimate goal of instruction on word recognition is to develop immediate pathways from print to meaning, the growth of young readers' visual vocabularies depends vitally on knowledge of spelling-sound relations. In keeping with this, research demonstrates that, when developed as part of a larger programme of reading and writing, phonics instruction leads to higher group achievement at least in word recognition, spelling, and vocabulary, at least in the primary grades, and especially for economically disadvantaged and slower students or pupils (see Adams, 1990, Chapter 3).

To be sure, there are lots of poor methods and materials (as well as some very good ones) in the phonics valise. However, what is (or should be) at issue on either side of this debate is not implementation of any particular methods and materials but realisation of the larger goals of the endeavour. Towards developing facility with words, there are two goals of phonics instruction: (1) to help students or pupils develop a productive understanding of the nature of spelling-sound correspondences in our writing system, and (2) to help them to learn to recognise frequent words and spelling patterns at a glance.

As its most obvious benefit, knowledge of spelling-sound relations enables independent word learning: Printed words that are in the child's oral vocabulary can be discovered by sounding them out. Yet spelling-sound knowledge serves another role for the learner that is still more important. As the child sounds the word out, the mind automatically makes a record of the links between the sequence of letters in attention and the sequence of sounds that are paired with them. In this way, the child's spoken image of the word serves to constrain, reinforce, and help her or him to remember its printed image.

Without such help, acquisition of an adequate visual vocabulary would be difficult if not impossible. To make this point compelling, it may be worth imagining how English print might be mastered without the help of spelling-sound correspondences. Imagine, instead, that the twenty-six basic symbols of our writing system were *unrelated* to the sounds of the words in whose representations they occur. Otherwise, let's keep the system the same. Let's assume that these symbols carry no meaning in themselves, that they are pictorially or iconically nondescript and hardly designed for discriminability – indeed, let's acknowledge that these twenty-six simple little symbols quite probably look more like each other than anything else the children have learned to date. Words, we would explain to the children, are to be represented by specific combinations and permutations of these twenty-six symbols – although 90 per cent of the time we'll rely on just fifteen of the set.

Fortunately for our students, half (but only half) of the words we expect them to learn will be fewer than seven symbols long. To attain the reading stature of the average American high school student (which, by the way, is functionally underwhelming), their challenge is to learn to recognise and spell – necessarily, that is, to rote memorise – the complete and infallibly ordered strings of symbols corresponding to at least 50,000 words. No wonder that among children who have learned or are successfully learning to read, all are found to appreciate the alphabetic nature of the language. Or conversely, no wonder that children who lack the alphabetic insight are inevitably found to be struggling with print.

Before phonics instruction can make any sense to children, they must come to understand that those seemingly strange little sounds that are paired with the letters are one and the same as the sounds of speech. To those of us who already know how to read and write, this realisation seems so very basic, almost transparent. Nevertheless, research shows that, initially at least, such phonemic awareness may qualify as a genuine insight. It is, moreover, an insight that eludes roughly 25 per cent of middle-class children in their first year at school and substantially more of those who come from less literacy-intensive backgrounds.

The problem, in large measure, is that people do not attend to the sounds of phonemes as they produce or listen to speech; instead, they process the phonemes automatically, directing their active attention to the meaning and force of the utterance as a whole. The challenge, therefore, is to find ways to get children to notice the phonemes, to discover their existence and separability. In fact, many of the activities that have long been enjoyed with preschool children are ideally suited to this. Yet, all such activities can be used with far more effectiveness toward helping children to develop pho-

:mic awareness if they are used with that goal in mind.

...le first step is to find ways to direct the children's attention to the sound structure of language. To this end, there are no better materials than the songs, chants, and word-sound games that are so familiar to all. By exaggerating the meter of the songs and poems, you are leading the children to discover the existence of syllables. Meanwhile, the rhyming words lead them to reflect on the sounds of syllables – and eventually you will want to move on to games and songs in which the children are challenged to produce rhymes on their own. By contrasting rhyming words and playing with alliteration, you are introducing the idea that syllables themselves can be analysed; you are, in other words, introducing the notion of phonemes.

As preliminaries, activities such as the above are invaluable. Yet, there is special power in linking phonemes to letters. So now it is time for the sorts of phonological awareness activities described by Peter Bryant in Chapter 6. Now, too, it is time for first-letter mystery bags and for playing games like 'I spy with my little eye.' Now, when you share books and language experience activities with your students or pupils, they are ready to explore the spellings and sounds of repeated words and of short soundable words. And now is the time to encourage the children to write independently, spelling each word as it sounds.

Early independent writing is a means of inviting children to explore communication and to reflect on their own thoughts and knowledge. Used well, it is a means of engaging children in many dimensions of print and literacy, in functional integration, and right from the start. With respect to phonics, it is a way of giving children that oh-so-critical message that the alphabetic system is not arbitrary, that it has a logic, and that it can and should be understood. Instead of just telling your students or pupils how the system works (and expecting them to listen!), you are challenging them to figure it out. You are, in effect, putting them in charge – and children cannot fail to attend when it is they who are doing the thinking.

For the learner, in other words, early independent writing and spelling creates a special motive for listening to the sound structure of language. It creates an incentive for noticing how words conventionally are spelled as well as the experience with print that is necessary for absorbing such detail. But for you, as the teacher, it is additionally invaluable as it gives you a means for coordinating your teaching with their needs and understanding: the children's written products offer on-going logs of their phonic growth. Many children will begin by representing whole words with first letters only, and you know these children are well on their way; those who don't, need extra attention. And more, as their spelling matures, you can monitor and assist their growing awareness of medial vowels, of consonant blends, of 'r's and 'l's; you can know when they are ready for information about digraphs, and long vowel patterns, and inflections. Before long (but very sensitively lest you inhibit their willingness to spell independently), their spelling should be exercised and refined in more systematic ways. Again, research indicates that, especially for children who have already started writing independently, this sort of attention to spelling results in exceptional progress in both reading and writing (Uhry and Shepherd, 1990).

In this way, through their thinking and your help, the students or pupils will develop a solid basic understanding of phonics. Even so, for purposes of reading, understanding is not enough. In addition, they need to develop ready perceptual familiarity with the spellings. The problem is that, in viewing words, children's natural tendency seems to be one of treating them more as holistic patterns than as any left-to-right sequence of symbols (Byrne and Fielding-Barnesley, 1989). (After all, this inclination is quite appropriate for virtually all else in their perceptual worlds.)

From this perspective, phonics instruction per se takes on a very special value. In order to sound a new word out as they read, children must attend to each and every one of its letters, in left to right order. Each time they do so, the printed word will become more strongly and completely represented in memory so that, very soon, it will be recognised at a glance (see Ehri, 1980, 1989). Indeed, work with seven- to eight-year-olds shows that once an unfamiliar word has been decoded and reread just a few times, its recognition remains speeded significantly and quite enduringly (Reitsma, 1983).

Of course, it is not just teaching children phonics that makes a difference, but persuading them to use it. Because a strong determinant of the latter lies in whether or not the children find it useful in their earliest efforts after print, there is strong motivation for ensuring that their first books consist largely of simple, short, and liberally repeated spelling patterns. Inasmuch as these short simple patterns are basic, they will effectively anchor the longer, more complex, and less frequent patterns that are yet to be mastered. Beyond that, the goal is to use the children's established understanding of the writing system as leverage; in reading as in writing, you want most of all for them to feel that they can understand, that they can succeed, and that they are growing. Indeed, when preprimers are designed in this way, children are shown to use and extend their phonics lessons on their own (Juel and Roper/ Schneider, 1985).

Through lots of reading and rereading, both independently and with guidance, they will soon move into books with more literary and informational challenge. Indeed, beyond the basics, the single most powerful means of furthering children's word recognition prowess is that of having them read. But that is not all: reading broadly and thoughtfully appears equally to be the most powerful means of furthering their vocabulary, writing abilities, and conceptual growth. The chapters in this book offer invaluable insights on ways to invite children into literacy in its fullest and most enriching sense.

Finally, for so cursorily overviewing these issues, I apologise both to you, the reader, and to the many whose work I have synthesised. Nonetheless, I hope that what you have read in this book whets your appetite to read more.

Literacy, after all, is enormously complex and children, much more so. Full participation in literacy depends on confidence and experience in exploring its larger forms, functions and values. Towards this end, developing a ready working knowledge of its code (which includes its syntax as well as the spellings and meanings of its words) is a relatively small but wholly necessary component of the challenge.

Meanwhile, towards reaching all of the children and students in your classrooms, I hope you will find the following list of recommendations useful. This list is a slightly edited version of those put together by my colleagues, Steven A. Stahl, Jean Osborn, and Fran Lehr, in producing the *Summary of Beginning to Read* (Stahl, Osborn and Lehr, 1990).

Predictors of reading acquisition

- Characteristics unrelated to linguistic skills or facility with print appear equally unrelated to early reading success. Examples of such poor predictors include IQ, mental age, perceptual-motor abilities, perceptual styles, and parental education or income.

- Children's general awareness of the nature and functions of print is a strong index of the ease with which they will learn to read.

- Children's familiarity with the letters of the alphabet is a strong predictor of success in learning to read.

- Children's awareness that spoken language is composed of simpler units – words, syllables, and phonemes – is an extremely important predictor of success in learning to read.

Before formal instruction begins

- The single most important activity for building the knowledge and skills eventually required for reading appears to be reading aloud to children regularly and interactively.

- Children learn a great deal about both the nature and functions of print through thoughtful interactions with adults.

- Language experience activities and the use of big books are excellent means of establishing print awareness (although they are less useful as primary vehicles for reading instruction itself).

- Some children have difficulty conceiving of spoken language as consisting of individual words. The concept of 'word' can be developed easily, though, through exposure to written text or through direct instruction.

Children should also be helped to appreciate the relationship between the lengths of spoken and written words.

- Activities designed to develop young children's awareness of words, syllables, and phonemes significantly increase their later success in learning to read and write. The impact of phonemic training on reading acquisition is especially strong when phonemes are taught together with the letters by which they are represented.

- Learning to recognise and discriminate the shapes of letters is a difficult process requiring support and encouragement. Ideally, letter knowledge should be well established before children reach first grade (year 2 in the UK).

- Among many preschool children in the United States who learn about letters at home, it is typically the names of the letters that are learned first, often through the alphabet song. Learning about their shapes comes later, and their sounds, later still.

- Children recognise a variety of environmental print that they encounter day to day, but environmental print does not seem to contribute to reading success unless a child has first begun to learn about the individual letters.

- Early encouragement of printing is both a way of developing letter recognition skills and of seeding children's inclination and ability to write independently.

Beginning to read

- Approaches in which systematic code instruction is included along with the reading and writing of meaningful text result in superior reading achievement overall, both for low-readiness and better prepared students.

- Matching children to different instructional programmes based on dominant perceptual modality or styles does not appear to improve the efficacy of instruction.

- Programmes for all children, good and poor readers alike, should strive to maintain an appropriate balance between phonics activities and the reading and appreciation of informative and engaging texts.

- The texts that children read influence the reading abilities they develop. Texts that contain a higher proportion of decodable words promote independent word recognition growth. As reflected by their writing, children also absorb the syntax, vocabulary, and conceptual structures of the texts they read.

- Writing and spelling activities, in general, are a means of developing and reinforcing knowledge of spelling and spelling-sound patterns.

- Independent writing activities are a means of developing children's deeper appreciation of the nature of text and of written communication.

Phonics instruction

- Phonics instruction is not only a means of teaching children to sound words out, but also of directing their attention to the spellings of words.

- To maximise word recognition growth, the wording of children's earliest texts should be carefully coordinated with the content and schedule of phonics lessons.

- The ability to recognise letters is extremely important to the development of word recognition.

- For children with little letter knowledge on entry to school, current learning theory suggests it is unwise to try to teach both upper case and lower case forms of all twenty-six letters at once. For children who do not know letter names on school entry, special care should be taken to avoid confusion of names and sounds.

- Classroom encouragement of invented spellings is a promising approach towards the development of phonemic awareness and knowledge of spelling patterns.

- The learning of regular spelling patterns and their phonic significance may be hastened through methodical use of onsets and rimes (see Chapters 4 and 6).

- Because most phonemes cannot be pronounced without a vowel, many reading programmes avoid or limit the use of isolated phonemes in their instruction. This practice often leads to potentially confusing instruction. Because phonemes are defined less by their sounds than by their proper place and manner of articulation, the advantages of asking students to articulate phonemes in isolation outweigh the disadvantages.

- Because children have special difficulty analysing the phonemic structure of words, reading programmes should include explicit instruction in segmenting and blending the sounds of words and syllables.

- Although rules and generalisations are no substitute for direct practice with the words to which they pertain, they may be useful for either directing students' attention to a particular spelling pattern or providing strategies for coping with difficult decoding patterns.

- Phonic rules and generalisations are, at best, of temporary value. Once a child has learned to read the spellings to which they pertain, they are superfluous.

• Reliance on special terminology may subvert the purpose of the lessons in which it occurs.

Beyond the basics

• Children should be given as much opportunity and encouragement as possible to practise their reading. Beyond the basics, children's reading facility, as well as their vocabulary and conceptual growth, depends strongly on the amount of text they read.

• Reading comprehension depends on the ability to perceive words relatively quickly and effortlessly.

• Reading comprehension also depends on the conviction that text is meant to be understood and thought about.

• To maximise achievement, children should be given texts that they can read orally with 90 per cent to 95 per cent accuracy.

• Given that a text is at an appropriate level of difficulty, it is preferable that children be encouraged not to skip words that are difficult for them. Instead, they should be encouraged to take the time to study a word and then to reread the entire sentence or phrase in which it appears.

• Repeated readings of text are found to produce marked improvement in children's word recognition, fluency, and comprehension.

• Encouraging children to learn to spell words correctly is important because spelling knowledge directly affects their reading ability.

bibliography

The numbers in brackets at the end of each entry indicate where the author in question has been referred to in this book.

Abramovici, S. and **Reid, J.F.** (in preparation) *The Role of Prediction in Skilled Reading.* **(28)**

Adams, M.J. (1990) *Beginning to Read: Thinking and Learning about Print.* Cambridge, Mass.: MIT Press. **(12, 29, 66, 68, 81, 96, 205, 207, 208)**

Adams, M.J. (1991) Why not phonics *and* whole language?, in **Ellis, W.** (ed.) *All Language and the Creation of Literacy.* Baltimore, Maryland: The Orton Dyslexia Society. **(3, 7, 69, 206)**

Anderson, J.R. (1982) Acquisition of cognitive skill, *Psychological Review,* **89**, 369–406. **(168)**

Anderson, J.R. (1983) *The Architecture of Cognition.* Cambridge, Mass.: Harvard University Press. **(158, 159)**

Applebee, A.N. (1978) *The Child's Concept of Story: Ages Two to Seventeen.* Chicago: University of Chicago Press. **(101)**

Baddeley, A.D.; Ellis, N.C.; Miles, T.R. and **Lewis, V.J.** (1982) 'Developmental and acquired dyslexia: a comparison', *Cognition,* **11**, 185–99. **(86)**

Ball, F. (1977) *The Development of Reading Skills.* Oxford: Basil Blackwell. **(145)**

Bannatyne, A. (1971) *Language, Reading and Learning Disabilities.* Springfield, Illinois: Charles C. Thomas. **(145)**

Bartlett, F. (1958) *Thinking: An experimental and social study.* London: Allen and Unwin. **(156)**

Beard, R. (1984) *Children's Writing in the Primary School.* London: Hodder and Stoughton. **(2)**

Beard, R. (1990) *Developing Reading 3–13,* 2nd edn. London: Hodder and Stoughton. **(107)**

Beers, J.W. (1980) Developmental strategies of spelling competence in primary school children, in **Henderson, E.H**

and **Beers, J.W.** (eds) *Developmental and Cognitive Aspects of Learning to Spell: Reflection of Word Knowledge*. Newark, Delaware: International Reading Association. (179)

Bereiter, C. (1980) Development in Writing, in **Gregg, L.W.** and **Steinberg, E.R.** (eds) *Cognitive Processes in Writing*. Hillsdale, New Jersey: Lawrence Erlbaum Associates. (165)

Bereiter, C. and **Bird, M.** (1985) Use of thinking aloud in identification and teaching of reading comprehension strategies, *Cognition and Instruction*, **2**, 131–56. (185)

Bereiter, C. and **Scardamalia, M.** (1983) Schooling and the growth of intentional cognition: Helping children to take charge of their own minds, in **Lamm, Z.** (ed.) *New Trends in Education*. Tel-Aviv: Yechdev Publishing Co. (173)

Bereiter, C. and **Scardamalia, M.** (1987) *The Psychology of Written Composition*. Hillsdale, New Jersey: Lawrence Erlbaum Associates. (2, 11, 155)

Biemiller, A. (1970) The development of the use of graphic and contextual cues as children learn to read, *Reading Research Quarterly*, **VI**, 1, 76–96. (32)

Blatchford, P. and **Plewis, I.** (1990) Pre-school reading-related skills and later reading achievement: further evidence, *British Educational Research Journal*, **16**, 4, 425–8. (78)

Bowerman, M. (1982) Reorganisational Processes, in **Wanner, E.** and **Gleitman, L.** (eds) *Language Acquisition: The State of the Art*. Cambridge: Cambridge University Press. (34)

Bradley, L. and **Bryant, P.E.** (1978) Difficulties in auditory organisation as a possible cause of reading backwardness, *Nature*, **271**, 746–7. (66)

Bradley, L. and **Bryant, P.E.** (1983) Categorising sounds and learning to read: A causal connection, *Nature*, **301**, 419–21. (66, 90)

Bradley, L. and **Bryant, P.E.** (1985) *Rhyme and Reason in Reading and Spelling*. Ann Arbor, Michigan: University of Michigan Press. (178, 183, 185)

Bruce, D.J. (1964) The analysis of word sounds, *British Journal of Educational Psychology*, **34**, 158–70. (85)

Bruner, J.S. (1957) *Contemporary Approaches to Cognition*. Cambridge, Mass.: Harvard University Press. (27)

Bruner, J.S. (1962) *On Knowing*. Cambridge, Mass.: Harvard University Press. (123)

Bruner, J.S. (1965) The growth of mind, *American Psychologist*, **20**, 17, 1007–17. (27)

Bruner, J.S. (1975) Poverty and Culture, in **Sants, J.** and **Butcher, H.J.** (eds) *Developmental Psychology: Selected Readings*. Harmondsworth: Penguin. (123)

Bruner, J.S. (1987) *Making Sense: The Child's Construction of the World.* London: Methuen. (124)

Bryant, P.E. and **Bradley, L.** (1985) *Children's Reading Problems.* Oxford: Basil Blackwell. (85)

Bryant, P.E.; Bradley, L.; Maclean, M. and **Crossland, J.** (1989) Nursery rhymes, phological skills and reading, *Journal of Child Language,* **16**, 407–28. (90)

Bryant, P.E.; Maclean, M.; Bradley, L. and **Crossland, J.** (1990) Rhyme, alliteration, phoneme detection and learning to read, *Developing Psychology,* **26**, 429–38. (90)

Byrne, B. and **Fielding-Barnesley, R.** (1989) Phonemic awareness and letter knowledge in the child's acquisition of the alphabetic principle, *Journal of Educational Psychology,* **81**, 313–21. (211)

Carbo, M. (1988) Debunking the great phonics myth, *Phi Delta Kappan,* **70**, 226–40. (2)

Cazden, C. (1974) Play with language and metalinguistic awareness: one dimension of language awareness, *The Urban Review,* **7**, 129–61. (54)

Chall, J.S. (1967) *Learning to Read: The Great Debate* (2nd edn 1983). New York: McGraw-Hill. (1, 142)

Chall, J.S. (1979) The Great Debate: Ten years later, with a modest proposal for reading stages, in **Resnick, L.B.** and **Weaver, P.A.** (eds) *Theory and Practice in Early Reading Vol. 1.* Hillsdale, New Jersey: Lawrence Erlbaum Associates. (72)

Chall, J.S. (1983) *Stages of Reading Development.* New York: McGraw-Hill. (204)

Chall, J.S. (1989) Learning to read: The great debate twenty years later. A response to 'Debunking the great phonics myth', *Phi Delta Kappan,* **71**, 521–38. (2)

Chall, J.S.; Jacobs, V.A. and **Baldwin, L.E.** (1990) *The Reading Crisis: Why Poor Children Fall Behind.* Cambridge, Mass.: Harvard University Press. (3, 133)

Chapman, L.J. (1987) *Reading: From 5–11 Years.* Milton Keynes: Open University Press. (127)

Chasty, H.T. (1979) Functional assymetry of the brain in normal children and dyslexics, *The Dyslexia Review,* **2**, 1, 9–12. (145)

Chomsky, C. (1969) *The Acquistion of Syntax in Children from Five to Ten.* Cambridge, Mass.: MIT Press. (34)

Chomsky, C. (1970) Reading, Writing and Phonology, *Harvard Educational Review,* **40**, 287–309. (180)

Chomsky, N. (1959) Review of Skinner, B.F. (1957) *Verbal Behaviour, Language,* **35**, 26–58. (24)

Clark, M. M. and **C.V.** (1971) *Psychology and language.* San Diego, USA: Harcourt, Brace, Jovanovich. (21)

Clark, M.M. (1976) *Young Fluent Readers.* London: Heinemann. (69)

Clay, M.M. (1969) Reading errors and self-correction behaviour, *British Journal of Educational Psychology,* **39**, 1, 47–58. (32, 46)

Clay, M.M. (1972) *Reading: The Patterning of Complex Behaviour.* London: Heinemann. (33, 34)

Clay, M.M. (1975) *What Did I Write? Beginning Writing Behaviour.* Auckland: Heinemann. (170)

Clay, M.M. (1979) *The Early Detection of Reading Difficulties: A Diagnostic Survey with Recovery Procedures,* 2nd edn. Auckland: Heinemann. (75, 144)

Commission on Reading, National Academy of Education (1985) *Becoming a Nation of Readers.* Washington DC: National Institute of Education. (204)

Cornman, O.P. (1902) *Spelling in the Elementary School.* Boston, Mass.: Ginn. (176)

Crowhurst, M. (1979) The writing workshop: An experiment in peer response to writing, *Language Arts,* **56**, 757–62. (170)

Crystal, D. (1985) *Linguistics* 2nd edn. Harmondsworth: Penguin Books. (21)

Crystal, D. (1986) *Listen to Your Child* Harmondsworth: Penguin Books. (21)

Crystal, D. (1987) *The Cambridge Encyclopedia of Language.* Cambridge: Cambridge University Press. (21)

Crystal, D. (1987) *Child Language, Learning and Linguistics,* 2nd edn. London: Edward Arnold. (15)

Crystal, D. (1988) *The English Language.* Harmondsworth: Penguin Books. (21)

DeCasper, A.J. and **Spence, M.J.** (1986) Prenatal maternal speech influences newborns' perceptions of speech sounds, *Infant Behaviour and Development,* **9**, 133–50. (31)

De la Mare, W. (1941) *Bells and Grass.* London: Faber. (114)

Department of Education and Science (1988) *Report of the Committee of Inquiry into the Teaching of English Language* (The Kingman Report). London: HMSO. (59)

Department of Education and Science (1989a) *English for ages 5 to 16*: National Curriculum Proposals of the Secretary of State for Education and Science and the Secretary of State for Wales (The Cox Report). London: HMSO. (127, 186)

Department of Education and Science (1989b) *A Survey of*

Support Services for Special Educational Needs. London: DES.
(149)

Department of Education and Science (1990) *English in the National Curriculum.* London: HMSO. (182)

Department of Education and Science (1991a) *The Teaching and Learning of Reading in Primary Schools*: A Report by Her Majesty's Inspectorate. London: DES. (67)

Department of Education and Science (1991b) *English Key Stage 1*: A Report by Her Majesty's Inspectorate on the First Year, 1989–90. London: HMSO. (127)

Department of Education and Science (1992) *Curriculum Organisation and Classroom Practice in Primary Schools*: A Discussion Paper by Robin Alexander, Jim Rose and Chris Woodhead. London: DES Information Branch. (3)

Diringer, D. (1962) *Writing.* London: Thames and Hudson. (190)

Doman, G. (1964) *How to Teach Your Baby to Read.* New York: Random House. (44)

Donaldson, M. (1978) *Children's Minds.* London: Fontana. (36)

Donaldson, M. (1989) *Sense and Sensibility: Some thoughts on the teaching of literacy* (Occasional Paper No. 3). Reading: Reading and Language Information Centre, University of Reading. (27, 133)

Donaldson, M. and **Reid, J.F.** (1982) Language skills and reading: a developmental perspective, in **Hendry, A.** (ed.) *Teaching Reading: The Key Issues.* London: Heinemann. (34)

Dowker, A. (1989) Rhymes and alliteration in poems elicited from young children, *Journal of Child Language*, **16**, 181–202. (89)

Downing, J. (1979) *Reading and Reasoning.* Edinburgh: Chambers. (31)

Du Pasquier-Grall, M.A. (1990) L'Evolution de l'Ecriture de l'Enfant: Point de Vue Clinique in **Sirat, C.** *et al. L'Ecriture: le Cerveau, l'Oeil et la Main.* Turnhout: Brepols. (190)

Dunn, J. (1987) Understanding feelings: the early stages, in **Bruner, J.** and **Haste, H.** (eds) *Making Sense: The Child's Construction of the World.* London and New York: Methuen. (43, 59)

Eckoff, B. (1983) How reading affects children's writing, *Language Arts*, **60**, 607–16. (95)

Ehri, L.C. (1980) The development of orthographic images, in **Frith, U.** (ed.) *Cognitive Processes in Spelling Development.* London: Academic Press. (209)

Ehri, L.C. (1989) The development of spelling knowledge and its role in reading acquisition and reading disability, *Journal of Learning Disabilities*, **22**, 6, 356–65. (183, 209)

Ellis, N. and **Large, B.** (1987) The development of reading: as you shall seek so shall you find, *British Journal of Psychology*, **78**, 1–28. (146)

Ellis, N. and **Large, B.** (1988) The early stages of reading: a longitudinal study, *Applied Cognitive Psychology*, **2**, 47–76. (66)

Fernald, G.M. (1943) *Remedial Techniques in Basic School Subjects*. New York: McGraw-Hall. (176, 177, 179)

Flower, L.S. (1979) Writer-based prose: A cognitive basis for problems in writing, *College English*, **41**, 19–37. (167)

Flower, L.S. and **Hayes, J.R.** (1980a) The cognition of discovery: Defining a rhetorical problem, *College Composition and Communication*, **31**, 21–32. (165)

Flower, L.S. and **Hayes, J.R.** (1980b) The dynamics of composing: Making plans and juggling constraints, in **Gregg, L.W.** and **Steinberg, E.R.** (eds) *Cognitive Processes in Writing*. Hillsdale, New Jersey: Lawrence Erlbaum Associates. (165)

Fowler, H.W. and **Fowler, F.G.** (eds) (1990) *The Concise Oxford Dictionary*. Oxford: Clarendon Press. (130)

Frith, U. (1980a) Unexpected spelling problems, in **Frith, U.** (ed.) (1980b) *Cognitive Processes in Spelling*. New York: Academic Press. (180)

Frith, U. (1985) Beneath the surface of developmental dyslexia, in **Patterson, K.; Coltheart, M.** and **Marshall, J.** (eds.) *Surface Dyslexia*. London: Lawrence Erlbaum Associates. (64)

Frith, U. and **Snowling, M.** (1983) Reading for meaning and reading for sound in autistic and dyslexic children, *British Journal of Developmental Psychology*, **1**, 329–42. (86)

Garner, R. (1987) *Metacognition and Reading Comprehension*. Norwood, New Jersey: Ablex Publishing Co. (71, 72)

Garton, A. and **Pratt, C.** (1989) *Learning to be Literate*. Oxford: Basil Blackwell. (27)

Gentry, J.R. (1981) Learning to Spell Developmentally, *Reading Teacher*, **34**, 4, 378–81. (182)

Gibson, E.J. and **Levin, H.** (1975) *The Psychology of Reading*. Cambridge, Mass.: MIT Press. (7, 180)

Gibson, E.J.; Pick, A.; Osser, H. and **Hammond, M.** (1962) The role of grapheme-phoneme correspondence in the perception of words, *American Journal of Psychology*, **75**, 554–70. (179)

Gilbert, L.C. (1935) Study of the effect of reading on spelling, *Journal of Educational Research*, **28**, 570–6. (177)

Gleitman, L.R.; Newport, E.L. and **Gleitman, H.** (1984) The current status of the motherese hypothesis, *Journal of Child Language*, **11**, 43–79. (59)

Gombert, J.E. (1992) *Metalinguistic Development.* Hemel Hempstead: Harvester Wheatsheaf. (85)

Goodman, K.S. (1967) Reading: a psycholinguistic guessing game, *Journal of the Reading Specialist*, **4**, 126–35. (22, 26, 28, 29, 83, 207)

Goodman, K.S. (1969) Oral reading miscues: applied psycholinguistics, *Reading Research Quarterly*, **V**, 1, 11–30. (22, 26, 28)

Goodman, K.S. (1972) Reading: the key is in children's language, *The Reading Teacher*, March, 505–8. (22, 23, 26, 28, 38)

Goodman, K.S. (1982) Miscue analysis: theory and reality in reading, in **Gollasch, F.K.** (ed.) *Language and Literacy: the selected writings of Kenneth S. Goodman.* London: Routledge and Kegan Paul. (83)

Goodman, K.S. and **Goodman, Y.M.** (1977) Learning about psycholinguistic processing by analysing oral reading, *Harvard Educational Review*, **47**, 3, 317–32. (145)

Goswami, U. (1986) Children's use of analogy in learning to read: a developmental study, *Journal of Experimental Child Psychology*, **42**, 73–83. (93)

Goswami, U. (1988a) Children's use of analogy in learning to spell, *British Journal of Developmental Psychology*, **6**, 21–33. (93)

Goswami, U. (1988b) Orthographic analogies and reading development, *Quarterly Journal of Experimental Psychology*, **40A**, 239–68. (93)

Goswami, U. and **Bryant, P.E.** (1990) *Phonological Skills and Learning to Read.* Hove: Lawrence Erlbaum Associates. (67, 85, 93, 184)

Gough, P.B. (1981) A comment on Kenneth Goodman, in **Kamil, M.L.** (ed.) *Directions in Reading: Research and Instruction*, pp. 92–5. Washington, DC: National Reading Conference. (7, 29, 33)

Gough, P.B. and **Hillinger, M.L.** (1980) Learning to Read: an unnatural act, *Bulletin of the Orton Society*, **30**, 179–96. (84)

Gough, P.B.; Alford, J.A. and **Holley-Wilcox, P.** (1981) Words and Contexts, in **Tzeng, O.J.L.** and **Singer, H.** (eds) *Perception of Print: Reading Research in Experimental Psychology.* Hillsdale, New Jersey: Lawrence Erlbaum Associates. (207)

Graves, D.H. (1975) An Examination of the Writing Processes of Seven-Year-Old Children, *Research in the Teaching of English*, **9**, 227–41. (2)

Graves, D.H. (1978) *Balance the basics: Let them write.* New York: Ford Foundation. (172)

Graves, D. (1983) *Writing: Teachers and Children At Work.* Exeter, New Hampshire and London: Heinemann. (2, 155, 163, 170, 181)

Gray, W.S. (1956) *The Teaching of Reading and Writing.* Paris: UNESCO. (195)

Haffner, L.E. and **Jolly, H.B.** (1982) *Teaching Children to Read.* New York: Macmillan. (145)

Halle, M. and **Vergnaud, J.-R.** (1980) Three-dimensional phonology, *Journal of Linguistic Research*, **1**, 83–105. (92)

Halliday, M.A.K. (1978) *Language as a Social Semiotic: The social interpretation of language and meaning.* London: Edward Arnold. (128)

Halliday, M.A.K. (1989) Context of Situation in **Halliday, M.A.K.** and **Hasan, R.** (eds) *Language, Context and Text: Aspects of language in a social-semiotic perspective.* Oxford: Oxford University Press. (130)

Harris, R. and **Coltheart, H.** (1986) *Language Processing in Children and Adults.* London: Routledge and Kegan Paul. (29)

Hasan, R. (1989) The Structure of Text in **Halliday, M.A.K.** and **Hasan, R.** (eds) *Language, Context and Text: Aspects of language in a social-semiotic perspective.* Oxford: Oxford University Press. (128)

Heath, S.B. (1986) The functions and uses of literacy, in **de Castell, S.; Luke, A.** and **Egan, K.** (eds) *Literacy, Society and Schooling.* Cambridge: Cambridge University Press. (53)

Henderson, E.H. (1980) Developmental concepts of words, in **Henderson, E.H.** and **Beers, J.W.** (eds) *Developmental and Cognitive Aspects of Learning to Spell: Reflection of Word Knowlege.* Newark, Delaware: International Reading Association. (180)

Hildreth, G.H. (1956) *Teaching Spelling.* New York: Henry Holt. (177)

Horowitz, W. (1985) Text Patterns: Part 2, *Journal of Reading*, **28**, 6, 534–41. (131)

Huey, E.B. (1968) *The Psychology and Pedagogy of Reading* (first published in 1908). Cambridge, Mass.: MIT Press. (60)

Hynds, J. (1988) In Pursuit of A Little Understanding, *Books for Keeps*, **52**, 4–5. (58)

Inner London Education Authority (1988) *The Primary Language Record*. London: London Centre for Language in Primary Education. (7)

Johnson, D.D. and **Baumann, J.F.** (1984) Word Identification, in **Pearson, P.D.** (ed.) *Handbook of Reading Research*. London: Longman. (67)

Juel, C. (1988) Learning to read and write: A longitudinal study of fifty-four children from first through fourth grade, *Journal of Educational Psychology*, **80**, 437–47. (202)

Juel, C. and **Roper/Schneider, D.** (1985) The influence of basal readers on first grade reading, *Reading Research Quarterly*, **20**, 134–52. (96, 211)

Kinneavy, J.L.; Cope, J.Q. and **Campbell, J.W.** (1976) *Writing – Basic Modes of Organisation*. Dubuque, Iowa: Kendall Hunt Publishing Co. (129)

Kirtley, C.; Bryant, P.; MacLean, M. and **Bradley, L.** (1989) Rhyme, rime and the onset of reading, *Journal of Experimental Child Psychology*, **48**, 224–45. (92)

Kyte, G.C. (1948) When spelling has been mastered in the elementary school, *Journal of Educational Research*, **xli**, 47–53. (177)

LaBerge, D. and **Samuels, S.J.** (1974) Towards a theory of automatic information processing in reading, *Cognitive Psychology*, **6**, 293–323. (147)

Lawson, A.E. and **Renner, J.W.** (1974) A quantitative analysis of responses to Piagetian Tasks and its implications for curriculum, *Science Education*, **58**, 545–59. (173)

Lenel, J.C. and **Cantor, J.H.** (1981) Rhyme recognition and phonemic perception in young children, *Journal of Psycholinguistic Research*, **10**, 57–68. (90)

Lenneberg, E. (1966) The natural history of language, in **Smith, F.** and **Miller, G.A.** (eds) *The Genesis of Language*. Cambridge, Mass.: MIT Press. (26)

Liberman, I.Y. and **Liberman, A.M.** (1990) Whole language vs. code emphasis: underlying assumptions and their implications for reading instruction, *Annals of Dyslexia*, **40**, 51–76. (Reprinted in **Gough, P.B.; Ehri, L.C.** and **Treiman, R.** (eds) (1992) *Reading Acquisition*. Hillsdale, New Jersey: Lawrence Erlbaum Associates.) (83, 207)

Liberman, I.Y.; Shankweiler, D.; Fischer, F.W. and **Carter, B.** (1974) Explicit syllable and phoneme segmentation in the young child, *Journal of Experimental Child Psychology*, **18**, 201–12. (85)

Liberman, I.Y.; Shankweiler, D. and **Liberman, A.** (1989) The alphabetic principle and learning to read, in **Shankweiler, D.** and **Liberman, I.Y.** (eds) *Phonology and Reading Disability*. Ann Arbor, Michigan: The University of Michigan Press. (85)

Littlefair, A.B. (1991) *Reading All Types of Writing*. Milton Keynes: Open University Press. (127, 129, 138)

Loban, W. (1976) *Language Development: Kindergarten through grade twelve* (Research Rep. No. 18). Urbana, Illinois: National Council of Teachers of English. (157)

Lowenthal, D. (1980) Mixing levels of revision, *Visible Language*, **14**, 383–7. (161)

Lundberg, I.; Frost, J. and **Peterson, O.** (1988) Effects of an extensive program for stimulating phonological awareness in preschool children, *Reading Research Quarterly*, **23**, 263–84. (86)

Lundberg, I.; Olofsson, A. and **Wall, S.** (1980) Reading and spelling skills in the first school years predicted from phonemic awareness skills in kindergarten, *Scandinavian Journal of Psychology*, **21**, 159–73. (86)

Lunzer, E. and **Gardner, K.** (eds) (1979) *The Effective Use of Reading*. Heinemann. (138)

Lyons, G. (1976) The Higher Illiteracy, *Harper's*. September, 33–40. (155)

Lyons, J. (1970) *Chomsky*. London: Fontana Books. (30)

Lyons, J. (1982) *Language and Linguistics*. Cambridge: Cambridge University Press. (21)

Mackay, D.G. (1972) The structure of words and syllables: evidence from errors in speech, *Cognitive Psychology*, **3**, 210–27. (92)

Mackay, D,; Thompson, B. and **Schaub, P.** (1970) *Breakthrough to Literacy: Teachers' Manual*. London: Longman. (2nd edn. 1979) (177)

MacLean, M.; Bryant, P.E. and **Bradley, L.** (1987) Rhymes, nursery rhymes and reading in early childhood, *Merrill-Palmer Quarterly*, **33**, 255–82. (90)

Malinowski, B. (1922) *Argonauts of the Western Pacific*. London: Routledge and Kegan Paul. (128)

Mann, V.A. (1986) Phonological awareness: the role of reading experience, *Cognition*, **24**, 65–92. (88)

Marland, M. (1991) Curse of the Vernacular, *The Guardian*, 28 May. (133)

Marsh, G.; Friedman, M.; Welch, V. and **Desberg, P.** (1980) The

Development of Strategies in Spelling, in **Frith, U.** (ed.) *Cognitive Processes in Spelling*. New York: Academic Press. (180)

Martin, J.R. and **Rothery, J.** (1981) *Writing Project* (Working Papers in Linguistics No. 2). Sydney: Linguistics Department, University of Sydney. (137)

Martin, J.R. and **Rothery, J.** (1986) *Writing Project* (Working Papers in Linguistics No. 4). Sydney: Linguistics Department, University of Sydney. (137)

Martin, J.R.; Christie, F. and **Rothery, J.** (1987) Social Processes in Education, in **Reid, I.** (ed.) *The Place of Genre in Learning: Current Debates*. Victoria: Deakin University. (128)

McAleavy, T. (1987) Conflict in Ireland, *History 13–16 Project*. Edinburgh: Holmes McDougall/School Curriculum Development Committee. (51)

McCloskey, M.; Caramazza, A. and **Green, B.** (1980) Curvilinear motion in the absence of external forces: Naive beliefs about the motion of objects, *Science*, **210**, 1139–41. (173, 175)

McCutchen, D. and **Perfetti, C.A.** (1982) Coherence and connectedness in the development of discourse production, *Text*, **2**, 113–39. (165, 167)

McNaughton, S. (1987) *Being Skilled: The socialisations of learning to read*. London: Methuen. (143, 150)

McNeill, D. (1966) Developmental psycholinguistics, in **Smith, F** and **Miller, G.A.** (eds) *The Genesis of Language*. Cambridge, Mass.: MIT Press. (24)

McNeill, D. (1987) *Psycholinguistics: A New Approach*. New York: Harper and Row. (40)

Meek, M. (1982) *Learning to Read*. London: The Bodley Head. (7, 37, 48)

Meek, M. (1988) *How Texts Teach What Readers Learn*. Stroud: Thimble Press. (12)

Meek, M.; Armstrong, S.; Auslerfield, V.; Graham, J. and **Plackett, E.** (1983) *Achieving Literacy*. London: Routledge and Kegan Paul. (12, 30)

Midgeley, M. (1985) *Evolution as Religion*. London and New York: Methuen. (35)

Mitchell, D.C. (1982) *The Process of Reading: A Cognitive Analysis of Fluent Reading and Learning to Read*. Chichester: Wiley. (68)

Montessori, M. (1967) *The Discovery of the Child*. New York: Ballentine. (191)

Morais, J.; Alegria, J. and **Content, A.** (1987) The relationship between segmental analysis and alphabetic literacy, *Cahiers de Psychologie Cognitive*, **7**, 415–38. (90)

Morais, J.; Bertelson, P.; Cary, L. and **Alegria, J.** (1986) Literacy training and speech segmentation, *Cognition*, **24**, 45–64. (87)

Morais, J.; Cary, L.; Alegria, J. and **Bertelson, P.** (1979) Does awareness of speech as a sequence of phones arise spontaneously? *Cognition*, **7**, 323–31. (67, 87)

Morris, J.M. (1979) New phonics for old, in **Thackray, D.V.** (ed.) *Growth in Reading*. London: Ward Lock. (7)

Moyle, D. (1976) *The Teaching of Reading* (7th edn). London: Ward Lock. (145)

Muller, H.J. (1967) *The Uses of English*. New York: Holt, Rinehart and Winston. (172)

Murray, D.M. (1978) Internal revision: A process of discovery, in **Cooper, C.R.** and **Odell, L.** (eds) *Research on Compsong*. Urbana, Illinois: National Council of Teachers of English. (161)

National Assessment of Educational Progress (1980a) *Writing achievement 1969–79: Results from the third national writing assessment (Vol. 1: 17 year olds)*, (Tech. Rep.). Denver, Colorado: National Assessment of Educational Progress (ERIC Document Reproduction Service No. ED 196 042). (167)

National Assessment of Educational Progress (1980b) *Writing achievement 1969–79: Results from the third national writing assessment (Vol. 2: 13 year olds)*, (Tech. Rep.). Denver, Colorado: National Assessment of Educational Progress (ERIC Document Reproduction Service No. ED 196 043). (167)

National Curriculum Council (1988) *Developmental Writing*. York: National Curriculum Council. (187)

Nell, V. (1988) *Lost in A Book: The Psychology of Reading for Pleasure*. Yale: Yale University Press. (116)

Newall, A. (1974) You can't play 20 questions with nature and win, in **Chase, W.G.** (ed.) *Visual Information Processing*. New York: Academic Press. (163)

Nisbet, S.D. (1941) The scientific investigation of spelling instruction in Scottish schools, *British Journal of Educational Psychology*, **11**, 150. (177)

Oakhill, J.V. and **Garnham, A.** (1988) *Becoming a Skilled Reader*. Oxford: Basil Blackwell. (7, 70)

Odell, L. (1974) Measuring the effect of instruction in prewriting, *Research in the Teaching of English*, **8**, 228–40. (169)

Odell, L. (1980) Business Writing: Observations and implications for teaching composition, *Theory into Practice*, **19**, 225–32. (155, 161)

Ogden, C.K. (1932) *Bentham's Theory of Fictions.* London: Kegan Paul, Trench, Trubner and Co. Ltd. (60)

O'Connor, J.D. (1973) *Phonetics.* Harmondsworth: Penguin Books. (21)

O'Hare, F. (1973) *Sentence combining: Improving Student writing without formal grammar instruction* (Research Rep. No. 15). Urbana, Illinois: National Council of Teachers of English. (170)

Olson, D. (1984) See! Jumping! Some oral antecedents of literacy, in **Goelman, H.; Obery, A.** and **Smith, F.** (eds) *Awakening to Literacy.* London: Heinemann. (42, 53)

Palincsar, A.S. and **Brown, A.L.** (1984) Reciprocal teaching of comprehension-fostering and monitoring activities, *Cognition and Instruction*, **1**, 117–75. (175)

Palmer, F.R. (1981) *Semantics* (2nd edn.). Cambridge: Cambridge University Press. (21)

Palmer, F.R. (1982) *Grammar* (2nd edn.). Harmondsworth: Penguin Books. (21)

Pearson, P.D. and **Gallagher, M.C.** (1983) The instruction of reading comprehension, *Contemporary Educational Psychology*, **8**, 317–44. (173)

Pederson, E.; Faucher, T.A. and **Ealon, W.W.** (1978) A new perspective on the effects of first-grade teachers on children's subsequent adult status, *Harvard Educational Review*, **48**, 1, 1–31. (80)

Perera, K. (1980) Review of Smith, F. (1978) *Reading, Journal of Linguistics*, **16**, 127–31. (7)

Perera, K. (1984) *Children's Writing and Reading: analysing classroom language.* Oxford: Basil Blackwell. (96, 131)

Peters, M.L. (1970) *Success in Spelling.* Cambridge: Cambridge Institute of Education. (178, 179)

Peters, M.L. (1985) *Spelling Caught or Taught? A New Look.* London: Routledge and Kegan Paul. (179)

Piaget, J. (1952) *The child's conception of number.* London: Routledge and Kegan Paul. (85)

Pumfrey, P.D. and **Reason, R.** (1991) *Sepcific Learning Difficulties (Dyslexia): Challenges and Responses.* Windsor: NFER–Nelson. (149)

Pyke, N. (1992) Warnock rethink on special needs, *Times Educational Supplement*, 10 July, p. 5. (149)

Quinsatt, M.G.; Levin, J.A.; Boruta, M. and **Newman, D.** (1983) The use of a word processor in classrooms. Paper presented at the meeting of the American Educational Research Association, Montreal. (170)

Read, C. and **Schreiber, P.** (1982) Why short subjects are harder to find, in **Wanner, E.** and **Gleitman, L.** (eds) *Language Acquisition: The State of the Art.* Cambridge: Cambridge University Press. (34)

Read, C.; Zhang, Y.; Nie, H. and **Ding, B.** (1986) The ability to manipulate speech sounds depends on knowing alphabetic spelling, *Cognition*, **24**, 31–44. (88)

Reid, J.F. (1958) An investigation of thirteen beginners in reading, *Acta Psychologica*, **XIV**, 4, 294–313. (32, 34, 46)

Reid, J.F. (1970) Sentence structure in reading primers, *Research in Education*, **3**, 23–37. (48)

Reid, J.F. (1974) *Breakthrough in Action: An independent evaluation of 'Breakthrough to Literacy'.* London: Longman for the Schools Council. (25, 44)

Reid, J.F. (1983) Into Print: Reading and Language Growth, in **Donaldson, M.; Grieve, R.** and **Pratt, C.** (eds) *Early Childhood Development and Education.* New York and London: The Guildford Press. (42)

Reitsma, P. (1983) Printed word learning in beginning readers, *Journal of Experimental Child Psychology,* **36**, 321–39. (211)

Rentel, V. and **King, M.** (1983) Present at the beginning, in **Mosenthal, P., Tamor, L.** and **Walmsley, S.** (eds). *Research on Writing: Principles and Methods.* New York: Longman Inc. (167)

Rice, J.M. (1897) The futility of the spelling grind, *Forum*, **23**. (176)

Richardson, M. (1935) *Writing and Writing Patterns: Teacher's Book.* London: Hodder and Stoughton. (195)

Samuels, S.J. and **Kamil, M.L.** (1984) Models of the reading process, in **Pearson, P.D.** (ed.) *Handbook of Reading Research.* New York: Longman. (7)

Sassoon, R. *et al.* (1986) An analysis of children's penholds, in **Kao, H.S.R.; Van Galen, G.P.** and *Graphonomics.* Amsterdam: North Holland. (191)

Sassoon, R. (1990a) *Handwriting: a new perspective.* Cheltenham: Stanley Thornes.

Sassoon, R. (1990b) *Handwriting: the way to teach it.* Cheltenham: Stanley Thornes. (193)

Sassoon, R. (1991) The Effect of Teachers' Personal Handwriting on their Reproduction of School Models, in **Wann, J.;**

Wing, A.M. and **Sovik, N.** (eds) *Development of Graphic Skills.* London: Academic Press. (196)

Saudek, R. (1932, reprinted 1991) *What Your Handwriting Shows.* Chesterfield: Nigel Bradley. (192)

Scardamalia, M. (1980) How children cope with the cognitive demands in writing, in **Frederiksen, C.H.** and **Dominic, J.F.** (eds) *Writing: The Nature, Development and Teaching of Written Communication.* Hillsdale, New Jersey: Lawrence Erlbaum Associates. (181)

Scardamalia, R. and **Bereiter, C.** (1982) Assimilative processes in composition planning, *Educational Psychologist,* **17**, 165–71. (172)

Schieffelin, B.B. and **Cochran-Smith, M.** (1982) Learning to read culturally: literacy before school, in **Goelman, H.; Oberg, A.** and **Smith, F.** (eds) *Awakening to Literacy.* Exeter, New Hampshire: Heinemann. (148)

Schonell, F.J. (1942) *Backwardness in Basic Subjects.* Edinburgh: Oliver and Boyd. (179)

Schools Examination and Assessment Council (SEAC) (1991) Assessment of Performance Unit Report on the 1988 APU Survey, in *Assessment Matters No. 4: Language and Learning.* London: HMSO. (127, 137)

Scottish Certificate of Education, Standard Grade (1987) *Revised Arrangements in English.* Scottish Examination Board. (53)

Sharron, H. (1987) Changing Children's Minds, *Times Educational Supplement,* 22 May, p. 20. (148)

Siegler, R.S. (1976) Three aspects of cognitive development, *Cognitive Psychology,* 8, 481–520. (86).

Simon, D.P. (1976) Spelling: A task analysis, *Instructional Science,* **5**, 277–302. (179)

Simon, D.P. and **Simon, H.A.** (1973) Alternative uses of phonemic information in spelling, *Review of Educational Research,* **43**, 115–37. (180)

Sloboda, J.A. (1980) Visual imagery and individual differences in spelling, in **Frith U.** (ed) *Cognitive Processes in Spelling.* New York: Academic Press. (178)

Smagorinsky, P. (1987) Graves Revisisted: A Look at the Methods and Conclusions of the New Hampshire Study, *Written Communication,* **4**, 4, 331–42. (2)

Smith, F. (1971) *Understanding Reading.* New York: Holt, Rinehart and Winston (4th edn 1988). (22, 23, 26, 29, 68, 204)

Smith, F. (ed.) (1973) *Psycholinguistics and Reading.* New York: Holt Rinehart and Winston. **(68)**

Smith, F. (1977) Making sense of reading and reading instruction, *Harvard Educational Review,* **47**, 3, 386–95. **(32)**

Smith, F. (1978) *Reading.* Cambridge: Cambridge University Press. **(40)**

Smith, F. (1982) *Writing and the Writer.* London: Heinemann. **(2)**

Smith, F. and **Miller, G.A.** (eds) (1966) *The Genesis of Language.* Cambridge, Mass.: MIT Press. **(24)**

Soderbergh, R. (1981) Early reading as language acquisition, *System,* **9**, 207–13. **(45, 60)**

Stahl, A. (1980) The structure of children's composition: Developmental and ethnic differences: Research in the teaching of English, in **Gregg, L.W.** and **Steinberg, E.R.** (eds) *Cognitive Processes in Writing.* Hillsdale, New Jersey: Lawrence Erlbaum Associates. **(181)**

Stahl, S.A.; Osborn, J. and **Lehr, F.** (1990) *Beginning to read: Thinking and learning about print – A summary.* Champaign, Illinois: University of Illinois Center for the Study of Reading. **(212)**

Stanovich, K. (1980) Towards an interactive-compensatory model of individual differences in the development of reading fluency, *Reading Research Quarterly,* **19**, 32–71. **(68)**

Stanovich, K.E.; Cunningham, A.E. and **Cramer, B.R.** (1984a) Assessing phonological awareness in kindergarten children: issues of task comparability, *Journal of Experimental Child Psychology,* **38**, 175–90. **(86)**

Stanovich, K.E.; Cunningham, A.E. and **Freeman, D.J.** (1984b) Intelligence, cognitive skills and early reading progress, *Reading Research Quarterly,* **19**, 278–303. **(86)**

Stein, N.L. and **Trabasso, T.** (1982) What's in a story: An approach to comprehension and instruction, in **Glaser, R.** (ed.) *Advances in Instructional Psychology.* Hillsdale, New Jersey: Lawrence Erlbaum Associates. **(165)**

Stott, D.H. (1981) Teaching reading: The psycholinguistic invasion, *Reading,* **15**, 3, 19–25. **(7)**

Strickland, R. (1962) The language of elementary school children: its relation to the language of reading textbooks and the quality of reading of selected children, *Bulletin of the School of Education, University of Indiana,* **38**, 2. **(48)**

Teale, W.H. and **Sulzby, E.** (1986) *Emergent Literacy: Writing and Reading.* Norwood, New Jersey: Ablex. **(7)**

Tenney, Y.J. (1980) Visual factors in spelling, in **Frith, U.** (ed.) *Cognitive Processes in Spelling.* New York: Academic Press. (179)

Thomatis, A. (1967). *La Dyslexie.* Paris: Centre du Langage. (145)

Tizard, B. and **Hughes, M.** (1984) *Young Children Learning.* London: Fontana. (43)

Tizard, B.; Blatchford, P.; Burke, J.; Farquhar, C. and **Plewis, I.** (1988) *Young Children At School in the Inner City.* London: Lawrence Erlbaum Associates. (9, 74, 78, 81)

Tizard, J; Schofield, W.N. and **Hewison, J.** (1982) Collaboration between teachers and parents in assisting children's reading, *British Journal of Educational Psychology,* **52,** 1–15. (150)

Treiman, R. (1983) The structure of spoken syllables: Evidence from novel word games, *Cognition,* 15, 49–74. (92)

Treiman, R. and **Baron, J.** (1981) Segmental analysis: development and relation to reading ability, in **MacKinnon, G.C.** and **Waller, T.C.** (eds) *Reading Research: advances in theory and practice, Vol. III.* New York: Academic Press. (86)

Trudgill, P. (1983) *Sociolinguistics: An introduction* (2nd edn.). Harmondsworth: Penguin Books. (21)

Tucker, N. (1981) *The Child and the Book.* Cambridge: Cambridge University Press. (114, 115, 122, 123)

Tunmer, W.E., Herriman, M.L. and Nesdale, A.R. (1988) Metalinguistic abilities and beginning reading, *Reading Research Quarterly,* 23, 134–158. (86)

Tyler, L.K. and **Marslen-Smith, W.D.** (1982) Speech Comprehension Processes, in **Mehler, J.; Walker, E.C.** and **Garrett, M.F.** (eds) *Perspectives on Mental Representation.* Hillsdale, New Jersey: Lawrence Erlbaum Associates. (29)

Uhry, J.K. and **Shepherd, M.J.** (1990) The effect of segmentation/ spelling training on the acquisition of beginning reading strategies. Paper presented at the annual meeting of the American Educational Research Association, Boston. (211)

Unsworth, L. (1990) Learning the culture through literacy development: information books for beginning readers. Paper presented to the thirteenth World Congress of the International Reading Association, Stockholm July 3–6, 1990 (134)

van Dijk, T.A. and **Kintsch, W.** (1983) *Strategies of Discourse Comprehension.* New York: Academic Press. (169)

Vellutino, F.R. (1991) Introduction to three studies on reading acquisition: Convergent findings on theoretical foundations of code-oriented versus whole-language approaches to reading instruction, *Journal of Educational Psychology*, **83**, 437–43. (207)

Venezky, R.L. (1970) *The Structure of English Orthography*. The Hague: Mouton. (1)

Ventola, E. (1987) *The Structure of Social Interaction: A systemic approach to the semiotics of service encounters*. London: Pinter. (128)

Vincent, D. and **Claydon, J.** (1982) *Diagnostic Spelling Test*. Slough: NFER–Nelson. (184)

Vygotsky, L.S. (1962) *Thought and Language*. Cambridge, Mass.: MIT Press. (39, 59)

Vygotsky, L.S. (1978) *Mind in Society* (Trans. Cole, M. *et al.*). Cambridge, Mass.: Harvard University Press. (155)

Wallach, M.A. (1963) Perceptual recognition of approximations to English in relation to spelling achievement, *Journal of Educational Psychology*, **civ**, 57–62. (184)

Wallin, J.E. (1910) Has the drill become obsolescent?, *Journal of Educational Psychology*, **1**, 200–13. (176)

Wanner, E. and **Gleitman, L.** (eds) (1982) *Language Acquisition: The State of the Art*. Cambridge: Cambridge University Press. (25)

Waterland, L. (1988) *Read With Me: An Apprenticeship Approach to Reading* (2nd edn). Stroud: Thimble Press. (7, 28)

Weber, R.M. (1970) A linguistic analysis of first-grade reading errors, *Reading Research Quarterly*, **V**, 3, 427–51. (32, 46, 96)

Wells, G. (1985) *Language, Learning and Education*. Windsor: NFER–Nelson. (150)

West, R.; Stanovich, K.; Feeman, D. and **Cunningham, A.** (1983) The effect of sentence context on word recognition in second- and sixth-grade children, *Reading Research Quarterly*, **19**, 6–15. (69)

Whitehead, A.N. (1932) *The Aims of Education*. London: Williams and Norgate. (55)

Wilkinson, A.; Barnsley, G.; Hanna, P. and **Swan, M.** (1980) *Assessing Language Development*. Oxford: Oxford University Press. (2)

Wise, B.W.; Olson, R.K. and **Treiman, R.** (1990) Subsyllabic units as aids in beginning readers' word learning: onset-rime versus post-vowel segmentation, *Journal of Experimental Child Psychology*, **49**, 1–19. (94)

Woodruff, E.; Bereiter, C. and **Scardamalia, M.** (1981) On the road to computer assisted compositions, *Journal of Educational Technology Systems*, **10**, 133–48. (171)

Woodruff, E. (1982) Computers and the composing process: An examination of computer-writer interaction, in **Lawlor, J.** (ed.) *Computers in Composition Instruction.* Los Alamitos, California: SWRL Educational Research and Development. **(171)**

Writers at Work: The Paris Review Interviews (2nd Series). (1963) New York: The Viking Press. **(160)**

Yuill, N.M. and **Oakhill, J.V.** (1991) *Children's Problems in Text Comprehension: An Experimental Investigation.* Cambridge: Cambridge University Press. **(72)**

Young, R.E.; Becker, A.L. and **Pike, K.E.** (1970) *Rhetoric: Discovery and Change.* New York: Harcourt, Brace and World. **(170)**

index